ASSESSMENT AND EVALUATION FOR TRANSFORMATION IN EARLY CHILDHOOD

Assessment and Evaluation for Transformation in Early Childhood establishes a new, democratic and participatory approach to assessment and evaluation in early childhood. By analysing the practice of assessment and evaluation within early childhood pedagogy, it provides a clear theoretical and methodological basis for this approach and a set of practical techniques for assessment and evaluation.

Structured into three parts – context and principles, approaches and techniques and case studies – the authors show how documentation and portfolios can be an ethical mode of conducting assessment and evaluation. The third part of the text provides educational snapshots of countries that use a participatory approach to learning and teaching, and which include the pedagogical dimension of assessment and evaluation. Each of the seven illustrative case studies from three different countries brings to life the theories, principles and techniques presented throughout the book.

Key points explored include:

- the nature and purpose of assessment and evaluation within a participatory pedagogy;
- participatory methods for assessment and evaluation;
- the search for a holistic approach to evaluation;
- pedagogic documentation: uncovering solidary learning;
- ethical principles for holistic pedagogic evaluation.

This book is a crucial read for anyone working in early childhood education who wishes to learn more about professional practice and policy development and all those interested in the pedagogical dimensions of assessment and evaluation.

Júlia Formosinho is Professor at the Portuguese Catholic University, Portugal, and President of the Childhood Association research centre in Braga, Portugal. She leads a team of researchers in early childhood working in Portugal, Brazil and Spain.

Christine Pascal is Director of the Centre for Research in Early Childhood (CREC) in Birmingham, UK, and President of the European Early Childhood Education Research Association (EECERA). She leads a team of researchers and trainers who work at policy and practice level across the UK and internationally to develop quality early education and care policy and practice.

EECERA

European Early Childhood Education Research Association

Written in association with the European Early Childhood Education Research Association (EECERA), titles in this series will reflect the latest developments and most current research and practice in early childhood education on a global level. Feeding into and supporting the further development of the discipline as an exciting and urgent field of research and high academic endeavour, the series carries a particular focus on knowledge and reflection, which has huge relevance and topicality for those at the front line of decision making and professional practice.

Rather than following a linear approach of research to practice, this series offers a unique fusion of research, theoretical, conceptual and philosophical perspectives, values and ethics, and professional practice, which has been termed 'Ethical Praxis'.

ASSESSMENT AND EVALUATION FOR TRANSFORMATION IN EARLY CHILDHOOD

Edited by
Júlia Formosinho and
Christine Pascal

LONDON AND NEW YORK

First published 2016
by Routledge
2 Park Square, Milton Park, Abingdon, Oxon OX14 4RN

and by Routledge
711 Third Avenue, New York, NY 10017

Routledge is an imprint of the Taylor & Francis Group, an informa business

British Library Cataloguing in Publication Data
A catalogue record for this book is available from the British Library

Library of Congress Cataloging-in-Publication Data
  Assessment and evaluation for transformation in early childhood/
  edited by Júlia Formosinho and Christine Pascal.
  pages cm
  1. Early childhood education—United States—Evaluation.
  2. Educational tests and measurements. I. Formosinho,
  Júlia. II. Pascal, Christine.
  LB1139.25.A84 2016
  372.21—dc23
  2015016577

ISBN: 978–1-138–90973–1 (hbk)
ISBN: 978–1-138–90974–8 (pbk)
ISBN: 978–1-315–69382–8 (ebk)

Typeset in Bembo
by Florence Production Ltd, Stoodleigh, Devon, UK

Printed in Great Britain by Ashford Colour Press Ltd

CONTENTS

List of illustrations   x
List of contributors   xiii

Foreword: presentation of the EECERA Book Series   xvii
TONY BERTRAM AND CHRISTINE PASCAL

Introduction   xxi
JÚLIA FORMOSINHO AND CHRISTINE PASCAL

*Our pedagogic creed for assessment and evaluation in
early childhood education*   xxv

PART I
Context and principles   1

  1 Pedagogy development: transmissive and participatory
     pedagogies for mass schooling   3
     João Formosinho and Júlia Formosinho

  2 Pedagogy-in-Participation: the search for a holistic praxis   26
     Júlia Formosinho and João Formosinho

PART II
Approaches and techniques   57

  3 The nature and purpose of assessment and evaluation
     within a participatory pedagogy   59
     Christine Pascal and Tony Bertram

4 Participatory methods for assessment and evaluation 74
  Christine Pascal and Tony Bertram

5 The search for a holistic approach to evaluation 93
  João Formosinho and Júlia Formosinho

6 Pedagogic documentation: uncovering solidary learning 107
  Júlia Formosinho

PART III
Portraits of practice: case studies **129**

7 Ethical principles for holistic pedagogic evaluation 131
  Júlia Formosinho, João Formosinho, Christine Pascal
  and Tony Bertram

8 Case study 1
  Why do the Omo River children paint themselves?
  A pedagogic evaluation 142
  Júlia Formosinho, Andreia Lima and Joana Sousa

9 Case study 2
  Pedagogical attunement: documenting toddlers' learning 168
  Júlia Formosinho, Sara Barros Araújo and Hélia Costa

10 Case study 3
   A case study on quality evaluation: a comparison between a
   traditional and a participatory pedagogic environment 181
   Inês Machado and Júlia Formosinho

11 Case study 4
   How to bring children's voices into assessment reports:
   working with teachers in two São Paulo public preschools 192
   Maria Malta Campos and Cristina Aparecida Colasanto

12 Case study 5
   The Effective Early Learning (EEL) Programme:
   evaluation and assessment in a private daycare setting 206
   Sue Ford and Christine Pascal

13 Case study 6
   Participatory assessment with parents: the Accounting
   Early for Lifelong Learning (AcE) Programme 220
   Donna Gaywood and Christine Pascal

14 Case study 7
A participatory model of assessment across a network
of children's centres 240
Elizabeth Fee and Christine Pascal

Index 259

ILLUSTRATIONS

Figures

1.1   The 'modern scientific management' of schooling to maximise
      mass production of education   6
1.2   The schoolification of early years   22
2.1   Praxis   27
2.2   Early childhood education centres as democratic spaces   29
2.3   Pedagogic axes of Pedagogy-in-Participation   32
2.4   Being, thinking, feeling   33
2.5   Belonging and participating   34
2.6   Exploring and communicating   35
2.7   Narrating and creating meaning   36
2.8   Experiential learning   38
2.9   Pedagogy-in-Participation learning areas   39
2.10 Integrated pedagogic dimensions   42
3.1   EEL conceptual framework for evaluating and developing quality
      in early childhood settings   68
3.2   EEL assessment and evaluation cycle   71
6.1   Axes of educational intentionality   113
6.2   Contextual/situated staff development   115
6.3   Pedagogic documentation   117
6.4   Pedagogy-in-Participation anchors for evaluation   118
6.5   Attunement in the revisitation of documentation   119
6.6   Solidary planning   121
6.7   Monitoring solidary learning through professional reflection   122
6.8   Uncovering learning for further learning   123
6.9   Uncovering solidary learning   124

8.1	Pedagogy-in-Participation	143
8.2	Group sharing	146
8.3	Natural fashion: tribal decoration from Africa/Ethiopia: people of the Omo Valley	147
8.4	The decorated faces of children of the Omo Valley	148
8.5	Children studying the faces of the Omo River children	149
8.6	Documenting children in action	150
8.7	Children's representations of their ideas	151
8.8	Family participation	153
8.9	Sharing knowledge and participating	154
8.10	A mother's contribution to children's research	155
8.11	A child's representation	156
8.12	A painted wooden statue	157
8.13	A father–teacher collaboration	159
8.14	Bringing nature and imagination together	160
8.15	Peer review and evaluation	164
9.1	Preschool, Pevidém, Portugal	169
9.2	Music baskets	172
9.3	Musical instruments	172
9.4	Children's experiential reactions	173
9.5	Exploring different properties of musical instruments	174
9.6	Teachers' professional understanding of actively waiting	175
9.7	João and the harmonica sequence	176
10.1	Well-being levels observed in each child integrated in the context that practises Pedagogy-in-Participation	187
10.2	Well-being levels observed in each child integrated in the context that practises a transmissive pedagogy	187
12.1	The quality evaluation and improvement cycle	212
12.2	Settings' Ofsted ratings after implementation of EEL programme	218
13.1	Impact report stay and play	225
13.2	Capturing the parents' voices	226
13.3	Using AcE to assess children's learning and development	228
13.4	Initial and final assessment of children's group using AcE	229
13.5	Assessment of individual 'distance travelled'	230
13.6	An AcE home learning plan	232
13.7	An example of an AcE family plan	235
14.1	AcE data analysis and visual presentation	248
14.2	The Pen Green loop	250

Tables

1.1	Transmissive versus participatory pedagogies: different views of the main goals of education	16

1.2   Transmissive versus participatory pedagogies: different views
       of the organisation of knowledge   17
1.3   Transmissive versus participatory pedagogies: different views
       of the organisation of teaching and learning   18
2.1   Pedagogy-in-Participation: a democratic solidary perspective   28
5.1   The characteristics of holistic evaluation: the aims of
       evaluation in early childhood   99
5.2   The characteristics of holistic evaluation: the processes
       of evaluation in early childhood   100
7.1   Ethical principles for pedagogic evaluation   133

CONTRIBUTORS

Sara Barros Araújo is Adjunct Professor at the School of Education of Polytechnic Institute of Porto, where she coordinates the Masters in Early Childhood Education. She holds a PhD in Childhood Studies from the University of Minho. She is a member of the Board of the Childhood Association and Country Coordinator for Portugal of European Early Childhood Education Research Association (EECERA). Her research interests are particularly focused on early childhood pedagogy, education of children under three years and praxeological research.

Tony Bertram, Director of the Centre for Research in Early Childhood, Birmingham, United Kingdom, was Founding President of EECERA, remains a Trustee and was elected Coordinating Editor of EECERJ in 2008. He is also the current President of Early Education (formerly the British Association for Early Childhood Education). He holds Visiting Professorships at both Birmingham City University and Wolverhampton University. He has written and researched extensively on early childhood education, nationally and internationally, and ensures all his work has implications for practice and policy. His working office is located in an integrated children's centre in Birmingham, UK.

Maria Malta Campos graduated in Pedagogy and has a PhD in Sociology, from the University of São Paulo. She is a senior researcher at the Carlos Chagas Foundation and a professor at the Catholic University of São Paulo. She was a visiting scholar at Stanford University (1987) and at the University of London (1990). She is the president of the NGO Ação Educativa and was the president of the National Association of Educational Research between 1995 and 1999. She has published many articles and book chapters in Brazil and in other countries. Her main interests are educational policies and early childhood education.

Cristina Aparecida Colasanto graduated in Pedagogy and has a Master's Degree in Applied Linguistics and Language Studies and a PhD in Education: Curriculum, both at the Catholic University of São Paulo. She works as a pedagogic adviser at the São Paulo municipal education system and as a teacher at a higher education institution. She has experience in the area of teacher training, evaluation in early childhood education and school management.

Hélia Costa has been an early childhood teacher at the Crèche and Pre-school Albano Coelho Lima (Guimarães), Portugal, for the past 20 years. She holds a bachelor's degree and a post-graduate diploma in Early Childhood Education from the University of Minho. She is a member of the Childhood Association and has been developing projects under Pedagogy-in-Participation, the pedagogical perspective of Childhood Association, some of which have been published.

Elizabeth Fee is an Early Years Improvement Officer, Bristol City Council, United Kingdom. She has extensive experience as a teacher in senior management roles and as headteacher of a large infant school with an attached education family centre. For the last twenty years Elizabeth has worked in a senior advisory capacity in the Improvement Services in Gloucestershire and Bristol local authorities as a primary and early years adviser, managing early years teams that support schools, children's centres, childminders and private, voluntary and independent (PVI) settings to improve provision and outcomes for all children. During this time, she also worked as a Registered Ofsted Inspector and was seconded to work part-time with the National Strategies as a regional Early Years Foundation Stage adviser. Elizabeth designs and delivers training for headteachers, senior managers, teachers and pre-school practitioners and has led many national and local early years quality improvement programmes and initiatives.

Sue Ford works as the Early Years Consultant for Workforce Development for Birmingham City Council in the United Kingdom, supporting and advising practitioners on continuing professional development (CPD) training and early years and childcare training and qualification pathways. She previously held the post of Quality Improvement Coordinator, coordinating the local authority Quality Improvement (QI) Programme. The Effective Early Learning Programme (EEL) formed part of the QI programme and Sue became a registered EEL trainer, supporting practitioners and settings. Before joining the city council in Birmingham she worked for 12 years as a coordinator for Magic Carpet Playbus Project, providing and promoting inclusive play for disabled children. Sue has worked on a variety of early years and childcare projects in the voluntary sector. She has a BA (Hons) in Education and an MSc in Early Years Management and Leadership.

João Formosinho is Professor at the Portuguese Catholic University, in Lisbon, and at the University of Minho. He is also President of Childhood Association. In a longtime partnership with Aga Khan Foundation, he developed, with Júlia

Formosinho, *Pedagogy-in-Participation* – a co-constructivist participatory approach to children and educators' development and learning. He is a member of the European Early Childhood Education Research Association (EECERA) as well as of ILADEI (Latin American Childhood Education Institute) and a consultant of the Brazilian Project on Integrated Early Childhood Centres of the Faculty of Education of the University of São Paulo. João publishes widely on childhood pedagogy, educational administration, teacher education and staff development and praxeological research.

Júlia Formosinho is a Professor at the Portuguese Catholic University in Lisbon and of the University of Minho. She is also Director of the Childhood Association Research Centre. In a long time partnership with Aga Khan Foundation, Júlia developed, with João Formosinho, *Pedagogy-in-Participation* – a co-constructivist participatory approach to children and educators' development and learning. Júlia is a member of the European Early Childhood Education Research Association (EECERA) Board of Trustees and coordinator of the special issues of EECERA Journal. She is also a member of the directory board of ILADEI (Latin American Institute for Childhood Studies) as well as of RELADEI (Latin American Childhood Education Journal). She is a Consultant to the Brazilian Project on Integrated Early Childhood Centres at the Faculty of Education of the University of São Paulo.

She publishes widely on childhood pedagogy, children learning, staff development, documentation-assessment-evaluation and praxeological research.

Donna Gaywood is a Children Centre teacher in the south-west of England. She has had an unconventional career as an educator spanning 25 years. Qualifying as a teacher in 1990, she spent the next ten years raising her five children. Donna has worked with children from birth to sixteen and has taught adults in a variety of roles during this time. She has worked for both the voluntary and charitable sector as well as for local authority and a private provider of daycare. Her passion is to use her skills as an educator to improve the life chances and choices of children and their parents who find themselves in adverse situations. She believes strongly that education is more far reaching and enduring than the current schooling experienced by many children in England and that the role of an educator is to empower rather than control.

Andreia Lima is an early years educator in Olivais Sul Children's Centre in Lisbon, Portugal, managed by the Aga Khan Foundation and pedagogically oriented by Childhood Association. Andreia has been developing Pedagogy-in-Participation in nursery and pre-school contexts. Currently Andreia is completing her Master's Thesis on educational planning in the perspective of Pedagogy-in-Participation at the Portuguese Catholic University.

Inês Machado is an early childhood educator working as an educator in Olivais Sul Children's Centre in Lisbon, Portugal, and since 2013 as a context-based educator at the development of Pedagogy-in-Participation in crèche and nursery contexts within the Early Childhood Development Programme, managed by the Aga Khan Foundation and pedagogically oriented by Childhood Association, a context-based staff development educator, developing Pedagogy-in-Participation in affiliate centres. She has a Master's Degree in Early Childhood Education from the University of Minho. She worked in Childhood Association in 2012, being a member of the 22nd EECERA Conference Local Organising Committee and collaborates in some of the Childhood Association's research.

Christine Pascal OBE is Director of Centre for Research in Early Childhood (CREC), an independent charitable research centre, based at the St Thomas Children's Centre in Birmingham, UK, and is also Director of Amber Publications and Training. She was a teacher in primary schools in Birmingham from 1976 to 1985, before moving into the university sector and specialising in professional development, early childhood research and evaluation projects. Currently she is President of the European Early Childhood Education Research Association (EECERA). She was President of the British Association for Early Childhood Education from 1994–1997, and is now Vice President. She has done extensive work at government level in the UK to support the development of early years policy, sitting on a number of national committees, has served as a ministerial adviser, and from 2000–2010 Early Years Specialist Adviser to the House of Commons Select Committee on Education. She was awarded an OBE for services to young children in 2001 and a Nursery World Lifetime Achievement Award in 2012.

Joana Sousa is an early years educator currently working as a context-based educator at the development of Pedagogy-in-Participation in crèche and nursery contexts within the Early Childhood Development Programme, managed by the Aga Khan Foundation and pedagogically oriented by Childhood Association. Since 2010 Joana has been co-authoring researches with the Childhood Association team. Currently Joana is completing a Master's Thesis on the role of pedagogical mediator for pedagogic transformation towards Pedagogy-in-Participation.

FOREWORD

Presentation of the EECERA Book Series

Tony Bertram and Christine Pascal

Underpinning aspirations

This book on assessment and evaluation in early childhood contexts provides the first book in an innovative new book series generated by the European Early Childhood Education Research Association (EECERA). The EECERA Book Series entitled 'Towards an Ethical Praxis in Early Childhood: From Research into Practice' offers an original and exemplary vehicle for the international early childhood sector to develop transformative pedagogy which integrates knowledge and practices for the development of ethical praxis. The book series is designed to complement and link with the European Early Childhood Education Research Journal (EECERJ), which is primarily an academic platform for publishing research according to the highest international standards of scholarship. The EECERA Book Series aims to combine rigorous practice based research with theoretically informed perspectives and to demonstrate how this knowledge can be used to develop and improve the quality of early education and care services to young children and their families. It is also intended to stimulate dialogue about the impact of such research studies.

Pedagogic approach

The approach taken in all the books in this series is not a linear one of research to practice but rather will be a realisation of a fusion of research, theoretical, conceptual and philosophical perspectives, values and ethics, which we term 'Ethical Praxis'. This fusion is embodied in all EECERA research and development activity, but in the book series there is a stronger focus on the development of practice and/or policy, as stimulated by research processes and outcomes. In addition to offering a forum for plural, multi-disciplinary and multi-method research approaches, we aim to offer a strong model of praxeological processes, which foreground issues of ethics and power in the development process. The aim through the series is to exemplify research informed, reflective, dialogic practice which has the capacity to secure deep improvements in the experience of cross national early childhood services.

The book series acknowledges pedagogy as a branch of professional/practical knowledge which is constructed in situated action in dialogue with theories and research and with beliefs (values) and principles. Pedagogy is seen as an 'ambiguous' space, not of one-between-two (theory and practice) but as one-between-three (actions, theories and beliefs) in an interactive, constantly renewed triangulation. Convening beliefs, values and principles, analysing practices and using several branches of knowledge (philosophy, history, anthropology, psychology, sociology amongst others) constitutes the triangular movement of the creation of pedagogy. Pedagogy is thus based on praxis, in other words, an action based on theory and sustained by belief systems. Contrary to other branches of knowledge which are identified by the definition of areas with well-defined frontiers, the pedagogical branch of knowledge is created in the ambiguity of a space which is aware of the frontiers but does not delimit them because their essence is in their integration.

Praxeological intentions

There is a growing body of practitioner and practice focused research which is reflected in the push at national and international levels to add research and analysis skills into the professional skill set of all early childhood practitioners. This is a reflection of the growing professionalism of the early childhood sector and its increased status internationally. The development of higher order professional standards and increased accountability are reflective of these international trends as the status and importance of early education in the success of educational systems is acknowledged.

Each book in the series is designed to have the following praxeological features:

- strongly and transparently positioned in the socio-cultural context of the authors;
- practice or policy focused but based on research and with strong conceptual/theoretical perspectives;
- topical and timely, focusing on key issues and new knowledge;
- provocative, ground breaking, innovative;
- critical, dialogic, reflexive;
- euro-centric, giving voice to Europe's traditions and innovations but open to global contributions;
- open, polyphonic, prismatic;
- plural, multi-disciplinary, multi-method;
- praxeological, with a concern for power, values and ethics, praxis and a focus on action research, the learning community and reflexive practitioners;
- views early childhood pedagogy as a field in itself, not as applied psychology;

- concerned with social justice, equity, diversity and transformation;
- concerned with professionalism and quality improvement;
- working for a social science of the social;
- *not* designed as a text book for practice but as a text for professional and practice/policy development.

This first book on assessment and evaluation exemplifies these underpinning philosophies, pedagogical ethics and scholarly intentions beautifully and sets the series off to a wonderful start. We believe it is topical and timely, focusing on key issues and new knowledge, and also provocative and critical, encouraging and opening polyphonic dialogue about our thinking and actions in developing high quality early childhood services internationally.

INTRODUCTION

Júlia Formosinho and Christine Pascal

Assessment and Evaluation for Transformation is the title of the first book of the EECERA Book Series. It sits right at the heart of the larger purpose of this series: to contribute to transformative processes in early years education aiming at the creation of an ethical praxis in childhood pedagogy.

We conceptualise pedagogy as a branch of professional/practical knowledge which is constructed in situated action in dialogue with theories and beliefs, values and principles. Pedagogy is seen as an 'ambiguous' space, not of one-between-two (theory and practice) but as one-between-three (actions, theories and beliefs) in an interactive, constantly renewed triangulation. Convening beliefs, values and principles, analysing practices and using several branches of knowledge (philosophy, history, anthropology, psychology, sociology amongst others) constitutes the triangular movement of the creation of pedagogy. Pedagogy is thus based on an ethical praxis, in other words, an action based on theory and sustained by belief systems. Contrary to other branches of knowledge which are identified by the definition of areas with well-defined frontiers, the pedagogical branch of knowledge is created in the ambiguity of a space which is aware of the frontiers but does not delimit them because their essence lies in their integration.

Through the specific glance of assessment and evaluation this book makes a journey that hopes to contribute to this understanding of childhood pedagogy.

The book is organised in three sections: Context and Principles (Chapters 1 and 2), Approaches and Techniques (Chapters 3 to 6), and Portraits of Practice (Chapter 7), which includes seven case studies from three countries, Portugal, Brazil and England (Chapters 8 to 14).

Chapter 1 sets out to deconstruct the pervasiveness of transmissive pedagogy used in mass schooling which has constituted mainstream education in the twentieth century. Since early childhood education is progressively joining in mainstream provision, this chapter calls attention to the risks of this inclusion and hopes to contribute to the preservation of the spirit of educational freedom that had always been present in early childhood settings. The chapter progresses to present participatory alternatives to this mainstream pedagogy through two authors – John Dewey and Paulo Freire, understood in dialogue with each other, calling attention to the wealth of participatory childhood pedagogies.

Chapter 2 presents a specific pedagogical approach – Pedagogy-in-Participation – that sits in the family of participatory pedagogies. This presentation of a specific approach to childhood pedagogy development is done through a journey that encompasses its democratic worldview followed by the identification of the pedagogic intentionality axes and the ethos of the educational environment as a "second educator". Pedagogic documentation as a basis for assessment and evaluation is highlighted.

Chapter 3 aims to critically explore the nature, purposes and value of assessment and evaluation processes within a participatory pedagogy. It begins with a clarification of the contribution of assessment and evaluation to developing and ensuring the quality of early childhood education and supporting sector accountability. It then goes on to explore the nature and focus of ethical and democratic participatory assessment and evaluation processes.

Chapter 4 builds on the conceptualisations set out in Chapter 3 and aims to offer exemplification of practical and ethically grounded assessment and evaluation methods and processes which may be used to support a participatory pedagogy. The methods presented are designed to document and assess pedagogic practice and its impact with the intention of reflecting critically on its power to transform learning and development for the children and adults involved.

Chapter 5 sets out to present theoretical and epistemological foundations of the holistic approach to evaluation which embodies an ethically principled and democratic perspective. This approach is interested in all aspects of children's learning with an intention to see the whole child, rather than fragmented elements of his/her identity and learning processes and progression.

Chapter 6 aims to analyse the role of pedagogic documentation in participative pedagogies, showing the relationship between children's and teacher's learning, as well as the relationship between documentation, assessment and evaluation. The chapter ends with a brief presentation of Andreia's classroom as an inspiration for how to develop individual and collective documentation as a basis for assessment and evaluation.

Chapter 7 expands upon a jointly developed 'Pedagogic Creed for Assessment and Evaluation' sustained in our images of children and educators, in our understanding of the nature of school and education, and of childhood pedagogy and pedagogic evaluation. It puts forward twelve principles that can inspire an ethically oriented assessment and evaluation.

These chapters are followed by a series of seven illustrative portraits of participatory assessment and evaluation practice.

The first case study, *Why do the Omo River children paint themselves? A pedagogic evaluation,* constitutes an illustration of the holistic approach to assessment presented in Chapter 5. This case study is contextualised in Pedagogy-in-Participation (described in Chapter 2) and sets out to present the journey of a project work where it is made visible the relationship between children's and teachers' learning, documentation and assessment.

The second case study, *Pedagogical attunement: documenting toddlers' learning,* is contextualised in Pedagogy-in-Participation (presented in Chapter 2) and illustrates the power of the approach to documentation (presented in Chapter 6). This praxe-ological case study aims at early education for diversity: starting with toddlers.

The third case study, *A case study on quality evaluation: a comparison between a traditional and a participatory pedagogic environment,* evaluates and contrasts a traditional crèche educational environment and a participatory one in what concerns the promotion of very little children's well-being, calling attention to the need for more research on the impact of different pedagogic approaches on children's learning.

The fourth case study, *How to bring children's voices into assessment reports: working with teachers at two São Paulo public preschools,* is based on data from an action research developed at two public preschools in the city of São Paulo, Brazil. The research questions were: how to change teachers' practices in order to make it possible to hear the children? How to make children's voices visible in the assessment reports? In this process successive layers of routine practices were explored and transformed.

The fifth case study, *The Effective Early Learning (EEL) Programme: assessment in a private daycare setting,* examines the challenges and benefits for quality of using a supported and participatory self-evaluation and improvement programme (explained in Chapters 2 and 3) within a private daycare setting located in a large, metropolitan city in England.

The sixth case study, *Participatory assessment with parents: the Accounting Early for Lifelong Learning (AcE) Programme* (explained in Chapters 2 and 3), reveals the challenges and benefits for parents and children of adopting a participatory model of assessment and evaluation within a network of children's centres in a semi-rural location.

The seventh case study, *A participatory model of assessment across a network of children centres,* examines the challenges and benefits for children, parents, practitioners, settings and local authorities of using a participatory child assessment programme (the AcE programme as explained in Chapters 2 and 3) for children from birth to three years within a large city in the southwest region of England.

Each of the seven illustrative case studies from three different countries brings to life the theories, principles and techniques presented throughout the book. Each one sits in the realm of participatory pedagogies.

This book answers the call for contributions to the EECERA Book Series and has been made possible due to the long standing dialogue of the Pascal and Bertram (CREC) team with the Formosinho and Oliveira-Formosinho (Childhood Association) team and sits in the crossroads of the collaboration of two of their central developments: the one from Pascal and Bertram on participatory theories and methods for assessment and evaluation and the one from Formosinho/

Oliveira-Formosinho and the Childhood Association team on the deconstruction of traditional pedagogies and co-construction of participatory pedagogies and specifically Pedagogy-in-Participation.

The local, situated participatory pedagogies in action require professional journeys on assessment and evaluation that allow the central actors (teachers, children, parents) to be empowered in the processes of quality development and pedagogic evaluation, giving them voice in matters that concern them – the development of the learners' identity connected with the development of professional identities.

OUR PEDAGOGIC CREED FOR ASSESSMENT AND EVALUATION IN EARLY CHILDHOOD EDUCATION

We believe that assessment and evaluation in early childhood education should:

1. better serve children and families following a philosophical principle of the greater good for all;

2. be democratic and participatory;

3. actively involve children;

4. take into account children's holistic learning;

5. seek participation of parents and of other primary carers of the children;

6. be ecological, that is, referred to contexts, processes and outcomes;

7. support individual learning journeys;

8. support the learning journeys of children and professionals;

9. be (inter)culturally relevant;

10. be documented, that is, informed by the documented learning of each child;

11. provide useful and usable information for children and families, professionals and schools, teacher educators and policy makers;

12. contribute to a civic spirit of accountability.

Júlia Formosinho, João Formosinho, Christine Pascal
and Tony Bertram

1. We believe that assessment and evaluation in early childhood education should better serve children and families following a philosophical principle of the greater good for all

We believe that assessment and evaluation in early childhood education should contribute to integrated holistic learning and development of children, should support children and families, mainly working parents, in their need and right to have a job and go to work with well-being feelings, and should contribute to the social fight against poverty through providing to all children and families, and especially to the more vulnerable, an empowering quality early education.

2. We believe that assessment and evaluation in early childhood education should be democratic and participatory

We believe that assessment and evaluation in early childhood education requires a democratic worldview as well as technical, professional, reflexive, critical competences in tune with the underlying educational philosophy.

Children have the right to be given voice in the pedagogic sphere of assessment. How to do this calls for a professional learning journey that should be travelled in companionable action and thinking within an organisation that supports ethical professionalism.

3. We believe that assessment and evaluation in early childhood education should actively involve children

We believe that assessment and evaluation in early childhood education should actively involve children in their own learning as well as in peers' and collective learning.

4. We believe that assessment and evaluation in early childhood education should take into account children's holistic learning

We believe that assessment and evaluation in early childhood education should take into account children's holistic learning informing about what the child does, what the child feels and what the child learns – making visible children's integrated ways of making meaning for learning experiences.

5. We believe that assessment and evaluation in early childhood education should actively seek participation of parents and of other primary carers of the children

We believe that assessment and evaluation in early childhood education should actively seek parents' and families' participation in their children's learning through participation in the pedagogic documentation.

6. We believe that assessment and evaluation in early childhood education should be ecological (contextualised and situated), that is, referred to contexts, processes and outcomes

We believe that assessment and evaluation in early childhood education should be ecological, that is, referred to contexts, processes and outcomes. The evaluation should be contextualised and situated encompassing the appreciation of all ecological dimensions – contexts, processes and outcomes and its interaction with other life contexts.

7. We believe that assessment and evaluation in early childhood education should support individual learning journeys

We believe that assessment and evaluation in early childhood education should support individual learning journeys helping each child to develop her/his possibilities as a competent, agent, participative learner.

8. We believe that assessment and evaluation in early childhood education should support the interdependent learning journeys of children and professionals

We believe that assessment and evaluation in early childhood education should support the interdependent learning journeys of children and professionals in order to create awareness of the deep relationship between teaching and learning in the context of a democratic organisation and to facilitate the development of further learning.

9. We believe that assessment and evaluation in early childhood education should be (inter)culturally relevant

We believe that assessment and evaluation in early childhood education should be (inter)culturally relevant calling for a pluralistic, integrated approach to life, learning and evaluation in the children's centre dealing daily and systematically with similarities and differences and supporting social cohesion.

10. We believe that assessment and evaluation in early childhood education should be informed by the documented learning of each child

We believe that assessment and evaluation in early childhood education should be informed by the documented learning of each child. A pedagogical approach to assessment and evaluation is conducted by reference to learning-teaching processes and searches for congruence with them. This documentation allows the children, the educators and the families to see and revisit children's learning processes, and support children as co-constructors of knowledge and ethics.

11. We believe that assessment and evaluation in early childhood education should provide useful and usable information for all involved

We believe that assessment and evaluation in early childhood education should provide useful and usable information for all involved – children and families, professionals and schools, teacher educators and policy makers – in order to sustain reflection on the quality of the educational environment, its learning opportunities and children's responses to these learning opportunities. We believe that assessment and evaluation should support professionals' awareness about their strategies, competences and motivations to serve each child's individual learning journey as well as the collective learning journey.

12. We believe that assessment and evaluation in early childhood education should contribute to a civic spirit of accountability

We believe that assessment and evaluation in early childhood education should be compatible with the central principles of democracy and participation and with children's competencies and motivations, interests and purposes. Its processes and outcomes should be shared with a democratic spirit of collaboration and an awareness about a professional, civic spirit of accountability.

PART I

Context and principles

1

PEDAGOGY DEVELOPMENT

Transmissive and participatory pedagogies for mass schooling

João Formosinho and Júlia Formosinho

The first level of education to become compulsory for all children was primary school education, beginning with five- to six-year-old children. It was then extended to the lower secondary school and, finally, compulsory secondary schooling was considered necessary for the education of children and adolescents eventually up to 18 years currently in most Western societies. More recently, mass schooling has been progressively extended to include pre-primary early years in mainstream education. Within Europe, this can mean that children from birth through to six years can find themselves in centre-based, out of home, education and care with compulsory attendance at four, five, six or seven years being dependent on the individual policies of different nations.

Chapter 1 of this book deconstructs the continuing pervasiveness of transmissive pedagogy used in most mass schooling which has constituted mainstream education in the twentieth century and asserts its inappropriateness for early childhood. Since early childhood education is progressively joining in mainstream provision, we call attention to the risks of this inclusion hoping to contribute to the preservation of the spirit of educational freedom always present in early childhood settings.[1]

The first section of this chapter expresses how the scientific 'management of education' prevailed in the building up of mass schooling during the twentieth century. Although John Dewey's ideas considering the school as a place to learn how to live and to build democracy developed exactly at the same time as Ford and Taylor's organisational ideas for industrial production, these latter were the ones which prevailed in educational expansion. This expansion of an education initially designed only for an elite to compulsory and universal entitlement was done with reference more to the dominant organisational theories of the industrial revolution than to pedagogical ones. Our analysis of the building of this segmented and compartmentalised mainstream education in the twentieth century underpins this chapter (Formosinho and Machado, 2007, 2012).

The second section of this chapter affirms that there are, and always have been, *participatory* alternatives to this mainstream pedagogy, even from the very start of mass schooling expansion. Two authors, especially, opened possible worlds for childhood pedagogy: John Dewey and Paulo Freire. These two pedagogues when considered in dialogue with each other help us to understand other possibilities, to develop the will to undertake change and to create networks of praxis that are respectful of the key actors of pedagogic development: children, educators and families.

To further help to create these networks of participatory praxis, the third section of this chapter aims to characterise the essential differences between these two basic perspectives, *transmissive* and *participatory*, explaining their respective rationale. Behind these two different approaches are different visions of teaching, learning and education. The aim of this section is to present these essential differences related to values and worldviews, goals and objectives, methods and operational principles, the organisation of knowledge and the organisation of curriculum, the role and image of teacher and learner, and the respective conception of assessment and evaluation. It is also our intention in this section to explain why the mainstream educational process is generally based on *transmissive* pedagogies.

The final section of the chapter analyses how the growing inclusion of early childhood education and care in compulsory education may tend to include it in the mainstream delivery mode, promoting the attendance of early childhood mainly as preparation for primary school. It would be contradictory and unethical that the growing acknowledgement of the importance of early childhood education in children's learning should promote the very characteristics which would limit its benefits.

The segmentation of education in the development of mass schooling

The 'scientific management of education': the contribution of Taylor and Ford

Traditional education aims to transmit to a next generation those skills, facts and standards of moral and social conduct that adults consider being necessary for the next generation's material and social success (Dewey, 1938). This transmission is often based on memorisation, rote learning (memorisation with no effort at understanding the meaning). The students are expected to obediently receive and believe these fixed answers; teachers are the instruments by which this knowledge is communicated. The main proposals of the *progressive education movement,* active since the last decades of the nineteenth century, were quite the opposite. They include an emphasis on learning by doing rather transmission, the selection of subject content based on the future needs of society rather than on internal academic continuity, an integrated curriculum focused on thematic units rather than a curriculum based on segmented knowledge, a pedagogy based on problem solving and critical thinking rather than aiming at rote learning, and based on group work and cooperation rather than promoting competition. And, finally, an assessment by evaluation of each child's projects and productions, rather than assessment of task completion or using tick box questionnaires.

John Dewey (1859–1952), one of the leading members of the progressive movement,[2] Frederick Taylor (1856–1915) and Henry Ford (1863–1947), the most influential proponents of the scientific management of industry and economy, were contemporaries and developed their main ideas and theoretical constructions in the last years of the nineteenth century and the first years of the twentieth century. The worldview and conception of humanity underpinning the progressive education movement and the scientific management theories were quite opposite. But the import to education of the industrialised organisational theories, that is, the 'scientific management of education', appeared to most Western governments as a more efficient tool for the development of mass education as it was already an indispensable mechanism for mass production in industry.

Taylor's theory of management aimed to transform craft production into mass production, improving efficiency, standardising the best practices. The agents of execution need not be 'smart' to execute their tasks. Ford's contribution was the development of an important mechanism for the standardisation of mass production through the breaking down of complex tasks into simpler ones, with the assembly line workers being merely executors of these simplified tasks.[3] On the assembly line, the manufacturing process is comprised of incremental different parts added in sequence as the semi-finished assembly moves from work station to work station until the final assembly is produced.

Thus the development of public school for all in Western societies seems to be, in the organisational dimension of schooling, more in debt to Taylor, Ford and Weber[4] than to Froebel, Montessori, Dewey, Steiner and other progressive pedagogues. For the educational mass production system to be efficient it was necessary to modernise the nineteenth century traditional education; the 'scientific management of education' appeared to serve more efficiently the traditional education aims through the standardisation of the content and the means (curriculum and pedagogy), thus maximising mass production of schooling. This standardisation demanded a single, unified curriculum for all students, regardless of motivation, developmental level or interest. It required that all students be taught the same materials at the same time and at the same rate. In order to achieve this, teaching groups should be homogeneous, with students matched by age and by ability; students that did not learn quickly enough failed, rather than being allowed to succeed at their natural speeds. The evaluation of students as control of knowledge acquisition was done through tests and final examinations.

The set up of the 'educational assembly line'

The standardisation of the content was obtained through the breaking down of the knowledge into different specific subject units (horizontal segmentation of the curriculum), dividing each subject unit into school grades (vertical segmentation

FIGURE 1.1 The 'modern scientific management' of schooling to maximise mass production of education

of the curriculum) and organising the curriculum through assembling these subject graded units into sequent school grades. The organisation of the teaching schedule for each week, month or school year is based on the same principles since it accommodates and organises both types of segmentation based on temporal teaching time units (typically the hour).

Students flow throughout the day according to these temporal teaching time units from one subject teaching unit to another, thus building, day by day and year by year, the educational assembly line.[5]

The 'bureaucratic management of education': the contribution of Weber

The State developed a bureaucratic model for the performance of its educational mission. Thus Weber is added to Taylor and Ford as an important contributor to the development of mass education.

In countries with administrative traditions based on centralisation, the State has conceived a unique way of ensuring the universality of education and, hence, of defining an *optimum pedagogy* which is set out in a school curriculum. When defining this curriculum, the central educational administration determines in uniform fashion for all the national territory and for all students *what* they should learn and, hence, what should be taught, while explicitly or implicitly assuming basic standards as regards educational conceptions and purposes. The definition of the curricular *corpus* is integrated into a conception of the school as a social place for formal education and social control, which has lent it legitimacy during the course of modernity and made it into an ideological apparatus of the State. At the same time, it incorporates conceptions and guidelines about the mode of structuring and materialising the curriculum as regards contents, methodologies and assessment.

The centralised bureaucratic model for formulating the curriculum cultivates uniformity and revolves around an abstract 'average' student. The role of each subject matter in the curriculum, the weekly workload and the programmatic contents are defined at a higher level. General methodological guidelines are formulated, with the purpose of recommending the best methods and techniques for transmitting the predefined curriculum contents in presumably uniform settings.

This led to a 'bureaucratic pedagogy' at both curriculum and classroom levels and uniformity in classroom practice was induced by strong normative control on all details of school management, while curriculum and pedagogical solutions were planned for the 'average able student' taught by the 'average teacher' in the 'average school'. This 'average able student' was the conforming, knowledgeable and motivated student. Curriculum remained uniform for all students and schools, regardless of previous learning experiences, of diverse capacities and motivations, of different interests and expectations. This 'ready to wear single size curriculum' (Formosinho, 1987, 2007) produced for all schools the same number of lecturing hours per subject, using the same syllabus, in the same teaching units, all determined by norms at central level. This 'one-size-fits-all curriculum' was taught to all students, regardless of their learning, ability, motivation, interests or expectations; in all classrooms, regardless of level of tracking; and, at all schools, regardless of the population and characteristics of the communities they served.

To teach the same content to all children at the same time in the same manner was seen not only as the most rational and 'scientific' mode but also the embodiment of educational equality of opportunity. This ideal was a blend of an ideological concept of equality seen as uniform treatment for all and of the centralised bureaucratic tradition of governing the educational system. This blend of bureaucratic reason and 'egalitarian' values is embodied in a conception of *equality as uniformity*, that equality of opportunity means the same treatment for all, regardless of their different competencies, interests, needs or learning progress.

The organisational and pedagogical instrument used to transform the teaching of several students into the teaching of the single abstract student assumed in the single size curriculum was the homogeneous classroom, that is, the permanent grouping of academically similar students.

The bureaucratic mode as mainstream education

In this bureaucratic mode, the *image of the child* is that of the 'tabula rasa', the blank sheet, and his/her activity is to memorise contents and reproduce them faithfully, to discriminate in response to external stimuli, to avoid mistakes and correct those which have not been avoided. The *image of the teacher* is that of a transmitter who will typically use structured materials for knowledge transmission, such as manuals, worksheets, workbooks. The child's motivation is based on extrinsic reinforcements, usually from the teacher (Oliveira-Formosinho and Formosinho, 2012). This bureaucratic mode is *blind to cultural differences* which explain why teachers in this mode are often blind to ethnic differences believing that children are also blind when confronted by colour or other social and cultural differences (Formosinho and Machado, 2012; Oliveira-Formosinho and Araújo, 2011).

In recent years, there has been a progressive integration of early years within this bureaucratic mode. As Formosinho and Oliveira-Formosinho (2008a) explain:

> Mainstream pedagogical practice in State pre-schools is becoming each time more influenced by the combined convergent impact of all these factors. They promote a pedagogical, professional and organisational culture in State pre-schools; encouraging the consolidation of a transmissive pedagogy and a bureaucratic practice influenced by primary school practice. This can be indicated by the introduction of bureaucratic formatted templates (planning models, curriculum projects, class registers, performance objectives, etc.), by the systematic reliance on commercial worksheets and activity books as the basis for daily activities.
>
> (Formosinho and Oliveira-Formosinho, 2008a, p. 20)

As will be better seen in Chapter 5, this is the traditional process of simplification of transmissive education beginning in the *organisational* dimension, through the building of an educational assembly line which reduces the complexity of any work to a sequence of very simple mechanic tasks, goes on to the *curricular* dimension through the systematic and sequential explication of the prescribed contents for each, and ends up in the *pedagogical* dimension, through the set up of homogeneous classrooms and standardisation of processes and outcomes in teaching.

The growing cultural diversity of public mass schools

The universal character of schooling induced not only quantitative but also important qualitative transformations in schools. Quantitative changes come from the increase in the number of students, teachers and school units; qualitative transformations come from the cultural diversity of students and local communities. Since the 1960s, the cultural diversity in mass schools has been growing due to the expansion of schooling to vulnerable suburban areas, to massive migrations and European Union work mobility.

Children from different geographic origins (rural, urban, suburban and inner city populations), from different socioeconomic backgrounds (poor and rich, unemployed and working class, low middle class and high middle class), from different national, linguistic and ethnic groups (immigrant populations, second generation families) compose the culturally diverse populations of mass schools today. This social diversity also encompasses academic diversity since the newly arrived children often come from families not aware of the values, norms and motivations of formal education systems. Some of these new populations may be less motivated to participate in formal instruction, some are even resistant to school culture; others adapt easily once they have overcome the initial linguistic barriers.

There was another important contribution to this diversity: the inclusion in regular classes of special needs children. The Salamanca Statement (UNESCO, 1994), to which most governments subscribed, proclaimed that special needs children should be allowed to attend regular schools. These special needs children represent a new student population in mass schools with specific requirements and demands.

For all these reasons, uniformity no longer flowed naturally within the tradition of schools based on (socio-academic) homogeneity. This new social and cultural diversity was often perceived by the school system (central educational adminis- trators, directors and teachers) as problematic, since teaching homogeneous academic groups had been the cornerstone of traditional school pedagogy refined by the 'scientific management of education'. This new social and cultural diversity was considered the kind of heterogeneity that broke the mould of traditional teaching practices. Applying the traditional homogeneity recipe to the culturally diverse schools led to difficulties and, in some cases, even to massive failure of the new student population.

Due to migration, globalisation, massive migrations and the free circulation of capital, goods, services and people, an intercultural dimension is present in most Western societies. The social and communitarian dimension of school has become as important as the intellectual one; schools both as communities of professionals and communities of learners are essential social and cultural assets of current societies.

Participatory approaches to education: Dewey and Freire

The second section of this chapter asserts that there are alternatives to the above described mainstream pedagogy through the presentation of two authors that promoted participatory approaches for education opposed to the traditional transmissive pedagogy. As said earlier, we chose the pedagogical ideas of John Dewey (1859–1952), the most prominent member of the *progressive* movement and one of the more influential educationalists, and Paulo Freire (1921–1997), a Brazilian educator and philosopher who was a leading advocate of critical pedagogy, in contrast to the widespread *modern scientific management* of schooling developed in the twentieth century. The growing cultural diversity of societies and the difficulties of the new populations in mass schools has given us the opportunity to revisit the question of how to organise schooling for all in current societies and to trouble the concept of *transmissive* pedagogy as the best solution to promote relevant learning and social cohesion.

Dewey and Freire are presented as pedagogues who created relevant and influent alternatives to the *transmissive* pedagogy, to the compartmentalisation of school education. They are chosen because they present participatory and holistic alternatives increasingly important for schools in current times. These pedagogues help us to understand other possibilities, to develop the will to undertake change and to create networks of *participatory* praxis that are respectful of the key actors of pedagogy development: children, educators, families.

John Dewey 'pedagogic creed'

John Dewey experienced through his lifetime three main scientific revolutions: the development of evolutionary theory, the development of relativity theory and the beginnings of the atomic era. Thus the debates around *the scientific method* were very important for the development of his educational thinking. John Dewey was a philosopher, psychologist and educational reformer whose ideas have been influential both in education and in social reform. Pedagogy is not a secondary focus for Dewey and is not seen as just an application of his philosophical, psychological or educational ideas, but on the contrary it is very central in his theoretical architecture revealed in a body of work comprising 12 books and around 150 other texts. Dewey's educational theories were presented in 'My Pedagogic Creed' (1897), *The School and Society* (1899), *The Child and the Curriculum* (1902), *Democracy and Education* (1916) and *Experience and Education* (1938).

Dewey was not a university man enclosed in an academic ivory tower. He was a democratic activist engaged in political participation, with involvement in social organisations and with contributions to progressive journals. It can be said that Dewey was a social, political and pedagogic thinker and activist. He was the leader of the progressive education movement, for a time director of the University Primary School (Laboratory School or Dewey School), a children's school annex to the University of Chicago. That school grew to be a pedagogic experiential centre. Dewey's conception of such a school is important for the understanding of his concept of pedagogy. This school was not a space for the student teachers application of the truth of the so-called scientific psychology or of the philosophical speculation. Since Dewey conceived the pedagogic sphere as a field of knowledge production, this experiential school was vital in the building up of his pedagogical theory.

Dewey was writing in times of oppressive school instruction that would only take into account the nature of knowledge and which rejected thinking about the nature of the child and even the nature of the teacher. The teacher was conceived merely as an instrument for the use of a ready-made curriculum designed to transmit ready knowledge and fixed morality.

The first text, 'My Pedagogic Creed' (1897), a ten-page article published in the *School Journal*, was a very comprehensive and challenging presentation of his pedagogic beliefs (using titles such as what is education, school, subject matter, method and the relationship between school and social progress). Most of these beliefs would be re-elaborated in later works. In 1938, in *Experience and Education*, his last book in the field of pedagogy, he pursued a small but very intense discussion of the key themes of his theory of education (and indeed of any theory of education): the continuous reconstruction of experience, the integration of processes and goals of education.

Throughout these writings, Dewey continually argued that education and learning are social and interactive processes, and thus the school itself is a social institution central to democratic societies through which social reform should take place. For Dewey (1897, p.16), 'education is a regulation of the process of coming to share in the social consciousness; and the adjustment of individual activity on the basis of this social consciousness is the only sure method of social reconstruction'.

For Dewey schools were not only places to gain content knowledge, but also places to learn how to live. Schools were not preparation for life, but were life itself. In his eyes, the purpose of education should not revolve around the acquisition of a predetermined set of skills, but rather the realisation of one's full potential and the ability to use those skills for the greater good. In his seminal *pedagogical creed* he declared that all students should have the opportunity to take part in their own learning since it is *impossible to prepare the child for any precise set of conditions.*

> With the advent of democracy and modern industrial conditions, it is impossible to foretell definitely just what civilization will be twenty years from now. Hence it is impossible to prepare the child for any precise set of conditions. To prepare him for the future life means to give him command of himself; it means so to train him that he will have the full and ready use of all his capacities.
>
> (Dewey, 1897, p. 6)

Already in 1902 (in *The Child and the Curriculum*), Dewey had discussed two conflicting schools of thought regarding educational pedagogy. The first is centred on the curriculum and focuses almost solely on the subject matter to be taught. The major error in this pedagogy is the inactivity of the student, 'the child is simply the immature being who is to be matured; he is the superficial being who is to be deepened' (1902, p.13). He argued that content must be presented in a way that allows the student to relate the information to prior experiences, thus deepening the connection with this new knowledge. The opposing school of thought is the *child-centred* pedagogy promoted by those who claimed to be his followers. He argued that too much reliance on the child could be equally detrimental to the learning process. The potential limitation of this line of thinking is that it minimises the importance of the content as well as the role of the teacher. In 1938 he summed up these two conflicting views,

> The history of educational theory is marked by opposition between the idea that education is development from within and that it is formation from without . . . At present the opposition tends to take the form of contrast between traditional and progressive education.
>
> (Dewey, 1938, p.17)

In *Experience and Education*, Dewey proceeded to the critical analysis of the kind of practices of the last three decades that would claim to be inspired by his theorisation and he developed a critical analysis of the progressive movement in which he had been a very central figure. This book showed how Dewey reformulated his ideas as a result of interventions in the children's 'laboratory school' based at the University of Chicago[6] and from which he discussed the relation of pedagogical thinking and its effects.

To sum up, Dewey developed in the last decade of the nineteenth century one pedagogical perspective based on participation of students in their own learning, valuing the community life as a context for social learning (not just as preparation for future life) and advocating an important role for education in social reform. Education was not just the transmission of content; it was participation in life and for life and for democracy (Dewey, 1916).

Dewey's thinking and work in the pedagogic experiential centre gave rise to progressive education practices which were an alternative to mainstream transmissive mass education. The core of Dewey's proposals are still inspiring many current participatory practices.

Freire's interpretation of the transmissive pedagogy as oppression

As Dewey was strongly critical of transmission of mere facts as the goal of education, Freire is critical of what he calls the 'banking concept of education' in which the student is viewed as an empty account to be filled by the teacher. Both acknowledge the political importance of mass schooling and that the building of knowledge is always a social action: as Dewey values education as the main mechanism of social change, Freire defends that education is a political act since it develops a critical consciousness. Freire sees the transmissive pedagogy as an oppressive social practice. In his *Pedagogy of the Oppressed,* first published in Brazil in 1970, Freire explains very clearly his ideas, drawing on his lived experiences as educator of adults in literacy programmes (Freire, 1970a). Freire develops his ideas in other books – books about the the pedagogy of freedom (Freire, 1970b, 1976, 1998), the pedagogy of hope (Freire, 2002), the pedagogy of the city (Freire, 1993), the pedagogy of heart (Freire and Freire, 1997) and many others, but his seminal *Pedagogy of the Oppressed,* in conjunction with the books about pedagogy of freedom, remain the main references for his thinking.

Freire sees the traditional role of the teacher in *transmissive* pedagogy as filling the students with the contents to be transmitted. These contents are transformed into lifeless and hollow words:

> The contents, whether values or empirical dimensions of reality, tend in the process of being narrated to become lifeless and petrified . . . The teacher talks about reality as if it were motionless, static, compartmentalized, and predictable. Or else he expounds on a topic completely alien to the existential

experience of the students. His task is to 'fill' the students with the contents of his narration, contents which are detached from reality, disconnected from the totality that engendered them and could give them significance. Words are emptied of their concreteness and become a hollow, alienated, and alienating verbosity.

(Freire, 1996, p. 52)

Freire sees the traditional role of the student in transmissive pedagogy as repeating the transmitted contents and the hollow words:

> The student records, memorizes, and repeats these phrases without perceiving . . . Narration (with the teacher as narrator) leads the students to memorize mechanically the narrated content. Worse yet, it turns them into 'containers', into 'receptacles' to be 'filled' by the teacher. The more completely she fills the receptacles, the better a teacher she is. The more meekly the receptacles permit themselves to be filled, the better students they are.

(Freire, 1996, pp. 52–53)

Freire presents his conception of (traditional) education as an act of 'depositing', building on his concept of 'banking' education.

> Education thus becomes an act of depositing, in which the students are the depositories and the teacher is the depositor . . . This is the 'banking' concept of education, in which the scope of action allowed to the students extends only as far as receiving, filing, and storing the deposits.

(Freire, 1996, p. 53)

Freire considers this transmissive pedagogy as an oppressive social practice since it is based on an oppressive power relationship:

> In the banking concept of education, knowledge is a gift bestowed by those who consider themselves knowledgeable upon those whom they consider to know nothing. Projecting an absolute ignorance onto others, a characteristic of the ideology of oppression, negates education and knowledge as processes of inquiry. The teacher presents himself to his students as their necessary opposite; by considering their ignorance absolute, he justifies his own existence.

(Freire, 1996, p. 53)

Freire's basic critique of the transmissive pedagogy is not new. John Dewey was strongly critical of transmission of mere facts as the goal of education. Freire's work updated the critique giving rise to a critical pedagogy that clearly connects knowledge and power relationships. This is why Freire values highly the dialogical practice as claiming a different perspective on this relationship.

> In order to understand the meaning of dialogical practice, we have to put
> aside the simplistic understanding of dialogue as a mere technique ... On
> the contrary, dialogue characterizes an epistemological relationship. Thus, in
> this sense, dialogue is a way of knowing and should never be viewed as a
> mere tactic to involve students in a particular task ... I engage in dialogue
> not necessarily because I like the other person. I engage in dialogue because
> I recognize the social and not merely the individualistic character of the process
> of knowing.
>
> (Freire and Macedo, 1995, p. 397)

This ideological critique of the traditional transmissive pedagogy came at a time
where knowledge was perceived and purposefully used as leverage for power in
education and in society. Dialogue and participation are viewed by Freire as an
essential social interaction and not a mere didactic resource. There lies one of his
main contributions for the development of participatory pedagogies.

Contrast between transmissive and participatory pedagogies

The second section of this chapter affirms that there were alternatives to the mainstream pedagogy, even from the very start of mass schooling expansion. As there
are several participatory approaches and even the transmissive perspective can take
more than one mode, this third section of our chapter aims to characterise the
essential differences between these two basic perspectives.[7] Behind the different
pedagogies are different visions of teaching, learning and education. The aim of
this third section is to present these essential differences related to goals and objectives, values and worldviews, methods and operational principles, the organisation
of knowledge and the organisation of curriculum, the role and image of teacher
and learner, and the respective conception of assessment and evaluation. This section
also seeks to explain why the mainstream educational process is generally based on
transmissive pedagogies.

Transmissive versus participatory pedagogies: two opposing views of the educational process

Transmissive pedagogies define a minimum set of essential and perennial information,
the transmission of which is supposed to enable the survival of a culture and of
every individual in that culture. The essence of the transmission mode is the passing
of this cultural heritage to each generation and individual. At the centre of
traditional transmissive education is knowledge considered essential and permanent.
The teacher is seen as a mere transmitter of what he or she has been told yesterday;
as the link between that perennial heritage and the child. The objectives of
education are based on the transmission of that permanent heritage and its translation
into the acquisition of (pre)academic skills, the acceleration of learning and the

compensation for deficits that hinder schooling. The transmissive teaching/learning process defines memorisation of content and its faithful reproduction as the core educational activity. Thus, the process feeds on an initiative that comes from outside the school, the teachers and the children, emphasising a respondent role for the child and opting for standardised proposals for the classroom.

Participatory pedagogies involve a break away from the traditional transmissive pedagogy to promote a different view of the learning process, and of the image and roles of children and educators. To develop participatory pedagogies it is necessary to deconstruct the traditional transmissive mode of doing pedagogy in order to create awareness about aims and goals, and about means and ends (Oliveira-Formosinho, 2007). The objectives of participatory pedagogies are the involvement of children in the experience and the construction of learning in continuous and interactive experience. The image of the child is that of an active, competent being; the motivation for learning is sustained by the intrinsic interest in the task and in the intrinsic motivation of children. The child's activity is understood as an essential collaboration with the learning process; the teacher's role is to organise the environment and to observe the child in order to understand and respond to it. The learning process is an interactive development between child and adult and the educational spaces and times are designed to enable this interactive education. The activities and projects are thought of as an opportunity for children to achieve meaningful learning.

Tables 1.1, 1.2 and 1.3 present a synthesis of the main differences between transmissive and participatory pedagogies.[8]

Table 1.1 presents the main differences between transmissive pedagogies and participatory pedagogies in reference to the main goals of education. The transmissive pedagogies aim at a rigorous provision of structured knowledge in academic format. The mission of transmissive schools is the correct acquisition of transmitted knowledge by the students, correction being evaluated by reproduction of the structured knowledge. The learner has a passive role of repeating the transmitted content (memorising and reproducing) and the teacher has also a passive role being reduced to mere transmitter of predefined contents. The school is a neutral space, closed and self-contained, for the organisation of knowledge and teaching.

The mission of participatory pedagogies is to develop responsible people and civic citizens, capable of being autonomous and taking initiative, through involving the students in their own learning and using the school as a platform for cultural transformation and social reform. The success of this pedagogy is not confined to academic success, but goes into the personal, social and civic success. Both teacher and student have an active role through involvement in meaningful learning experiences. The school is a committed organisation, ecological and contextualised, open to parental and local community involvement.

Table 1.2 presents the main differences in the organisation of knowledge between transmissive pedagogies and participatory pedagogies. The operational principle of transmissive education is one of reductionisms and simplification of

TABLE 1.1 Transmissive versus participatory pedagogies: different views of the main goals of education

	Transmissive pedagogies	*Participatory pedagogies*
Main goal of education	• transmission of knowledge for the next generation • rigorous provision of structured knowledge in academic format	• involving students in their own learning • developing responsible persons and civic citizens • social reform and cultural transformation
Image of the learner	• passive role of repeating the transmitted content (memorising and reproducing)	• active role of participation in the process of learning
Image of the teacher	• passive role of mere transmitter, filling the students with the contents to be transmitted	• active role of promoting meaningful learning experiences involving the students
The educational role of participation	• the participation of the student in the educational process is minimised or ignored	• the participation of the student in the learning process is an intrinsic component of the educational process
The conception of school	• self-contained • closed to parental or local interaction	• ecological and contextual • open to parental and local community involvement
Prevalence in mass schools	• mainstream pedagogy in mass schools	• alternative and minority in mass schools

knowledge which is presented compartmentalised and fragmented. In transmissive pedagogies curriculum and teaching are aimed at the abstract student of average ability, average motivation and average family culture, thus assuming the social and academic uniformity of students, viewing this uniformity as the epitome of equity.

Participatory pedagogies are comprehensive and respect the complexity of knowledge, aiming at a holistic, integrated and connected presentation of contents. Participatory pedagogies start from the diversity of the students, plan the curriculum considering the concrete students with their different characteristics, needs and interests, viewing equity as the respect for these differences within same equal status. As Boaventura Sousa-Santos says,

> We have the right to be equal when our difference makes us inferior; and we have the right to be different when our equality can mischaracterize us. Hence the need for an equality that acknowledges differences and a difference that does not produce, promote or reproduce inequalities.
>
> (Sousa-Santos, 2003a, p. 56)[9]

TABLE 1.2 Transmissive versus participatory pedagogies: different views of the organisation of knowledge

	Transmissive pedagogies	Participatory pedagogies
Epistemological principle	• reductionism, simplification	• comprehensiveness, respect for complexity • analysis of the relationship between whole and parts
Organisation of the knowledge	• compartmentalisation, fragmentation, disjunction	• holistic, integrated, connected
Main character of curriculum and teaching	• abstractness • curriculum and teaching are aimed at the abstract student of average ability, average motivation, average family culture, etc.	• concrete character of curriculum and teaching • situated in place and time • contextualised for the community and the concrete students
Assumptions about students' background – uniformity versus diversity	• assume social and academic uniformity of students	• assume social and academic diversity of students (both cultural differences and individual differences)
Concept of human equity	• equity as uniformity	• equity as respect for plural identities

Table 1.3 presents the main differences in the organisation of the educational processes, of the organisation of learning and teaching between transmissive pedagogies and participatory pedagogies.

The operational principle of transmissive education is based on a closed and self-contained process where teaching is the transmission of contents and skills (from simple to complex and from concrete to abstract) and learning is obtained by listening and reproducing. Evaluation is based on the accuracy of this reproduction.

The operational principle of participatory education is based on an ecological and contextual process, situated on a concrete time and place, where teaching is the creation of learning situations and the support of students throughout the learning process, and evaluation is done through the documentation of the learning realised by doing, experiencing and discovering.

The differentiated status in the educational system of transmissive and participatory pedagogies: mainstream education has been based on the most predictable pedagogy

There is one clear differentiation of status within the educational system: traditional transmissive approaches constitute the basis of mainstream education and

TABLE 1.3 Transmissive versus participatory pedagogies: different views of the organisation of teaching and learning

	Transmissive pedagogies	Participatory pedagogies
Organisation of the educational process	• closed, self contained	• ecological, contextual, situated in time and place
Concept of teaching	• transmission of contents and skills	• creation of meaningful learning experiences involving the students
Concept of learning	• learning by listening and reproducing	• learning by doing, experiencing and discovering
Student activity	• the student sits, listens and reproduces	• the student actively participates in the learning process
Teacher activity	• the teacher transmits contents and skills	• the teacher creates learning situations and supports the student throughout the learning process
Organisation of the teaching and learning settings	• sets up of an optimum pedagogy based on the 'scientific management of education' • set up of an educational assembly line	• sets up contexts and processes which facilitate doing, experiencing and discovering
Concept of evaluation	• centred in the results • centred in comparing individual realisation with the norm • repeating the transmitted content	• centred both in the processes and results • centred both in individual learning and group learning • reflecting on the acquisitions and realisations

participatory approaches had always constituted an alternative. The essential intrinsic differences above presented tell us that one pedagogical mode is much more controllable and predictable than the other.

The rationale of transmissive pedagogy is as follows. The mass production based on the industrial mode demands a totally planned pedagogy, based in single units of knowledge sequentially chained and coupled together on preset stages of learning progression throughout the compulsory school years. The mass production demands a pedagogy where the different needs and interests of the students, their different competencies and even different progress rates are devalued or ignored. The rate of teaching is determined by the learning expected from the average abstract student and not by the actual learning of the concrete classroom students. Since learning is mainly a sole responsibility of the students, the pace of the delivery of content is predetermined and irrespective of its success.

Compartmentalising school life from social life and family life, separating learning from living, allows the school to assume academic and social uniformity thus sustaining the transmissive mode. This planned pedagogy can be bureaucratically controlled and is expected to follow according to plan most of the time. State bureaucracies favour such a system since it is much more predictable and controllable (Formosinho, 1987). Such a system is based on conformity as a means and as an end, that is, it works largely through conformist behaviour of both students and teachers and so inculcates passivity and conformity. The kind of conformity that is expected to be reproduced in economic, social and cultural units.

In contrast, a participatory pedagogy reduces the gap between school life and social life, since it takes into account the needs, interests and projects of the students and their life outside the school, and acknowledges the other contexts where the students live. A participatory pedagogy is by definition less compartmentalised and more holistic than a transmissive one. As participatory pedagogies involve students in their own learning, aiming at the development of responsible persons and civic citizens, the concept of school is different. The self-contained and closed school of transmissive perspectives is transformed into an ecological and contextualised organisation, promoting parental involvement and interacting with the local community. In such pedagogy, learning may take unexpected developments based on the competencies and interests of all. It is not controllable by the pre-allocated time planned for each matter and, in short, it is much less predictable. Since it promotes involvement in the development of classroom activities it sets a civic model of participation in economic and social units.

In most societies mainstream education has always been based on the most predictable, controllable and conformist pedagogy.

Early childhood education: from the dual system to mainstream delivery

This last section presents a brief analysis of the emergence and development of early childhood education and care in the twentieth century, from the dual system of care versus education to the current trend of unification as educational provision in (quasi) compulsory schooling mode.

The dual system: care versus education

The initial industrialisation process demanded a cheap and unqualified labour force which meant, in some working class communities, the employment of both father and mother. The demand for proper care for the working class children gave rise to institutions that answered to this social demand – *crèches* and *daycare nurseries*. A care system was thus developed.

On the other hand, philosophers and pedagogues of the nineteenth century and early twentieth century, like Pestalozzi, Froebel, Montessori, Dewey, Steiner and many others, went beyond this concern for proper care and stressed the importance of the formative years for the educational development of each person and for society. They created all over Europe and America progressive kindergartens. Progressive kindergartens promoted holistic approaches, education for social responsibility and democracy as opposed to rote knowledge. They placed an emphasis on free play and friendly, natural materials, on learning by doing, on cooperative learning projects, on problem solving and critical thinking, on group work and development of social skills, on integrated curriculum and on assessment by evaluation of children's projects and realisations. An early years educational system was gradually built around the idea of the competence of the child and pedagogic freedom.

Most countries of the European Union gradually built their early childhood services around these two systems: the care system and the educational system. The *care system* was predominantly based on private or public charities. These care contexts usually provided extended hours of permanency, fewer holidays and school meals. They were usually orientated towards enabling parents (especially women) to enter or maintain employment. There were generally fewer qualified members of staff, which meant that children were often attended by non-professionally qualified staff. The staff was generally less qualified, worked more hours and earned less than in educational settings. This care system operated under government departments such as the Ministry of Welfare, Employment, or Health or under non-government organisations such as religious or charitable bodies.

In the *educational system* children had fewer hours of provision, often a break of service at lunch time and longer holidays. The educational early childhood centres had always more qualified staff, often specifically qualified for early childhood education (pre-school teachers); in many countries these centres adopted the name of kindergartens or school nurseries or classes. Many times these centres offered a practice based in progressive education ideas, with free play and child-centred activities, often based on specific pedagogical perspectives.[10] This educational system operated generally under the Ministry of Education departments' supervision and was focused primarily on the child's development rather than giving parents access to employment.

So daycare nurseries and kindergartens/school nurseries had different missions and visions, were regulated by different norms and were generally dependent on different governmental departments. This dual system prevailed for the most part of the twentieth century. But in the last quarter of the twentieth century, many countries began gradually promoting unification of care and education systems and, at the same time, extending mass schooling to the last years of early childhood education, thus including early years in compulsory education (Moss, 2013, 2014).

Inclusion of early childhood education in mainstream delivery: pre-schooling as preparation to primary school

As early childhood education and care is focused on the very young, authorities did not consider them as students. States, therefore, did not feel the need to present this as an educational level, a necessary step to ascend to primary education. Many conservative groups claim that early childhood education should be only a concern of the families, not an institutionalised process. Thus, in many instances, ideological concern and benign neglect allowed the kindergartens to develop independently from the mainstream delivery mode.

The pedagogy in educational early childhood schools, mainly at the level of kindergarten, was clearly distinctive of the compartmentalised education of mainstream primary schools based on a transmissive pedagogy (Formosinho and Oliveira-Formosinho, 2008b).

Evidence began to mount of the importance of pre-school attendance for success in school and in life (OECD 2011, 2012), many parents began to demand from early childhood some of the characteristics of mainstream mass education. The terminology of 'pre-school education' rather than 'early childhood education and care' was used by governments; kindergarten, now defined as pre-school, began to be seen mainly as a preparation for primary school. The gradual contamination of early childhood education by the characteristics of traditional education in primary school followed. This contamination came also through the combined pre-school and primary school teacher education programmes and the general trend to make teacher education a strict academic endeavour rather than a professional project[11] (Formosinho, 2002a), thus transforming the professionality of the early childhood educator (Oliveira-Formosinho, 2001).

As Peter Moss (2013, 2014) recognises, the relationship between early childhood education and care and compulsory schooling is the subject of increasing research and policy attention, as the discourse of lifelong learning emphasises that learning begins at birth. Investment in early childhood is increasingly advocated for the returns it brings in later education.

Mainstream school based pedagogy devalues participatory planning based on the encounter with children. It promotes instead planning based on transmissive principles. This progressive immersion of pre-schools in the bureaucratic climate of primary and secondary education, the *schoolification* of early years (Bennett, 2006; see Figure 1.2), makes more important the development of participatory pedagogies as a children's rights approach, in which children and professionals are seen as constantly developing their learners' identities and having the right to professional support (Pascal and Bertram, 2009).

FIGURE 1.2 The schoolification of early years

The preservation of educational freedom in early childhood education

This chapter hopefully contributes to deconstruct the transmissive ethos of mainstream pedagogy and aims at preserving the spirit of educational freedom which until now allowed several pedagogical models to co-exist in early childhood education and care. The growing acknowledgement of the importance of early childhood education in the development of children and in their preparation for school and work, for economic life and for social life, should not promote the very characteristics which would limit these benefits.

Notes

1. See Giardello (2013), Nutbrown and Clough (2014).
2. The inspirational progressive manifesto of John Dewey – *My Pedagogical Creed* – dates from 1897.
3. Reducing worker autonomy was one of Taylor's aims as he believed the worker left to his own devices and not controlled through task specification, would do as little as possible.
4. Max Weber (1864–1920) was a key proponent of methodological antipositivism, arguing for the study of social action through interpretive (rather than purely empiricist) means, based on understanding the purpose and meaning that individuals attach to their own actions. His concern was to understand the processes of rationalisation and secularisation, which he associated with the rise of modernity. His bureaucratic theory (the 'Legal-Rational' model) was appropriated by many State administrations as prescriptive rather than an interpretative model.
5. To facilitate this process there existed different tracks (assembly lines) for different types of students – vocational tracks and academic tracks, normal tracks and special tracks for the then called normal children and handicapped children. This compartmentalised system sometimes created specific school paths for specific social groups.
6. Dewey reformulated his ideas also analysing the experience of other progressive schools and the criticism that his theories have received (p. 7).
7. Transmissive pedagogy and participatory pedagogy are presented as ideal types (pure types) using Max Weber concept – it is a description and interpretation which stresses elements common to most case of the given phenomenon, a synthesis of many diffuse individual phenomena arranged according to a specific viewpoint built into a unified analytical construct. This specific viewpoint is presented in the tables provided. There are many variants of the participatory pedagogy and some of the transmisssive pedagogy.
8. See Oliveira-Formosinho (2007), Oliveira-Formosinho and Formosinho (2012).
9. See also Sousa-Santos (2003b).
10. There were early childhood education centres based on the perspectives of Pestalozzi, Froebel, Montessori, Dewey, Steiner, Kilpatrick, Freinet, Malaguzzi and others.
11. The *academicisation of teacher education,* seen as prevailing academic tendencies in professional certification programmes, is the progressive subordination of teacher training institutions to the logic of the traditional university in the organisational structure (feudal fragmentation of power centred on academic disciplines), the organisation of teaching, the design and curriculum development, rather than the logic inherent to professional training. It is the process of building a predominantly academic logic in a professional certification programme and the enforcement of a positivist applicationist view of education (see Chapter 5) – Formosinho (2002a, 2002b, 2009).

References

Bennett, J. (2006) *Schoolifying early childhood education and care: accompanying pre-school into education.* Public lecture given at the Institute of Education University of London, 10 May 10 2006.

Dewey, J. (1897) My pedagogic creed. *School Journal* 54: 77–80. Available at: https:// archive.org/stream/mypedagogiccree00dewegoog#page/n10/mode/2up (accessed 26 May 2015).

Dewey, J. (1899) *The School and the Society.* Chicago: The University of Chicago Press.

Dewey, J. (1902) *The Child and the Curriculum.* Chicago: The University of Chicago Press.

Dewey, J. (1916) *Democracy and Education: An Introduction to the Philosophy of Education.* New York: Macmillan.

Dewey, J. (1938) *Experience and Education*. Indiana: Kappa Delta Pi.

Formosinho, J. (1987) *Educating for passivity: a study of Portuguese education*. Ph.D. Dissertation, London: University of London, Institute of Education.

Formosinho, J. (2002a) Universitisation of teacher education in Portugal. In O. Gassner (ed.), *Strategies of Change in Teacher Education – European Views*, pp. 105–127. Feldkirch, Austria: ENTEP, European Network on Teacher Education Policies.

Formosinho, J. (2002b) A universidade e a formação de educadores de infância: potencialidades e dilemas. In Maria Lúcia de A Machado (ed.), *Encontros e Desencontros em Educação Infantil*, pp. 169–188. São Paulo, Cortez Editora.

Formosinho, J. (2007) *O currículo uniforme pronto-a-vestir de tamanho único*. Cadernos de Políticas Educativas e Curriculares. Mangualde: Edições Pedago. First edition in *O Insucesso Escolar em Questão, Cadernos de Análise Social da Educação*, ed. J. Formosinho. Braga: Universidade do Minho, 1987.

Formosinho, J. (2009) A academização da formação de professores. In J. Formosinho (ed.), *Formação de professores. Aprendizagem profissional e acção docente*, pp. 287–302. Porto: Porto Editora

Formosinho, J. and Machado, J. (2007) Autor anónimo do século XX. A construção da pedagogia burocrática. In J. Oliveira-Formosinho, T.M. Kishimoto and M.A. Pinazza (eds), *Pedagogia(s) da Infância. Dialogando com o passado, construindo o futuro*, pp. 293–328. Porto Alegre: Artmed Editora.

Formosinho, J. and Machado, J. (2012) Democratic governance of public mass schools in Portugal. In J. Paraskeva and J.T. Santome (eds), *Globalism and Power: Iberian Educational and Curriculum Policies*, pp. 25–41. New York: Peter Lang Publishing.

Formosinho, J., and Oliveira-Formosinho, J. (2008a). *System of Early Education/Care and Professionalization in Portugal*. SEEPRO Project. Pamela Oberhuemer (ed.). München: Staatsinstitut für Früpädagogik. Available at: www.ifp.bayern.de/imperia/md/content/stmas/ifp/commissioned_report_portugal.pdf (accessed 26 May 2015).

Formosinho, J. and Oliveira-Formosinho, J. (2008b) Working with young children in Portugal. In P. Oberhuemer (ed.), *Working with Young Children in Europe*, pp. 353–365. München: Staatsinstitut für Früpädagogik.

Freire, P. (1970a) *Cultural Action for Freedom*. Cambridge: Harvard Educational Review.

Freire, P. (1970b) *Pedagogy of the Oppressed*. New York: The Continuum Publishing Company.

Freire, P. (1976) *Education, the Practice of Freedom*. London: Writers and Readers Publishing Cooperative.

Freire, P. (1993) *Pedagogy of the City*. New York: The Continuum Publishing Company.

Freire, P. (1996) *Pedagogy of the Oppressed*. London: Penguin Books.

Freire, P. (1998) *Pedagogy of Freedom: Ethics, Democracy and Civic Courage*. Lanham: Rowman & Littlefield Publishers.

Freire, P. (2002) *Pedagogy of Hope: Reliving Pedagogy of the Oppressed*. New York: The Continuum Publishing Company.

Freire, P. and Freire, A.M.A. (1997) *Pedagogy of the Heart*. New York: The Continuum Publishing Company.

Freire, P. and Macedo, D. (1995) A dialogue: culture, language, and race. *Harvard Educational Review* 65, 3: 377–403.

Giardello, P. (2013) *Pioneers in Early Childhood Education: The Roots and Legacies of Rachel and Margaret McMillan, Maria Montessori and Susan Isaacs*. London: Routledge.

Moss, P. (2013) *Early Childhood and Compulsory Education: Reconceptualising the Relationship*. London: Routledge.

Moss, P. (2014) *Transformative Change and Real Utopias in Early Childhood Education: A Story of Democracy, Experimentation and Potentiality*. London: Routledge.

Nutbrown, C. and Clough, P. (2014) *Early Childhood Education: History, Philosophy and Experience*. London: Sage.

OECD (2011) *Investing in High Quality Early Childhood Education and Care (ECEC)*. Available at: www.oecd.org/edu/school/48980282.pdf (accessed 26 May 2015).

OECD (2012) *Starting Strong III – A Quality Toolbox for Early Childhood Education and Care*. Paris: OECD.

Oliveira-Formosinho, J. (2001) The specific professional nature of early years education and styles of adult/child interaction. *European Early Childhood Education Research Journal* 9, 1: 57–72.

Oliveira-Formosinho, J. (2007) Pedagogia(s) da infância: Reconstruindo uma práxis de participação. In J. Oliveira-Formosinho, T.M. Kishimoto and M. Pinazza (eds), *Pedagogias(s) da Infância. Dialogando com o passado, construindo o futuro*, pp. 13–36. São Paulo: Artmed Editora.

Oliveira-Formosinho, J. and Araújo, S. B. (2011) Early education for diversity: starting from birth. *European Early Childhood Education Research Journal* 19, 2: 223–235.

Oliveira-Formosinho, J. and Formosinho, J. (2012) *Pedagogy-in-Participation: Childhood Association Educational Perspective*. Porto: Porto Editora.

Pascal, C. and Bertram, T. (2009). Listening to young citizens: the struggle to make real a participatory paradigm in research with young children. *European Early Childhood Education Research Journal* 17, 2: 249–262.

Sousa-Santos, B. (2003a) Introdução: para ampliar o cânone do reconhecimento, da diferença e da igualdade. In B. Sousa-Santos (ed.), *Reconhecer para Libertar: Os caminhos do cosmopolitanismo multicultural*. Rio de Janeiro: Civilização Brasileira.

Sousa-Santos, B. (2003b) Por uma Concepção Multicultural de Direitos Humanos. In B. Sousa-Santos (ed.), *Reconhecer para Libertar: Os caminhos do cosmopolitanismo multicultural*, pp. 429–461. Rio de Janeiro: Civilização Brasileira.

UNESCO (1994) *The Salamanca Statement and Framework for Action on Special Needs Education*. Salamanca, Spain, 7–10 June 1994. Paper: E D-94/WS/ 1 8 United Nations Educational, Scientific and Cultural Organisation, Special Education, Division of Basic Education, Paris.

2

PEDAGOGY-IN-PARTICIPATION

The search for a holistic praxis

Júlia Formosinho and João Formosinho

Introduction

This chapter sets out to present *Pedagogy-in-Participation,* an educational pedagogical perspective that sits in the family of participatory pedagogies. This presentation of a specific approach to pedagogy development is done through a journey that encompasses a democratic worldview, on which it is primarily founded. This is followed by the identification of the pedagogical axes that inspire the creation of educational intentionality for children's daily experiential learning. The acknowledgement of the educational environment as a *second educator* takes us to the analysis of some of the criteria we use for its organisation and unfolds the pedagogic dimensions that are constituents of the learning context and form its educational tapestry. For the purpose of this book, among those dimensions we highlight pedagogic documentation that supports pedagogic assessment and evaluation as fully presented in Chapter 6.

We hope that those who will keep us company in this journey will uncover the highly related concept of *pedagogic isomorphism* as the key for our understanding of the complex and interactive nature of children's and adult's learning.

Pedagogy-in-Participation: a Childhood Association educational perspective

Pedagogy-in-Participation is the educational perspective of the Childhood Association (*Associação Criança*).[1] This is a co-constructive participatory pedagogy for early childhood education under development since the late 1990s (Formosinho and Oliveira-Formosinho, 1996, 2008; Oliveira-Formosinho and Formosinho, 2001, 2012), and used in several early childhood centres in Portugal and abroad. The Childhood Association has been supported since its creation by the Aga Khan

Foundation based in Portugal. Pedagogy-in-Participation is currently used in partnership with the Aga Khan Foundation Portugal in various contexts in the Greater Lisbon area, namely in the Olivais Sul Children's Centre.

Praxis as the locus of pedagogy

Pedagogy is organised around knowledge built on situated action and infused with theories and beliefs (beliefs, values and principles). As Bruner (1996) says, pedagogy is never innocent and is never neutral. Pedagogy is an 'ambiguous' space, not the one-of-two kind, that is, theory and practice, as some say, but a one-of-three kind: action, theories and beliefs in an interactive and constantly renewed triangulation. This triangular movement in the creation of pedagogy results from convening beliefs, values and principles; reflecting on practices; and using knowledge and theories. Thus, pedagogy is sustained on a *praxis*, that is, on *action impregnated in theory and supported by a belief system*. Being praxis the locus of pedagogy, it becomes the locus for pedagogical knowledge development (see Figure 2.1).

Pedagogy is defined as the construction of praxeological knowledge in situated action. As such it refutes both the reductive academicism in which the logic of

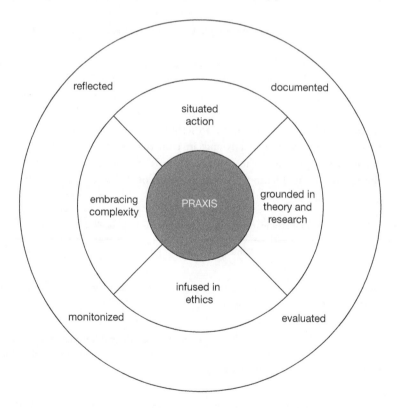

FIGURE 2.1 Praxis

knowledge constitutes a single criterion for knowing and knowledge development, and also the empiricism in which the unreflected primary experience of everyday life constitutes the central reference (Formosinho, 2002a, 2002b). Unlike other scientific domains identified by the establishment of well-defined borders, pedagogical knowing and knowledge is created in the ambiguity and complexity of a space that knows its boundaries but does not define them, because its essence lies in integration.

Pedagogy-in-Participation

There are two basic ways for developing pedagogy as explored in Chapter 1: the *transmissive* mode and the *participatory* mode (Oliveira-Formosinho, 1998, 2004, 2007).[2] Transmissive pedagogy focuses on the knowledge that is to be conveyed, while participatory pedagogies focus on the actors who co-construct knowledge by participating in the learning process. As said, Pedagogy-in-Participation sits in the family of participatory pedagogies.[3] It is essentially *the creation of pedagogic environments in which interactions and relationships sustain joint activities and projects*; this enables the child and the group to co-construct their own learning and celebrate their achievements (Formosinho and Oliveira-Formosinho, 2008; Oliveira-Formosinho, 1998).

We will use the structure shown in Table 2.1 to present our pedagogic perspective.

According to Dewey (1939), democracy is more than a form of government. It is primarily a form of living together, of communicative shared experience, a way of life controlled by a working faith in the possibilities of human nature.

Democracy is at the heart of Pedagogy-in-Participation's system of beliefs, values and principles. Early childhood education settings and centres should be organised so that democracy is both a means and an end, that is, it is present as a major educational goal, as well as in the context of a participatory daily life experienced by all the central actors. Democracy is at the heart of Pedagogy-in-Participation's

TABLE 2.1 Pedagogy-in-Participation: a democratic, solidary perspective

a)	theoretical support: beliefs, values and knowledge
b)	pedagogic axes
c)	experiential learning (the creation of experiential situations for the development of pedagogic axes)
d)	areas of learning
e)	organisation of the educational environment for experiential learning (spaces and times, pedagogic materials, learning groups, adult-child(ren) interactions, planning with the child, activities and projects)
f)	parents' involvement
g)	pedagogic documentation and connected evaluation procedures

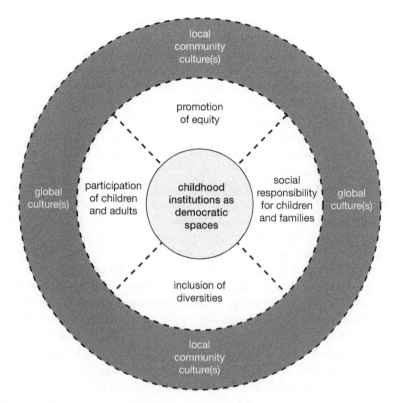

FIGURE 2.2 Early childhood education centres as democratic spaces

beliefs also because it stresses the promotion of equity for all and the inclusion of all diversities (see Figure 2.2).

These principles should imbue all levels of educational intervention: the definition of educational objectives, the choice of methods for the development of everyday learning and its evaluation, the organisation of educational institutions, the organisation of staff development and the development of research. Learning goals, for children and adults alike, should be permeated by ideals of democracy and participation. The congruence of values, beliefs and principles for all actors is the requirement for an isomorphic dynamic as an ethical proposal. This implies the need for a coherent quotidian that analyses praxis by the principles that should sustain it, with respect for children's learning as well as adult learning, and at the level of organisation, pedagogy and research.

To begin from the concept of democracy as the belief and founding value of this set of principles is to begin from a certain view of the world. This is not naive optimism, but rather a hard challenge to create conditions for humans, both children and adults, to use the ability at their disposal. It is this 'agency' that makes us free and collaborative human beings, capable of thinking and of reflexive, intelligent and solidary action.[4] Solidary learning (to be presented in Chapter 6) develops through solidary teaching in a deep interconnectedness of children's and teachers' thinking, feeling and doing.

This set of starting points leads to the assertion of respect for all individuals and groups involved in educational processes. Pedagogy-in-Participation promotes the intercultural dialogue between groups and individuals involved in pedagogical processes; it endorses collaborative learning in looking for educational success for all. The concept of democracy develops in a context of respect for human rights (including the rights of children, namely the right to learn) and of identity development for children and professionals which is also an educative process of self-identity development of themselves and others as learners.

Pedagogy-in-Participation finds it necessary and indispensable to exercise consciousness (Freire, 2005) of what traditional pedagogy is, deconstructing it in its essential features (Formosinho and Machado, 2007; Formosinho, 2007a, 2007b) and in its process of educating for passivity (Formosinho, 1987), as seen in Chapter 1. Pedagogy-in-Participation faces the dual challenge of enduring hope and permanent construction and reconstruction that is required by participatory pedagogies in the context of critical reflexive deconstruction (Freire, 2002).

The roles of student and teachers (both learners) in Pedagogy-in-Participation are based on the re-conceptualisation of the person (the person of the student and the person of the teacher) as possessing competence and agency and the ability and taste to collaborate, and as having the right to participate. Children and adults developing activities and projects (through joint thinking, joint doing and joint reflecting) assert themselves as co-authors of learning as a basis for knowing.

The educational objectives in Pedagogy-in-Participation are to support the child's involvement in the experiential continuum, and the construction of learning through interactive and continuous experience, in which the child has the right to participate as well as the right to sensitive, empowering and stimulating support from the educator (Bertram, 1996). Joint attention (Tomasello, 1998, 2009) has been conceptualised within Pedagogy-in-Participation as *learning in companionship (aprender em companhia)*. It is known that children's and teachers' joint attention to objects, actions and situations creates attunement and is a base for inter-subjectivity.

The child's activity is exercised in collaboration with its peers and with the educator at all levels, and very specifically in the area of planning, doing and reflecting about the activities and projects. In Dewey's terms, these collaboration processes lead to the development of togetherness and facilitate the encounter of minds.

The child's motivation for experiential learning is developed through a process of identifying interests, motivations and hopes, creating intentionality and purpose, and dialoguing with the educator's professional motivations whose professionalism and identity is projected when meeting with the child. The educator's central role is to co-organise the educational environment and to observe, listen and document in order to understand and respond, extending the interests and knowledge of the child and the group towards culture(s). Learning develops in cultural encounters of children and adults together.

The teaching method centred on learning gives the child, the collaboration among peers and the educator's collaboration an important role, developing a constructive, interactive and collaborative methodology as a pathway to knowing, sustained by the development of a local educational community (Formosinho, 1989; Formosinho et al., 1999) and a learning community (Wenger, 1998). Pedagogy is seen as an encounter of cultures.

In this context it becomes essential to carry out a constant professional self-monitoring of the adult-child interactions through reflexive questioning: do these interactions develop attunement with the child? Do they favour autonomy and simultaneously create interdependence? Do they promote listening, accept decisions, organise processes and provide stimulation? Do they contribute to the well-being, involvement and learning of the children, the parents and the educators?

Pedagogy-in-Participation is essentially the *creation of educational environments in which the ethics of relationships and interactions enable the development of activities and projects* that allow children to live, learn, mean and create, because they value the children's and families' experience, knowledge and culture dialoguing with the educator's knowledge and culture.

Pedagogy-in-Participation's pedagogical axes

Pedagogical axes inspire the process of creating educational intentionality; they define the central lines guiding think-do-think processes in everyday educational life and learning (Formosinho and Oliveira-Formosinho, 1996, 2008). These axes indicate the fields in which one aspires to negotiate and develop purposes, objectives, means, processes, documentation, evaluation and research. They constitute mediators between theory and praxis.

Figure 2.3 shows the pedagogic axes (anchors) of Pedagogy-in-Participation defined by the processes of theory development, intervention and research that have been developed by the Childhood Association team.

These axes are deeply interdependent and meant to inspire and organise educational processes that aim to collaborate in the construction and development of socio-cultural-historical identities. This is pedagogy as a process for strengthening identities: to cultivate humanity through education, making it a process for cultivating the being, the bonds, the learning and the meaning.

We conceptualise pedagogy as a process for strengthening identities: to cultivate humanity through education, making it a process for cultivating the relational holistic *being* in context(s) and culture(s), the *competent* learner in communication, dialogue and participation, the *meaning maker* in progress.

Edgar Morin's thinking (1986, 1999a, 199b) has been an inspiration for Pedagogy-in-Participation to look at the whole child as unity and diversity in processes that weave together identities and communities, senses and intelligences, exploration and communication, creation of meaning through multiple narrations developed in the comfort of belonging and the right to participate in learning, immersed in a welcoming educational context.

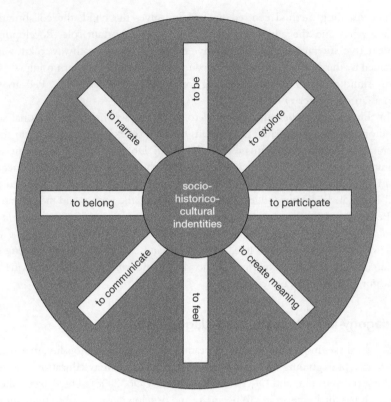

FIGURE 2.3 Pedagogic axes of Pedagogy-in-Participation

The journey to develop these intentionalities clearly shows dialogic processes that weave together the thinking and the research of many of the members of Childhood Association.[5]

Being/feeling/thinking

Exploring Figure 2.3, the *first pedagogical axis – being/feeling/thinking* – provides intentionality to a *pedagogy of identities' development* in which learning emerges, from birth, focused on the development of identities that share similarities and differences (see Figure 2.4). We hope to develop plural identities because we aim to include all diversities, emphasising humans as inherently plural social beings. Children's individual identities in social educational contexts begin to learn from birth to engage with educators' and peers' plural identities that can help them to be plural themselves (Oliveira-Formosinho and Araújo, 2011). If the educational environment is designed to promote plural identities and the inner-social-plural identity of the self, the other's difference is not a barrier; the conviviality of rainbows of identities helps to learn to develop permeable boundaries. Our first pedagogical concern is the creation of a climate of well-being for children and families alike where children's

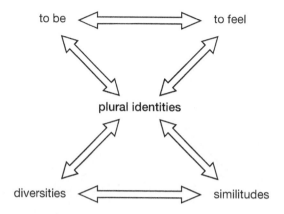

FIGURE 2.4 Being, thinking, feeling

plural selves are welcomed and respected. The socio-cultural process of identity development starts with personal identity development in relationships.

This first central axis of plural identities in development through relationships and interactions, in educational contexts interactive with other life contexts, has been inspired in Oliveira-Formosinho (1987, 1992). Learners' identities need to have space to develop as personal, social identities. Learners in their processes of identity development in interaction with peers and teachers need educators that tune with them, challenge and provoke them, support and scaffold them (Oliveira-Formosinho, 1998, 2001; Araújo, 2011; Wertsch, 1985).

Belonging and participation

The *second pedagogical axis, the belonging and participation axis*, provides intentionality to the *pedagogy of bonds* and connectedness in which the recognition of belonging to the family is progressively broadened to recognition of belonging to the early childhood centre and to the educational community. This axis also gives intentionality to learning the differences and similarities in the human process of developing bonds, relationships and belongings (see Figure 2.5). Participation gains meaning in these contexts of belonging where one can participate. The growth in participation is facilitated when the child feels that he/she 'belongs here' because she/he is respected and responded to. The wish to belong is there as a social impulse; the educational environment needs to be designed to read signals, to listen, to tune in, to respond; to make visible the respect for children and families; to include funds of knowledge (Moll et al., 1992) of the families to which children belong.

'Belonging here' (to the early childhood centre) is made easier when children feel the respect for their families' belonging (Formosinho, 1989). The connectivity between belongings, the promotion of ties with the families facilitates the

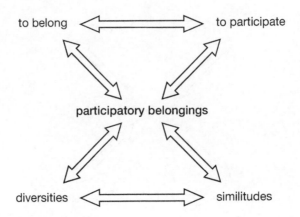

FIGURE 2.5 Belonging and participating

development of feelings of belonging to the early childhood centre. Families' involvement in their children's centre helps them to learn to be strong in participation in the centre daily life (Whalley, 1994, 2001), and helps them to participate with their inner strengths and their families' funds of knowledge (Moll et al., 1992).[6] These funds represent cognitive and cultural resources for children's education in a democratic pedagogical approach.

A central inspiration for this axis has been João Formosinho's PhD thesis *Education for passivity: a study of Portuguese education* presented at the Institute of Education, London University (1987). Formosinho with his research on education for passivity has deconstructed the Portuguese traditional educational system of Salazar's dictatorship showing that it was designed for cultural passivity through pedagogic conformity and administrative bureaucratic control. With this piece of research he points to a new approach to education centred on participation. One of the first anchors for the development of the educational intentionality of Pedagogy-in-Participation is participation in learning and in the life of the educational community. This contribution helps to develop feelings of belonging and promotes further participation.

The bureaucratic control of central government can be also exerted though the curriculum as another piece of Formosinho's (1987, 2007a) research evidences: the *ready to wear single size curriculum*, through the promotion of a one-size-fits-all educational proposal, takes away the participation both from teachers and students. This makes very difficult the creation of a school educational community (Formosinho, 1989) and even the educators-children learning communities (Oliveira-Formosinho, 1987; Kohlberg, 1987).

João Formosinho's deconstruction of pedagogic passivity shows that the creation of educational communities starts with a pedagogical proposal that puts forward the right for all to participate in a shared project.[7]

Languages and communication

The *third pedagogical axis*, the *languages and communication axis*, defines an *experiential learning pedagogy* in which the intentionality is that of doing – experiencing in continuity and interactivity, in reflection and in communication, in autonomy and collaboration. To explore, experience, reflect, analyse and communicate is a process that enables learning to think and learning to know. As in the other pedagogical axes, it enhances learning and knowing, in a spiralling manner, understanding similarities and differences (Oliveira-Formosinho and Araújo, 2011) (see Figure 2.6). Freire (2005) asserts that only through communication can human life hold meaning. The communication of explorations of the world using intelligent senses and sensitive intelligences (Formosinho and Oliveira-Formosinho, 2008) opens up for the child possible worlds of meaning. The educational environment seeks to develop attunement with each child's modes of exploration and communication. This is achieved through its pedagogical organisation, its pedagogical mediation styles and strategies, its approach to pedagogical documentation as narration and celebration of plural learning journeys and its respectful evaluation.

Malaguzzi (1998) has been a central inspiration for this third axis, to explore/to communicate, when we refer to children in communicative exploration using *one hundred languages* and having the right to see their learning documented and by that mean facilitating re-visitation, communication, memory, narration and metacognition.

Narration and learning journeys

The *fourth pedagogical axis* (see Figure 2.7), the *narration of learning journeys axis*, enables another order of intentionality and understanding that becomes a basis for learning about learning and learning about oneself as a learner. This axis of pedagogic intentionality aims at seeing the learner in the learning and the 'learning in the

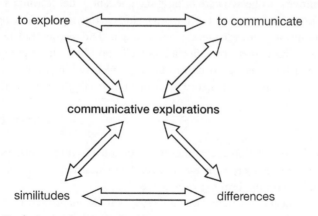

FIGURE 2.6 Exploring and communicating

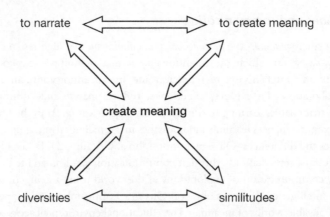

FIGURE 2.7 Narrating and creating meaning

making' (Carr and Lee, 2012). Children's access to pedagogical documentation about their own and their peers' learning gives them access to the multiple forms of creating the reality of learning – through the stories of their own learning. Pedagogic documentation is a form of narration of learning journeys that allows children's conversations with their processes of learning and its achievements (Bruner, 1996). Pedagogic documentation facilitates the distance and the proximity of the learner from him/herself through narration. This duality of distance and proximity from the doing that is facilitated by the documentation supports the children to create meaning for their learning and to see themselves learning, remembering and thinking, creating knowledge and knowing.

Bruner (1990, 1996) provided inspiration for this axis in his understanding of:

> modern pedagogy as moving increasingly to the view that the child should be aware of her own thought processes, and that it is crucial for the pedagogical theorist and teacher alike to help her to become more meta-cognitive – to be as aware of how she goes about her learning and thinking as she is about the subject matter she is studying. Achieving skill and accumulating knowledge are not enough. The learner can be helped to achieve full mastery by reflecting as well upon how she is going about her job and how her approach can be improved. Equipping her with a good theory of mind – or a theory of mental functioning – is one part of helping her to do so.
>
> (Bruner, 1996, p. 64)

Pedagogic documentation as a narration of individual learning journeys is a natural vehicle for the organisation of experience. The narrative is very appropriate for framing and telling the learning experience.

Bruner's concept of narrative thought (1996) can be understood as an instrument of social negotiation of meaning. Bruner (1990, 1996) has been inspirational for this axis in his understanding of young children's search for meaning through early narratives. For Bruner (1990) the narrative is a natural vehicle for the organisation of experience. The narrative is seen as typical for the frame of experience.

The understanding of the axes of Pedagogy-in-Participation's educational intentionality borders between the ideology of rights in which it is sustained and the action fields in which it develops.

Experiential learning: the creation of experiential situations for the development of pedagogical axes

Pedagogy-in-Participation creates educational intentionality around these axes and cultivates identities and relationships that sustain the recognition of similarities and diversities. Pedagogy-in-Participation develops *experiential learning* and the construction of meaning through the use of intelligent senses and sensitive intelligences, creating conversations and dialogues which are expressed in the richness of plural languages that serve the organisation and narration of the learning experiences. The interconnection of the intentionality axes requires the promoting and documenting of learning experiences in each of these axes, involves their integration for the advance of a holistic pedagogy that values holistic identities. Experiential learning is transversal. The work around the four axes contributes to a new understanding of intercultural pedagogy, one that weaves together the four central intentionality dimensions creating a bond between them and raising awareness about the unity of the multiple and the multiplicity of the one (Morin, 1999b).

Pedagogy-in-Participation proposes the creation of experiential situations for the development of identities and relationships (relational identities), and for the development of belonging and participation (participatory belongings). It proposes the creation of a complex pedagogy (Morin, 1999a), in which the experiential learning of the 'hundred languages' integrates with the experiential learning of identities development and participatory belongings. Thinking, reflecting and communicating throughout this learning pathway enables meaning making about the world of objects and persons, of nature and culture, of knowing and ethics, of rights and duties.

The educational *objectives* need a method that does not reduce reality – the reality of being, relating and experiencing; so this is the support for learning. The meaning for learning lies in the creation of relationships within reflected narrated experience.

Figure 2.8 shows experiential learning as the co-construction of knowing and knowledge through experience and reflection on that experience. Experiences create boundaries between the child and the world, turning them into a relational experiential continuum. The reflexive documented manner of living such a holistic experience makes it a possible vehicle of narration and meaning.

An educator who uses Pedagogy-in-Participation organises the educational environment so as to create opportunities that are rich in experiential possibilities and the narratives which flow from it. This allows the development of

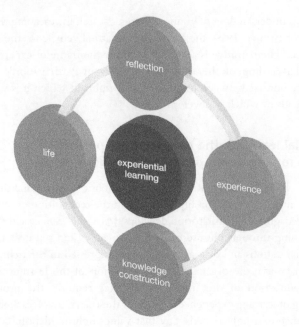

FIGURE 2.8 Experiential learning

manipulation, exploration and representation; and allows communication about manipulation, exploration and representation experiences and narrative experiences supported by documentation and aiming at the creation of meaning.

Pedagogy-in-Participation: learning areas

The interactivity within each pole of the educational intentionality axes and the interconnectivity between the axes indicate four central experiential learning areas: identities, relationships, languages and meanings. The learning opportunities of the educational environment should provide experiential learning in the development of identities and relationships, as well as in the learning of one hundred languages and the construction of meaning. The experience of exploring the world with access to cultural instruments such as the *hundred languages* (Malaguzzi, 1998) opens opportunities to participate in the socio-historical cultural inheritance. It is vital to negotiate with the children purposes, trajectories and learning journeys in these four areas (identities, relationships, languages and meanings). It is also vital to make sure that learning is integrated with learning to learn, as the mode of teaching in a participatory pedagogy is essentially concerned with the mode of learning. Pedagogy is a mode that carries messages and meanings.

Figure 2.9 shows the four areas of intentionality for learning and their relationship to the pedagogic axes.

The two first learning areas, *identities and relationships*, are the result of the intersection of two pedagogical axes: being-feeling-thinking and belonging-

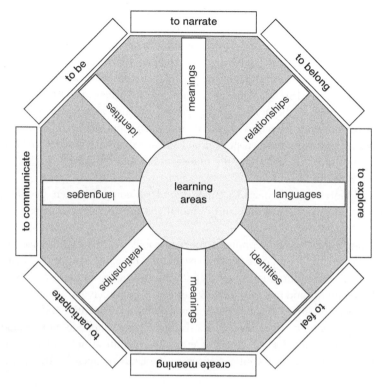

FIGURE 2.9 Pedagogy-in-Participation learning areas

participation. Both promote the development of plural identities and multiple relationships, and lead to learning about me (body, mind, spirit) (Morin, 1999a), about others (bodies, minds, spirits) and also to learning about relationships, bonds, connectedness and participation. These are areas of learning that are vital for children, so it is necessary for the educational context to provide experience in these areas. This experience is gathered from birth onwards, throughout the childhood education period, and is as important as the experience of communicative and meaningful ownership of cultural languages and of curriculum content.

The two other areas of learning, *languages and meanings*, are the result of the intersection of two other pedagogical axes (exploring and communicating, and creating and narrating the learning journeys), projecting the cultural learning of one hundred languages, of cultural content and of psychological functions (Vygotsky, 1998).

From birth and throughout life, children need and want to answer central questions such as:

> Who am I? Who is she/he? How do we relate? How do I feel? How does she/he feel? How do they see me? How do I see them? Where do I belong? How do I contribute? Am I allowed to use my sensitive intelligences and

intelligent senses? What do I learn? How do I learn to be a learner? How do I answer? How can I get an answer? How can I engage in this process of developing the self, the other, the subjectivity and inter-subjectivity? Do I feel I belong? Am I growing in participation? Am I using the available cultural instruments (plural languages)? Am I regarded as a meaning maker? Am I observed in my signs? Am I heard in my questions? Am I respected in my need to be a learner that grows on skills and factual knowledge integrated with reflection, thinking, and meta-cognition? Am I treated as an active, agent, intentional person and learner that co-construct knowledge about the world and about the understanding of each other?

Early childhood centres need to support understanding between people as a condition and protection of humanity's moral and intellectual solidarity:

> Human understanding implies subject-to-subject knowledge. If I see a child crying, I am not going to understand his tears by measuring their salt content but by finding my own childish distress deep inside, by identifying him with me and me with him. We do not only perceive others objectively, we perceive them as other subjects with whom we identify and whom we identify with ourselves, an ego alter that becomes an alter ego. Understanding necessarily includes a process of empathy, identification, and projection. Understanding, always inter-subjective, demands an open heart, sympathy, generosity.
>
> (Morin, 1999b, p. 50)

Children's experiential learning opportunities are the vehicle for learning cultural tools such as the hundred languages and for the development of higher psychological functions such as attention, memory, imagination and reflection (Vygotsky, 1998).

The learning of cultural tools and the development of higher mental functions take place in reflected use and thoughtful action – they are learned in action. As Malaguzzi (1998) reminded us, the same is true for intelligence, i.e. intelligence is developed by using it in reflection required by experience, during and after the action it causes. Communication with others supports this development and human understanding (Formosinho and Oliveira-Formosinho, 2008).

Organisation of the educational environment for experiential learning

The nature/nurture debate is very important for pedagogic thinking. We know that children's learning and development is both a natural phenomenon that is dependent on nature and a nurturing phenomenon depending on culture where pedagogy occupies a central space. The conception of the child as a personal and cultural subject forces us to rethink their living environments, specifically their educational contexts. Recent understanding about young children as cultural beings, with agency and rights, stresses that schools should be quality nurturing contexts. Children as socio-cultural beings have the right to educational contexts that are respectful, welcoming of children and families alike, and provocative in what concerns the development of plural learners' identities.

Bettelheim and Zelan (1982) ask, 'Do we make the environment or does the environment makes us?' The second half of the twentieth century brought many contributions to the understanding of life contexts and their interactions in the processes of children's learning and development, emphasising the importance of lived experience in contexts and its interpretation. Lewin (1948) sustains the idea that the social climate where children live is as important for the development of feelings of security as the air she/he breathes. Foucault (1975) analyses the processes of space and time organisation for the formation of certain habits and behaviours. Bronfenbrenner (1979) studies the influence of the micro and macro environments and their interactions in children's learning and development.

Integrated pedagogical dimensions

The available knowledge regarding the importance of life contexts as spaces and times for the development of identities and learning is so challenging for educators and researchers alike that we need an in-depth question raising process regarding how to conceptualise and create them in the quotidian of children's centres. This requires a research journey that goes from an implicit to an explicit view of a pedagogic approach to the development of learning contexts. This means to reconceptualise pedagogical understandings about the organisation of the educational environments as living-learning multidimensional contexts whose dimensions are interdependent.

Within Pedagogy-in-Participation the thinking about the educational environment never ends; the creation of educational environments is for us a constant *experiment in democracy* because its primary purpose is the inclusion of all voices and the answers to each and all of them (Pascal and Bertram, 2009).

The educational environment is a delicate and dynamic texture. The educational environment conveys messages, collaborates (or not) in the development of the educational project and its objectives. It supports (or not) the educators and the centre's educational ideology. It respects (or not) children's rights to co-author their learning.

The construction of knowledge by the child requires a social and educational context that supports, promotes, facilitates and celebrates participation, i.e. a context that participates in the construction of participation because ultimately learning means growing in participation (Rogoff, 1990). Pedagogy-in-Participation wants to develop contexts that participate in participation, educational contexts that facilitate and promote co-construction of learning.

To develop Pedagogy-in-Participation as a responsive listening process it is necessary to consider several dimensions of pedagogy (see Figure 2.10) – pedagogical spaces, materials and times; the organisation of groups; the quality of relationships

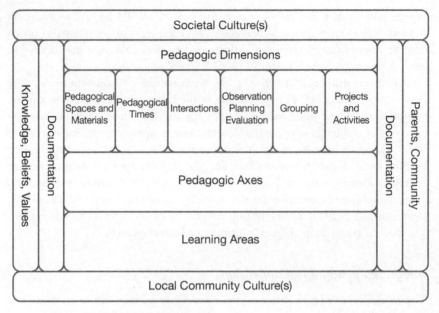

FIGURE 2.10 Integrated pedagogic dimensions

and interactions; the observation, planning and evaluation of learning; the activities and projects that bring to life the co-construction of learning; pedagogical documentation that creates memory, learning and meta-learning and sustains evaluation; the involvement of parents, families and communities. The quality of the several pedagogical dimensions impact differently on the co-construction of children's learning. The quality of the delicate tapestry formed by the interconnectivity of these dimensions conforms one or other type of educational context.

Organisation of pedagogical space

There is an indisputable pedagogicity in the materiality of space says Paulo Freire regarding his visit to schools in São Paulo, Brazil's municipal schooling system as São Paulo State Secretary of Education.

> In 'Education in the City,' I drew attention to this fact . . . How is it possible to ask of the children the minimum of respect for their material surroundings when the authorities demonstrated such absolute neglect of and indifference to the public institutions under their care? It's really unbelievable that we are unable to include all these elements in our 'rhetoric' about education. Why does such 'rhetoric' not include hygiene, cleanliness, beauty? Why does it neglect the indisputable pedagogical value of the 'materiality' of the school environment?
>
> (Freire, 1998, p. 48)

Pedagogy-in-Participation acknowledges the indisputable pedagogicity in the materiality of educational spaces. In Pedagogy-in-Participation the space is seen as a place of well-being, joy and pleasure; a space open to plural experiences and interests of children and communities. A pedagogical space is for us open to the outside that features the communicative power of nature, the ethical power of respect for every personal and social identity, turned safe and friendly haven, open to play and to culture, and a guarantor of cultural learning. The creation of different areas with their own materials (library, artistic expressions area, symbolic play area, science and experiments area, games and construction area, etc.) facilitates the co-construction of meaningful learning. As the areas are plural territories for life, experience and learning, the organisation of space is not permanent: it must adapt to the development of activities and projects over the year, and should incorporate materials produced by the children.

Organisation of pedagogical materials

The classroom space gains pedagogical density with the educator's professional decisions in the selection of pedagogical materials, toys and multicultural artefacts. It gains ethical density when children and families are respected and involved in the selection of pedagogic materials. *Pedagogical materials* are central to promotion of play and games, similarities and differences, learning with well-being (Laevers, 2005; Araújo, 2011). The pedagogical materials are a central mainstay for the educator's pedagogic mediation with the children in order to facilitate play and learning.

A pedagogic approach that promotes plural identities, such as Pedagogy-in-Participation, is inspired by this plurality in the selection of the learning materials. They are utilised for an in-action view of the activities they enable to develop and to ask in reflection: Is this doll a sexist instrument? Does this doll contribute to an aggressive image of masculinity? Do these books contain stories about other cultures? Do the materials for symbolic play (materials of the make believe area) represent only the national cultural traditions or are they open to the realities of other nations, continents and cultures? Is the pedagogicity of materials a vehicle for intercultural education?

The plurality of experiences that are created when mediated by the pedagogical dimension of the materials strengthens the consistency of the founding theoretical proposal for everyday learning. The image of a competent child as the subject of rights and, specifically, of the right to participate in collaboration with peers and adults finds differentiated support depending on the choice of the pedagogic materials. Methods are not neutral, rather they are instruments riddled with ideology (Morin, 1999a). The pedagogical materials, which in early childhood education are allies to educators because they mediate the professional's mediation, are an integral part of the method. They are loaded with ideology. The one hundred languages, the multiple intelligences and senses, all the diversities (personal, social and cultural), may or may not be present though their mediation. They are the key for the development of the specific educational participatory ideology.

In the scope of Pedagogy-in-Participation, the selection, availability and use of materials are conceived upstream and downstream: upstream as the initial choice should be consistent with the educational theory that supports the pedagogical perspective; downstream as their continued use in everyday life should be based on an evaluative reflection about the persistence of this consistency. Since praxis integrates theory and beliefs into action, Pedagogy-in-Participation must systematically assess the humanising pedagogicity of the materials it makes use of, because the experiences of children with the objects constitute transactions in which learners' identities are constituted as a reality in constant change.

Organisation of pedagogical times

Pedagogical time organises the day with a daily routine that respects the children's rhythms, taking into account well-being and learning. Pedagogical time is asked to include polyphony of rhythms: that of the individual child, that of the small groups and that of the entire group. Pedagogical time is also asked to include a number of purposes, multiple experiences, cognition and emotion, plural languages, and different cultures and diversities.[8] The spaces and times lived are relational, i.e. the organisation, diversity, beauty and wealth of the space, of the time and of the materials gain meaning through relationships and interactions that humanise life and learning.

Organisation of learning groups

The meaning of participation is sometimes presented in simplistic and opposing perspectives. There is a *restrictive perspective* that says that each child must be allowed to influence the decision-making process. Thus, the pedagogical proposal is for teaching individual children, based on the assertion of the knowledge of their rights, to develop confidence, including the right to participate in the decision-making processes regarding matters that concern them. The main objective is that each child will develop the power to influence learning processes.

The *collaborative perspectives* emphasise the idea of a group or of a class (and of the education centre) as a learning community where interactions and relationships are central, and where the sense of belonging and participation is cultivated as a manner for attaining community. John Dewey's concept of togetherness is very inspiring here as well as Lawrence Kohlberg's (1985) concept of a just community within a school. It is desirable to educate children to be assertive in what concerns their participation rights using their powers, but we understand that individual affirmation should not be sought without a communitarian sense of affirmation. On the other hand, this communitarian sense will not be fulfilled in an integrated manner if the individuals in the learning community are not able to be affirmative. Transformative participative pedagogy must ensure that it supports both the social actor in context, with multiple ways of participation, and the growing up personal actor, an autonomous subject with its own expression and initiative. Pedagogy is again revealed in all its complexity, integrating the individual autonomy of exercising power and influence with the social, reciprocal and relational exercise of collective participation.

Throughout the daily routine as a sequence of systems there are several manners of participation and involvement of children in the co-construction of experiential learning – individually, in pairs, in small groups, in a large group. Pedagogy-in-Participation favours the organisation of heterogeneous groups (concerning age, psychological and social characteristics), reflecting the surrounding cultural diversity.

Developing interactions, activities and projects

The organisation of the educational environment sustains the development of relationships and interactions and promotes activities and projects.

Interacting with the child(ren)

Adult-child interactions are such an important dimension of pedagogy that the analysis of the style of these interactions allows us to determine whether it is a transmissive pedagogy or a participative pedagogy (Oliveira-Formosinho, 2007). The *relationships and interactions* are the central means for achieving a participative pedagogy (Oliveira-Formosinho, 1998, 2001; Araújo, 2011). Developing inter-actions, reflecting on them, thinking them and reconstructing them is a *habitus* (Bourdieu, 1990) that the professionals who develop Pedagogy-in-Participation need to develop.

Mediating learning in which the child has agency requires self-monitoring of interactive styles (Bertram and Pascal, 2004, 2006), because not all are equal promoters of the exercise of the child's agency. The teacher's agency as the power to make a difference in pedagogy requires transforming structures, systems, processes and interactions that may eventually constitute a hindrance to the children's agency and to participatory experiential learning. Mediating the child's agency requires an understanding of the interdependence between the child who is learning and the context of learning where adult-child(ren) interaction(s) are central (Oliveira-Formosinho, 2001). Mediating the child's agency requires ethics to recognise that the active participation of children in learning depends on the educational context and the processes it develops.

Pedagogy-in-Participation is a proposal that honours the relational identities as a precondition for experiential learning; it incorporates the co-construction of learning in the flow of pedagogical interactions. The construction of pedagogical interactions as mediators of the right of every child to be respected and to participate has been theoretically developed, empirically researched and day-to-day reflected upon by cooperating professionals.

Planning with the child(ren)

Transformative childhood pedagogy emphasises pedagogic planning which conceptualises the child as a person not someone waiting to be a person, a person with agency, a person who reads and understands the world, who builds knowledge and culture, who participates as an individual and as a citizen in family life, school and society. The 'trades' of child and teacher are reconstructed based on the reconceptualisation of the person with agency: the person of the learner and the person of the teacher.

Planning in Pedagogy-in-Participation creates moments in which children have the right to listen to themselves defining their intentions, and moments in which children listen to the intentions of others, or to those of the teacher. One important role of the adults is to create space for the child to listen to him/herself. Planning is intended to give the child the power to listen to her/himself and to communicate this listening; it is a humanising process – the child knows that listening to her/himself and to others is guaranteed. The child who listens creates a *habitus* of including intentions and purposes, and making decisions; the educator creates the corresponding *habitus* of including the purposes of the child and of negotiating the activities and projects, promoting a cooperative experiential learning. This is a process of negotiating the curriculum with children through the negotiation of educational planning. This process requires observation as an on-going process, because it requires the knowledge of each individual child in his/her learning journey in the making, his/her creation of meaning from experiential learning, necessarily different from the assignment of meaning of another individual child who, although of the same age, has another life story, another experience, another family culture.

This requires a symbiosis between theory and practice. Therefore it requires the observation of 'child-in-action': not the observation of the isolated child but the child situated in a number of contexts – family, school and community. It requires listening as a process of hearing the children's thoughts on their collaboration in the co-construction of knowledge, i.e. on their collaboration in the co-definition of their learning journey. Beyond the discussion of listening modes, it is important to access the integrated holistic understanding of listening. Listening, like observation, must be a continuous process in everyday education, a process of seeking knowledge about children, their interests, motivations, relationships, knowledge, intentions, desires, life worlds, in the context of an educational community that is seeking an ethics of reciprocity. Thus, listening or observing should be a safe haven for contextualising and designing educational situations; it requires negotiation as a process of debating and achieving consensus with each child and the group. It is a guided participation of the class in the co-definition of educational experiences. It is an instrument of participation which further disconnects the co-constructivist perspective from the traditional perspective, as it leads learners to access the 'holy of holies' of transmissive pedagogy, the curriculum. It creates solidary planning.[9]

Developing activities and projects

Revisiting Dewey (1910) and Kilpatrick (2006) to deconstruct and reconstruct the project work, we relearned that activities and projects are both intentional acts – the basic unit that brings activities and projects together is intentionality. Children listening to themselves, discovering their interests and motivations, progressively unravel the intentionality they confer to the situated actions. Children discover themselves as people with motivational dynamics and with the ability to act intentionally and rationally within these living dynamics that are their interests, creating purposes or experiential scripts for the development of purposes.

Children in Pedagogy-in-Participation develop, in the company of peers and adults, activities and projects that enable experiential learning at the levels of content and learning how to learn. The experience of the educational environment, with the flow of interactions and relationships that this experience holds, mediates the learning constructed through activities and projects. Activities and projects both imply the involvement of children and the same motivational dynamics; however projects imply necessarily a more persistent and enduring involvement based on supported problem-solving research by a group of children.

Pedagogy-in-Participation is concerned with the symbiosis of learning between content and method, that is, the ways to construct this content. On Dewey's and Morin's heels, it flees from the empty formalism of those who emphasise only one of the poles of the duality of the learning process: either the methods or the contents. The integration and interactivity of method and content redeems the learning of reductionism which represents a mere accentuation of the method or the mere accentuation of content, and ventures us into a pedagogy of complexity (Morin, 1999a) and significance (Bruner, 1990). The child is redeemed as an active and competent subject, and the learner is redeemed as a participatory pedagogical subject who, in the company of others, develops the powers to participate in the experiential learning script and in its acquisitions. The image of the competent child and its participatory role in the learning process is redeemed. An epistemology of participation and integration is created.

There are no neutral dimensions in pedagogy. The way one thinks and materialises the core dimensions of pedagogy is imbued with a vision of the world, of life, of man and of society, of knowledge and specifically of the relationship between child and knowledge. In line with Dewey and Kilpatrick, it implies redeeming knowledge-in-action, i.e. the practical knowledge as a living expression of the rational and ethical connection of the transactions between the subject and the world (Freire, 2005). The goal is to redeem democracy in early childhood education, allowing the child to exercise its powers in the situation in which experiential learning is developed.

In transmissive education, the children's activities are pre-programmed by the teacher. The project, if and when it appears, emerges as something different but is often assimilated and accommodated in the traditional way of performing activities. Pedagogy-in-Participation proposes that, in an educational context that promotes the participation of children and the discussion of issues, activities and projects are born of the same motivational dynamics and gain intentionality for and in the action.

Pedagogic documentation

Pedagogic documentation as a process of constructing meaning for pedagogic situations

Pedagogic documentation is developed through an interconnection of processes for the study of children's learning, and also the learning of professionals and parents. Pedagogy-in-Participation places documentation at the centre of the learning process, as documenting allows description, analysis and interpretation of the learning experience and the narration of learning. It also supports meaning making about the learning experiences and about the development of the learner. It is a sound basis for assessment and evaluation (Azevedo and Oliveira-Formosinho, 2008). Documentation enables the professional community to describe, understand and interpret the everyday pedagogic life experience and learning of children (Azevedo, 2009) and the professional life experience of educators. Documentation allows children to see themselves learning, allows educators to see their contribution to children's learning. One of the great values attributed to pedagogical documentation is that it brings pedagogical practices out of anonymity, making them visible and allowing cultures and identities to dialogue: the culture of the child and the culture of the adult, the identity of the child and the identity of the educator. These processes create evidence for the understanding of children as beings who feel, think, act, explore, communicate, narrate, that is, who live and learn.

Documentation is currently understood as a process of constructing meaning for pedagogic situations. This (re)meaning of the concept is due essentially to the fact that the teaching and learning process has been reconceptualised and dreamed as more democratic, assuming the participation of central actors (teachers, children, families). Learning is understood as a co-construction process that requires the involvement of its key players, and documentation enables a crossing of glances (from children, parents, educators) on the markers of the educational acts that became organised and the educational situations that were experienced. The documented relations between teaching and learning create evidence for the processes of assessment and evaluation; these processes reveal solidary learning.[10]

We conducted a piece of research about children's views of their own portfolios – this research reveals that when children look at their learning history narrated in the individual portfolios, they recognise themselves in it, they are pleased and seek to communicate, interpret and signify their routes to learning, thus entering meta-cognition processes (Azevedo and Oliveira-Formosinho, 2008).

In Pedagogy-in-Participation's perspective one seeks to understand, in the History of Pedagogy, the emergence of different modes to document and, with the lessons learned, reconstruct a contextual and situated documentation format.

Serving the purpose of seeing and understanding the children's learning, the format allows:

- reconstructing the child's image as a person and as a learner;
- supporting the development of individual identities and of group identity;
- 'seeing' learning, talking about learning, reflecting about learning;
- supporting the planning which creates an educational intentionality that is bidirectional in nature, i.e., that reconciles interests, motivations and purposes of the children with the educational requirements of society and its educational project;
- supporting monitoring and evaluation of children's and adults' learning;
- answering three key questions: what is the child doing, how she is feeling and what she is learning.

In our approach, pedagogical documentation is a strategy to create descriptions, analyses, interpretations and understanding that enable us to identify progress in learning (Azevedo, 2009). In Pedagogy-in-Participation documentation allows us to see if our intentionalities are being developed in daily praxis, meaning that it allows us to analyse if children are developing holistic learning experiences.

Narrative is a pathway to meaning. When the teacher is a 'collector' of children's cultural artefacts, she or he can easily bring out conversation, communication, dialogues around these artefacts and the experience that created them, making available to the child the edited documentation that helps them to revisit the learning, to identify processes of learning how to learn (the processes of knowing), to celebrate achievements. The children are co-constructing themselves as learners when they have access to their learning journeys through documentation. The complexity of this process enables the creation of meaning which, in turn, drives creativity (Formosinho and Oliveira-Formosinho, 2008). The narratives of children about documented learning experiences represent a second order analysis about learning. While they narrate learning, they discover processes and achievements, and discover themselves and others in these processes and these achievements (Azevedo and Oliveira-Formosinho, 2008). They discover the psychological energy of their self-presentation as a learner. They are in the process of constituting their learner identities so listening to them is very important (Oliveira-Formosinho and Araújo, 2004). The way we learn and see ourselves as learners has an influence on the personal, social, civic and cognitive construction of the learner.

Pedagogic documentation and the co-construction of learning with parents

Parents and families are our key partners in the development of children's learning. Right from day one of their visit to the centre we discuss our foundational intentionalities and our modes of enacting them in the centre and in the classrooms. It is very rewarding to share a rights based approach and to open to parents and families feelings and intents. Our aim of developing the circularity of children's well-being and parents' well-being is central for the development of the other educational intentionalities. Children's perception about their parents' well-being and happiness is very important for children's own well-being (Formosinho and Oliveira-Formosinho, 2008) and vice versa. Daily life experience of families' involvement in the centre and centre involvement with families is demanding and rewarding. The open doors to the theoretical foundations and to the classrooms is highly appreciated by families. Pedagogic documentation is a very special means to facilitate involvement, collaboration, partnership. It is as well a very special means to empower parents in their support of children's transition to primary school (Monge, 2015).

Pedagogic documentation as a process for sustaining Pedagogy-in-Participation

Pedagogic documentation is built around children's learning and adults' learning. Documentation as a description, analysis and interpretation of a child's thinking-doing-feeling-learning requires documentation of the adult's parallel processes. Professional development portfolios, reflective portfolios constructed by educators around their praxis are very important for the development and complex understanding of their children's learning portfolios, but also for educators' professional development.

Thus, pedagogical documentation is not only a process central to the (meta)-learning of children and professionals, it is also a process central to the (meta)learning of the educators (teachers, pedagogic mediators, supervisors, researchers). It serves to monitor, supervise, evaluate and research the flow of activities and projects, processes and achievements, that is, the flow of learning and knowing (Formosinho and Oliveira-Formosinho, 2008). As Pedagogy-in-Participation wishes to be a coherent perspective, it requires such a documentation that makes visible the principles that sustain it, or which disclose the absence of such principles in certain situations; in this last eventuality, it helps to promote the resolution of problems of incoherence and lack of integration possibly revealed through documentation.

On Morin's heels (1986), as the whole is in every part, documentation about any part is revealing of the whole. Documentation as an integral part of praxis is very useful to analyse and transform this same pedagogy, namely very useful in analysing the theoretical coherence of the educational proposal. Through this, the pedagogical documentation allows meta-learning for all who will be (re)constructing Pedagogy-in-Participation. Consequently it is a central process for sustaining the praxis, through triangulation between interactive intentions, actions and achievements; therefore it is also a central process for (re)creating the pedagogy as an *action fecundated in theory and sustained by an ethical system.*

In Pedagogy-in-Participation, the creation of documentation was a long evolutionary process and was Childhood Association's way to experiment in dialogues with other pedagogic cultures. Chapter 6 presents in detail our approach to pedagogic documentation, its relationship with solidary learning through solidary teaching, and its relationship with pedagogic evaluation.

Notes

1. From now on *Associação Criança* will be referred as Childhood Association. Childhood Association (www.childhoodassociation.com) is a civic association of professionals of human development created in the early 1990s. The central aims are: the development of change and innovation processes with childhood institutions, the development of quality as equity. Childhood Association developed a socio-constructivist pedagogical approach – Pedagogy-in-Participation – aiming at the collaborative development of childhood institutions as democratic spaces and encompassing: childhood pedagogy, context based teacher education, parental involvement in their children's learning, professional and organisational development, research. Childhood Association supports the development of Pedagogy-in-Participation in several early childhood contexts across Portugal, namely Lisbon, Braga, Oporto, Guimarães, and develops dialogues with academic and pedagogic institutions in Brazil, England and Spain among others.
2. Morin (1999b) quoting Bachelard clearly shows that *methods carry ideologies*. The learning-teaching method materialises into processes, and these qualify the type of epistemology present, making it transmissive or participatory. The consciousness (Freire, 2005) of the method's role is necessary when one aims for an epistemology that respects the rights of children to learn by participating in the process.
3. Pedagogy-in-Participation has been developed within the partnership between Childhood Association (*Associação Criança*) and the Aga Khan Foundation Portugal.
4. Our starting points are deeply inspired by Dewey and by the entire pedagogical richness of the twentieth century (Dewey, Freinet, Piaget, Vygotsky, Malaguzzi, Bruner). The book we published together with Tizuko Kishimoto and Mônica Pinazza (2007) expresses our conviction that we need to better understand our pedagogical belonging so we may invent a present and a future which will better serve children, families and society. The constant deconstruction process that is required for the development of praxis is deeply indebted to Paulo Freire. The hope for the possibility of a new construction is deeply indebted to the children we have been working with and presented us with evidence about their inventiveness in the co-construction of knowledge.
5. Namely Oliveira-Formosinho (1998), Oliveira-Formosinho and Formosinho (2001), Azevedo (2009), Oliveira-Formosinho, Andrade and Gambôa (2009), Oliveira-Formosinho, Costa and Azevedo (2009a, 2009b), Araújo (2011), Machado (2014), Sousa (in press).
6. According to these authors, the concept of funds of knowledge refers to 'the historically accumulated and culturally developed bodies of knowledge and skills essential for household or individual functioning and well-being' (Moll et al., 1992, p. 133).
7. The methodology of his PhD thesis (London Institute of Education) is centred on the analysis of four decades of text books (1932–1968) produced during the Salazar dictatorship and the detailed analysis of the administrative mechanisms to exert bureaucratic control over school directors, teachers and students.
8. An example of a typical daily routine – welcome time, planning time, realisation of projects or/and activities, reflection time, recreation, intercultural time, moment of small group work, council, time of departure.
9. See Chapters 6 and 8.
10. See Chapters 5, 6, 7 and 8.

References

Araújo, S.B. (2011) *Pedagogia em creche: Da avaliação da qualidade à transformação praxiológica*. Tese de Doutoramento em Estudos da Criança – Especialização em Metodologia e Supervisão da Educação de Infância. Braga: Universidade do Minho.

Azevedo, A. (2009) *Revelando a aprendizagem das crianças: a documentação pedagógica*. Tese de Mestrado em Educação de Infância. Braga: Instituto de Estudos da Criança, Universidade do Minho.

Azevedo, A. and Oliveira-Formosinho, J. (2008) A documentação da aprendizagem: A voz das crianças. In J. Oliveira-Formosinho (ed.), *A escola vista pelas crianças*, pp. 117–143. Coleção Infância, nº 12. Porto: Porto Editora.

Bertram, A.D. (1996) *Effective early educators*, Unpublished PhD thesis, Coventry University.

Bertram, T. and Pascal, C. (2004) *The Effective Early Learning Programme*. Birmingham: Amber Publications, Centre for Research in Early Childhood.

Bertram, T. and Pascal, C. (2006) *The Baby Effective Early Learning Programme: Improving Quality in Early Childhood Settings for Children from Birth to Three Years*. Birmingham: Amber Publications, Centre for Research in Early Childhood.

Bettelheim, B. and Zelan, K. (1982) *On Learning To Read: The Child's Fascination with Meaning*. New York: Knopf.

Bourdieu, P. (1990) *The Logic of Practice*. Cambridge: Polity.

Bronfenbrenner, U. (1979) *The Ecology of Human Development*. Cambridge, MA: Harvard University Press.

Bruner, J. (1990) *Acts of Meaning*. Cambridge, MA: Harvard University Press.

Bruner, J. (1996) *The Culture of Education*. Cambridge, MA: Harvard University Press.

Carr, M. and Lee, W. (2012) *Learning Stories: Constructing Learner Identities in Early Education*. London: Sage Publications.

Dewey, J. (1939) *Creative Democracy: The Task Before Us*. Available at: www.philosophie.uni-muenchen.de/studium/das_fach/warum_phil_ueberhaupt/dewey_creative_democracy.pd f (accessed 26 May 2015).

Dewey, J. (1910) *How We Think*. Boston: D.C. Health & Company Publishers.

Formosinho, J. (1987) *Educating for passivity – a study of Portuguese education, 1926–68*. PhD dissertation. London: University of London, Institute of Education.

Formosinho, J. (1989) De serviço de estado a comunidade educativa: uma nova concepção para a escola portuguesa. *Revista Portuguesa de Educação (Universidade do Minho, Braga)* 2, 1: pp. 53–86.

Formosinho, J. (2002a) Universitisation of teacher education in Portugal. In O. Gassner (ed.), *Strategies of Change in Teacher Education – European Views*, pp. 105–127. Feldkirch, Austria: ENTEP, European Network on Teacher Education Policies.

Formosinho, J. (2002b) A academização da formação de professores de crianças. *Infância e Educação: Investigação e Práticas (Revista do GEDEI – Grupo de Estudos para o Desenvolvimento da Educação de Infância)* 4: 19–35.

Formosinho, J. (2007a) *O currículo uniforme pronto-a-vestir de tamanho único*. Cadernos de Políticas Educativas e Curriculares. Mangualde: Edições Pedago. First edition in J. Formosinho (ed.), *O Insucesso Escolar em Questão, Cadernos de Análise Social da Educação*. Braga: Universidade do Minho, 1987.

Formosinho, J. (2007b.) Modelos curriculares na educação básica – Um referencial de qualidade na diversidade (Prefácio). In J. Oliveira-Formosinho (ed.), *Modelos curriculares para a educação de infância: Construindo uma praxis de participação*, pp. 9–12. Coleção Infância no. 1, 3rd edn. Porto: Porto Editora.

Formosinho, J. and Machado, J. (2007) Anónimo do século XX: A construção da pedagogia burocrática. In J. Oliveira-Formosino, T. M. Kishimoto and M. A. Pinazza (eds), *Pedagogia(s) da Infância: Dialogando com o Passado, construindo o futuro*, pp. 292–328. Porto Alegre: Armed.

Formosinho, J. and Oliveira-Formosinho, J. (1996) *The Search for Participatory Curricular Approaches for Early Childhood Education*. Research Report, Aga Khan Foundation, Lisbon.

Formosinho, J. and Oliveira-Formosinho, J. (2008) *Pedagogy-in-Participation: Childhood Association's Approach*. Research Report, Aga Khan Foundation, Lisbon.

Formosinho, J., Sousa Fernandes, A. Sarmento, M.J. and Ferreira, F.I. (1999) *Comunidades educativas: Novos desafios à educação básica*. Braga: Livraria Minho.

Foucault, M. (1975) *Surveiller et punir: Naissance de la prison*. Paris: Gallimard.

Freire, P. (1998) *Pedagogy of Freedom: Ethics, Democracy, and Civic Courage*. Maryland: Rowman & Littlefield Publisher, Inc.

Freire, P. (2002) *Pedagogy of Hope: Reliving Pedagogy of the Oppressed*. New York: The Continuum Publishing Company.

Freire, P. (2005) *Pedagogy of the Oppressed*. New York: The Continuum International Publishing Group Inc.

Kilpatrick, W. (2006) *O método de projecto*. Viseu: Livraria Pretexto e Edições Pedago.

Kohlberg, L. (1985) The just community approach to moral education in theory and practice. In M. Berkowitz and F. Oser (eds), *Moral Education: Theory and Application*, pp. 27–87. Hillsdale, NJ: Lawrence Erlbaum.

Kohlberg, L. (1987) Democratic moral education. *Psicologia (Revista da Associação Portuguesa de Psicologia* V, 3: 335–341.

Laevers, F. (ed.) (2005) *Well-being and Involvement in Care. A Process-oriented Self-evaluation Instrument*. Leuven University, Belgium: Kind en Cezin and Research Centre for Experiential Education.

Lewin, K. (1948) *Resolving Social Conflicts*. New York: Harper and Row Publishers.

Machado, I. (2014) *Avaliação da qualidade em creche: um estudo de caso sobre o bem-estar das crianças*. Tese de Mestrado em Educação de Infância, Instituto de Educação da Universidade do Minho, Braga, Portugal.

Malaguzzi, L. (1998) History, ideas, and basic philosophy: an interview with Lella Gandini. In C. Edwards, L. Gandini and G. Forman (eds), *The Hundred Languages of Children: The Reggio Emilia Approach – Advanced Reflection*, pp. 49–97. Greenwich, CT: Ablex.

Moll, L., Amanti, C., Neff, D. and Gonzalez, N. (1992) Funds of knowledge for teaching: using a qualitative approach to connect homes and classrooms. *Theory into Practice* 31, 2: 132–141.

Monge, G. (2015) As transições das crianças na Pedagogia-em-Participação: o cruzamento das diversas vozes. In G. Monge and J. Formosinho (eds) *As transições das crianças na Pedagogia-em-Participação*. Porto: Porto Editora.

Morin, E. (1986) *O Método 3 – O Conhecimento do Conhecimento*. Lisbon: Europa América.

Morin, E. (1999a) *L'intelligence de la complexité*. Paris: L'Harmattan.

Morin, E. (1999b) *Seven Complex Lessons in Education for the Future*. Paris: UNESCO.

Oliveira-Formosinho, J. (1987) Fundamentos psicológicos para um modelo desenvolvimentista de formação de professores. *Psicologia (Revista da Associação Portuguesa de Psicologia* V, 3: 247–257.

Oliveira-Formosinho, J. (1992) A formação de professores para a formação pessoal e social: relato de uma experiência de ensino. In Sociedade Portuguesa de Ciências de Educação, *Formação pessoal e social*, pp. 151–163. Porto: Sociedade Portuguesa de Ciências de Educação.

Oliveira-Formosinho, J. (1998) *O desenvolvimento profissional das educadoras de infância: Um estudo de caso*. Dissertação de Doutoramento em Estudos da Criança. Braga: Universidade do Minho.

Oliveira-Formosinho, J. (2001) The specific professional nature of early years education and styles of adult/child interaction. *European Early Childhood Education Research Journal* 9, 1: 57–72.

Oliveira-Formosinho, J. (2004) A participação guiada – coração da pedagogia da infância? *Revista Portuguesa de Pedagogia – Infância: Família, comunidade e educação (Revista da Faculdade de Psicologia e Ciências de Educação da Universidade de Coimbra)* 38, 1, 2 and 3: 145–158.

Oliveira-Formosinho, J. (2007) Pedagogia(s) da infância: Reconstruindo uma praxis de participação. In J. Oliveira-Formosinho, T. Kishimoto and M. Pinazza (eds), *Pedagogia(s) da Infância: Dialogando com o passado construindo o futuro*, pp. 13–36. São Paulo: Artmed.

Oliveira-Formosinho, J. and Araújo, S.B. (2004) Children's perspectives about pedagogical interactions. *European Early Childhood Education Research Journal* 12, 1: 103–114.

Oliveira-Formosinho, J. and Araújo, S.B. (2011) Early education for diversity: starting from birth. *European Early Childhood Education Research Journal* 19, 2: 223–235.

Oliveira-Formosinho, J. and Formosinho, J. (eds) (2001) *Associação Criança: Um contexto de formação em contexto*. Braga: Livraria Minho.

Oliveira-Formosinho, J. and Formosinho, J. (2012) *Pedagogy-in-Participation: Childhood Association Educational Perspective*. Porto: Porto Editora.

Oliveira-Formosinho, J., Andrade, F.F. and Gambôa, R. (2009) Podiam chamar-se lenços de amor. In J. Olivera-Formosinho (eds), *Podiam chamar-se lenços de amor*, pp. 15–53. Lisbon: Ministérios da Educação e Direcção-Geral de Inovação e de Desenvolvimento Curricular (DGIDC).

Oliveira-Formosinho, J., Costa, H. and Azevedo, A. (2009a) A minha árvore: Leonor. In J. Olivera-Formosinho (eds), *Limoeiros e laranjeiras: Revelando as aprendizagens*, pp. 15–27. Lisbon: Ministérios da Educação e Direcção-Geral de Inovação e de Desenvolvimento Curricular (DGIDC).

Oliveira-Formosinho, J., Costa, H. and Azevedo, A. (2009b) A minha laranjeira: Sofia. In J. Olivera-Formosinho (eds), *Limoeiros e laranjeiras: Revelando as aprendizagens*, pp. 29–42. Lisbon: Ministérios da Educação e Direcção-Geral de Inovação e de Desenvolvimento Curricular (DGIDC).

Oliveira-Formosinho, J., Kishimoto, T. and Pinazza, M. (2007). *Pedagogia(s) da Infância: Dialogando com o passado construindo o futuro*. São Paulo: Artmed.

Pascal, C. and Bertram, T. (2009) Listening to young citizens: the struggle to make real a participatory paradigm in research with young children. *European Early Childhood Education Research Journal* 17, 2: 249–262.

Rogoff, B. (1990) *Apprenticeship In Thinking: Cognitive Development in Social Context*. Oxford: Oxford University Press.

Sousa, J. (in press). Mediação pedagógica: Um estudo de caso. In J. Formosinho and J. Oliveira-Formosinho (eds), *Desenvolvimento profissional em contexto*. Porto: Porto Editora.

Tomasello, M. (1998) The role of joint attentional processes in early language development. *Language Sciences* 10, 1: 69–88.

Tomasello, M. (2009) *Why We Cooperate*. Cambridge: A Boston Review Book & The MIT Press.

Vygotsky, L.S. (1998) *A formação social da mente*. São Paulo: Livraria Martins Fontes Editora.

Wenger, E. (1998) *Communities of Practice: Learning, Meaning and Identity*. Cambridge: Cambridge University Press.

Wertsch, J.V. (1985) *Vygotsky and the Social Formation of Mind*. Cambridge, MA: Harvard University Press.

Whalley, M. (ed.) (1994) *Learning to Be Strong: Setting up a Neighbourhood Service for Under-fives and Their Families*. Sevenoaks, Kent: Hodder & Stoughton Educational.

Whalley, M. (ed.) (2001) *Involving Parents in Their Children's Learning*. London: Paul Chapman Publishing.

PART II

Approaches and techniques

3

THE NATURE AND PURPOSE OF ASSESSMENT AND EVALUATION WITHIN A PARTICIPATORY PEDAGOGY

Christine Pascal and Tony Bertram

Introduction

This chapter aims to critically explore the nature, purposes and value of assessment and evaluation processes within a participatory pedagogy. It will begin with a clarification of the contribution of assessment and evaluation to developing and ensuring the quality of early childhood education and supporting sector accountability. It will then explore the nature and focus of participatory assessment and evaluation processes.

In a participatory paradigm, pedagogic approaches are favoured which are co-constructed, where the learners (practitioners, parents and children) actively lead their own learning and development, and are seen as active and equal partners in the construction of the curriculum and the learning environment and processes adopted. Learning and development are seen as a socio-cultural processes (Vygotsky, 1978; Bruner, 1996; Rogoff, 2003) in which those who are within the context (teacher, child, parent) are viewed as citizens, or subjects with democratic rights to have a voice in its realisation (Pascal and Bertram, 2009, 2012). In this paradigm pedagogic and andragogic (Knowles, 1973; Mezirow, 2006) learning approaches for both children and practitioners are favoured which are dynamic, co-constructed and socially situated, viewing the child's and the adult's overall developmental outcomes holistically. Learning and development are thus seen as complex, non-linear processes, and learning experiences are not compartmentalised into rigidly defined areas with linear, pre-programmed steps through which learners progress but rather as a set of 'affordances' (Gibson, 1977) or opportunities from which the learner constructs their own meanings and developmental journey. Assessment and evaluation processes are therefore required which match this complex, democratic, dynamic and multi-dimensional educational reality. Participatory assessment and evaluation processes in early childhood settings are fundamentally characterised by those involved within an educational context systemically gathering evidence to gain greater knowledge, understanding and confidence to make constructive changes for the better. It is an internally led, subjective and deeply attached process rather than an externally driven, objective, detached process.

A further quality of participatory assessment and evaluation is that it is based on a strong ethical code of action with the express aim of actively encouraging the participation of those involved in the early years context, including children and parents, giving them voice and power in the evaluation process.

Through our work for the Effective Early Learning (EEL) Programme and the Accounting Early for Life Long Learning (AcE) Programme we have learned a lot about the challenges of listening well and operating to enhance child and parent participation in assessment and evaluation processes. This work has revealed that:

- there is a strong demand for more open dialogues from parents, practitioners and children in all communities;
- there is a clear awareness by parents, practitioners and children of the inequity in the relationships in many early childhood settings and a desire to challenge this through more dialogue and training.

These findings, which are derived from our analysis of the views expressed in our evaluative focus group dialogues, have challenged us to develop a strategy for opening and deepening equitable and respectful dialogues in early childhood settings. We have taken these messages into the next phase of work which offers training materials and activities that aim to change practice by encouraging more open interaction and equitable dialogues between the children, parents, practitioners and researchers in our richly diverse communities. The idea of 'Opening Windows' comes from a quote by Mahatma Ghandi (speech given 1 June 1921):

> I do not want my house to be walled in on all sides, and my windows to be closed. Instead, I want the cultures of all lands to be blown about my house as freely as possible. But I refuse to be blown off my feet by any.
>
> (Gandhi, 1981, p. 170)

We were inspired by the idea of opening our early childhood institutions and practices to feel and breathe the diversity of cultures and world views that prevail in twenty-first century communities, and how this openness to difference and diversity might actually strengthen community cohesion and identity for all. This is the intention of the participatory paradigm which we hope to embed in early childhood research and practice.

Our work has also been inspired by Freire's dialogic and reflexive action in a *Pedagogy of the Oppressed* (1972) where he promotes the challenge of working with those who are *domesticated* or *silenced* with the clear aim of *liberation*. His work of course was with adults but we have applied these radical ideas to our work as researchers and practitioners with children. The first step in this process of liberation is 'consciousness raising' and the development of selfhood in the oppressed (practitioners and children) with the intention of helping them to name their world and to begin to shape it, that is, it is an empowerment approach. The capacity of young children to adopt and participate actively in such encounters has been shown in the popularity of 'circle time' which has become a predominant activity in early childhood settings. The key difference is that we are aiming to create listening circles in which children are given the floor to initiate and generate their own ideas and where dialogues are symmetrical in terms of power distribution.

In these projects we have trained researchers and practitioners to use a variety of techniques/approaches which encourage the voices, dialogues and narratives from children and parents to be listened to, given status and acted upon. This model of symmetrical dialogue was initially modelled by the research team, but increasingly practitioners and parents have been encouraged and empowered to take over this role and embed it into their daily ways of working and being with children. The development process has been fully documented, and participants were encouraged to keep journals, so that the impact of the project intervention could be fully evaluated. A key finding was that practitioners and parents needed to develop new confidence, competences and commitment before symmetrical dialogues could begin. The process of redistributing power was harder than we had anticipated. This difficulty was expressed in many ways, with many practitioners and parents resisting the opportunities to allow children to 'name their world' and shape their dialogue with it (Freire, 1970). Many showed a reluctance to 'take the lid off' the existing status quo in the fear that they would not be able to control or handle what followed. We have found this resistance or internalised oppression (Freire, 1970) has to be acknowledged and worked through respectfully and compassionately.

Our experimentation and innovations in this project have led to a programme with the express aim of developing strategies and practices which support democratic, equalising and participative encounters within early childhood settings and also primary schools for researchers, practitioners, parents and children. This has meant initial work to enhance the skills of participants, both researchers and practitioners, in understanding diversity, clarifying values, supporting open dialogues, handling conflict and developing active listening approaches.

At the heart of this work is a process of critical self-evaluation, reflection and action (praxis) with the guiding purpose of advancing practice and supporting practitioners to develop a more profound understanding of their work and, therefore, a more effective delivery of services to children and families. In short, it is action based and transformational for the settings and the people involved in the delivery and receipt of services. As J. McNiff points out, it involves,

> a strategy that helps you to live in the way you feel is a good way. It helps you to live out the things you believe in (your values); and it enables you to give reasons every step of the way.
>
> (McNiff, 2010, p. 6)

This culturally and socially located, insider led, participatory approach has a number of strengths. It is fundamentally focused on finding out more about practice and exploring what works and why from the front line, and using this knowledge to transform realities. To date, much of the evaluation evidence that has informed practice in early childhood education has been generated from external sources but this alternative approach radically shifts this perspective and attempts to gain from evidence that originates within the real world of practice, through the active and authentic participation of those involved generating their own agendas and data for further exploration, enquiry and change. Key strengths in this approach are that those involved in practice themselves identify ways to improve their world and take responsibility for this action, inspiring and generating collaborative learning and action. It is able to give a close account of what works, how and why, thus ensuring credibility and utility in the real world of practice. And finally, and critically for those who work with young children and families, it has an ethical and values transparent stance.

The purpose of participatory assessment and evaluation

The fundamental purpose of assessment and evaluation in early childhood educational settings is to interrogate, document and make informed judgements about the quality and effectiveness of early learning experiences offered to young children. The intention is to provide those involved in the creation of learning opportunities with rigorous evidence which can be used to direct and further develop the pedagogic offer to ensure all children have access to a continuously improving, high quality educational programme. The organisational aspiration is that responsibility for self-directed and continuous development, through established assessment and evaluation processes, resides with those inside, rather than outside of the organisation, as this will ensure that the education offered is appropriate, challenging and fit for purpose. Within a participatory pedagogy, assessment and evaluation are viewed as two, mutually interdependent processes which together ensure that the co-constructed learning experiences offered to, and experienced by, children within early education contexts have value and impact for the child, the family and the wider social community or society in which they are located i.e. they are of quality. In this sense, assessment and evaluation are essential pedagogic tools for ensuring that the education offered is culturally situated, empowering and transformational for all those involved.

Assessment and evaluation are also the key means by which accountability for educational inputs are realised. Accountability is another key aim of assessment and evaluation processes and this is seen as having three aspects or facets. Firstly, assessment and evaluation evidence can feed accountability by providing a narrative or 'account' of the educational process and its outcomes. Secondly, the evidence can provide an explanation or 'account' of why and how learning occurred. Thirdly, the evidence can provide a quantitative or qualitative 'measure' or 'count' of what has been achieved. In a participatory paradigm, all three senses of accountability are achieved through the adoption of rigorous assessment and evaluation processes and are seen as desirable and necessary responsibilities towards those involved for ensuring high quality educational experiences are available for all.

In this approach, it is also argued that to realise these intentions of accountability for, and improvement of, quality fully, it is essential that those involved in creating, experiencing and benefiting from the education offered are viewed as active partners and participants in all assessment and evaluation processes (Bertram and Pascal, 2006, 2009, 2012). This movement is part of a slow but growing acknowledgement of the centrality of the rights of children as citizens and recognition of Articles 12 and 13 of the UNCRC (1989; ratified by UK in 1991) which state that:

> *Article 12*: The Governments of all countries should ensure that a child who is capable of forming his or her own views should have the right to express those views freely in all matters affecting that child, and that the views of that child should be given due weight in accordance with the age and maturity of the child;

> *Article 13*: (which includes the right to freedom of expression): This right shall include freedom to seek, receive and impart ideas of all kinds, regardless of frontiers, either orally, in writing or in print, in the form of art, or through any other media of the child's choice.

Progress towards embedding these rights continues, but the deeper changes in values and attitudes required to realise this commitment for all children in all early childhood settings are hard to make a reality. In many settings these hard fought for rights of children are not yet evident in practice. Many children are not listened to in their daily lives, whether at home or in schools, and the development of their capacity to participate effectively as citizens is thus restricted. This situation particularly characterises the reality of our youngest children, who can remain 'silenced' and often excluded from the decisions which shape their lives with the rationale that they are 'too young' to express their rights and voice and that we, as adults, have to act on their behalf. We have also found that in 'crossing the border' from home to school, children from migrant, travelling, asylum-seeking and refugee families across a range of diverse communities and backgrounds are even less likely to be heard (Bertram and Pascal, 2006, 2008). It is our view that if all our children are to enjoy the rights enshrined in the UNCRC then research and practice needs to fundamentally reshape its paradigm to become more inclusive and participatory.

Our own work, and that of many other researchers and practitioners in the field, has documented the challenges to making this paradigm shift happen (Woodhead, 1999; Lloyd-Smith and Tarr, 2000; Lewis and Lindsay, 2000; Clark and Moss, 2001; Oliveira-Formosinho and Barros, 2006; Dahlberg et al., 2006). These initiatives reflect a growing acceptance of the view of young children as citizens with rights and voice in our services, with the underpinning notion, well expressed by Lloyd-Smith and Tarr (2000), that 'reality experienced by children and young people in educational settings cannot be fully comprehended by inference and assumption'. At the heart of this view is that the actual experiences perceived by the child cannot be inferred by others and so practitioners must include their voices as they speak and not as we infer or interpret. It is our belief that our task as practitioners is to meet this challenge and open our eyes and ears and minds to these voices; to become expert and active listeners to children and to recognise the many ways in which children skilfully communicate their realities to us (Malaguzzi, 1998).

Perhaps in response to this body of work which promotes children's perspectives, we can also trace a growing recognition in the early years' sector of the import- ance of listening to young children's perspectives within assessment and evaluation processes. This collective participation in assessment and evaluation processes ensures shared responsibility and ownership, and helps to ensure that the evidence gathered has relevance and utility for quality improvement, another essential goal in creating high quality education for all. In this sense assessment and evaluation become highly attached, embedded and culturally located within the educational context and are viewed as an ongoing, internally driven and continuous process, rather than as an externally owned, detached, objective event. This approach also acknowledges that children, parents and practitioners have agency, capacity and the democratic right to shape, name and influence their world for the better. In this sense, assessment and evaluation processes can be seen as highly political, liberating and transforming forces for those involved (Freire, 1970; Bertram and Pascal, 2006; Pascal and Bertram, 2009, 2012; Formosinho and Oliveira- Formosinho, 2012). Finally, in this account of participatory assessment and evaluation practices, we are seeking to offer a means of establishing robust and practice based evidence which may be used for critical reflection and action (praxis) which we believe is at the heart of quality early education.

In summary, participatory assessment and evaluation has two key objectives. Firstly, it aims to produce relevant and practical knowledge and actions which are directly useful for improving the quality of early education offered within an early education setting. Secondly, assessment and evaluation seeks to empower those within an early education setting to seek social transformation through a process of constructing and using their own knowledge.

The generation of knowledge

Participatory assessment and evaluation is always situated within a specific context and so embraces localism but it is also democratic and participatory in the wider sense of society. Wenger's (1998) ideas on *communities of practice*, for example, can be seen to underpin and support this social and collaborative approach to knowledge generation. But philosophically and politically, individual liberty as set against the greater good of universalism and the power of the State carries political dangers on the right of neo-liberalism, and on the left of anarchy. A participatory approach therefore takes the middle ground and foregrounds participation, voice and democracy, in which individuals are acknowledged but as members of a wider community. Because there is nothing as culturally and individually located, nothing as central to our concept of identity and belonging as how we rear our young children, early educational settings must recognise and be sensitive to these core and localised significances and cultural diversities. Participatory assessment and evaluation is careful of generalisations and universals and of reducing these complexities to numerical representations which deny people's plurality. In this approach, knowledge is viewed as soundest and most trustworthy when it is co-constructed and validated by those who are in the field of inquiry. It purports that knowledge can be localised and yet still be authentic, genuine and meaningful and have transferability.

Liberation and transformation

Freire's (1970) concept of 'praxis' is essentially political in that it seeks to explore 'the study of practice' with all its concomitants of avoiding 'domesticity' in thinking by establishing a critical stance of self-awareness and self-critique. This allows the creation of highly relevant but personalised and individualised libraries of the world's knowledge and thinking. Participatory assessment and evaluation embraces this emphasis on the importance of inclusionary paradigms and methodologies which recognise the value of the polyphonic, multi-perspective approach which leads to perceiving practitioners, parents and children as co-constructors of knowledge about the services and their development. Like McNiff's (2010) action researchers, this approach involves an intellectual story of adventurers, encouraging leaders, explorers and risk takers working at the cutting edge of understanding and knowledge creation in a Vygotskyian *zone of development*, embedded in a culture of transformation, which is forged by new integrated and cross-cultural, cross-paradigm and cross-disciplinary collaborations. The wider understandings which grow from these fertile participatory conditions is often messy but this 'chaos', as Gladwell (2006) suggests, permits the creative emergence of new methodologies and concepts. Much of this road has been travelled before but Reason and Bradbury (2008) suggest an added resonance recently, claiming we are witnessing,

> an emerging worldview, more holistic, pluralist and egalitarian that is eventually participative. This worldview sees human beings as co-creating their reality through participation, through their experience, their imagination and intuition, their thinking and their action. This participative worldview is at the heart of inquiry methodologies that emphasise participation as a core strategy.
>
> (Reason and Bradbury, 2008, p. 324)

In many countries we can see a new concern for grounded early childhood evaluation practices emerging from the 'bottom-up, not top-down'. As Martha Zaslow, Director of the Office of Policy and Communications for the Society for Research in Child Development stated,

> We're in the middle of a conceptual shift. We've had a very long-standing assumption that knowledge-focused professional development – meaning coursework and training – would suffice to yield changes in practice and quality. We're standing it on its head now, and beginning to say: if you want to change practice and quality, you need to begin by directly intervening with practice.
>
> (Zaslow et al., 2010, p. 6)

We suggest that there are many possibilities for 'intervening with practice' in order to transform and improve people's lives but we feel that profound change should and does grow from experience to conceptualisation and not the other way round. For example, Barnett's (2011) work examining what had and had not worked in state-funded early intervention programmes in the USA which aimed to transform children's life chances suggests that the nature of professional development offered to early childhood practitioners was a key factor in the success of an intervention. His work showed that initiatives which focused on developing practitioner knowledge, within a participatory approach, led to specific shifts in practice and these had the greatest impact in enhancing children's life chances. The potential role and power of participatory evidence generation is being to be realised.

The nature of participatory assessment and evaluation

The nature of participatory assessment and evaluation practice is shaped by three key concepts, which were central to the approach taken in the Effective Early Learning Programme (Bertram and Pascal, 2006):

1. *A democratic approach*: the assessment and evaluation process adopts a 'democratic approach', in which quality evaluation is viewed as a value laden enterprise, which is best achieved through the active involvement of participants in the process.
2. *An inclusionary approach*: this approach adopts an 'inclusionary model', in which the evaluation process is viewed as something 'done with' participants and not 'done to' them.
3. *Multiple perceptions and voices*: the subjectivity of the definition is thus acknowledged and the shared perceptions of quality are celebrated as central to the debate about quality in each particular setting. Quality is defined by the shared reflections and agreement of experienced practitioners, parents/ carers and children within the framework of the programme. It is validated and scrutinised for accuracy by those closest to the learning experiences being evaluated.

This approach is therefore firmly founded on democratic principles and proponents have to work hard to establish a feeling of partnership and shared ownership of the whole process and must keep reflecting on the distribution of power within these relationships. A philosophical commitment to this approach is reinforced with the hope that it will also help the assessment and evaluation process become a major vehicle for the professional development of the practitioners involved. It aims to ensure that the individual settings become more responsive, better fit for purpose and that those within them would be empowered by the process. The process of review and implementation thus becomes part of the definition.

This approach to quality assessment and evaluation is not static or finite but is locally situated and responsive to time, culture and place. We make no attempt to give it a fixed definition but rather to provide a framework of reflective questions which encourage the individuals within each setting, including the parents/carers and children, to document and review how they experience the quality and effectiveness of the learning process. The aim is to support practitioners to improve on 'previous best' through gradual, incremental change and development, not through revolution. This approach has an underpinning philosophy which accepts that:

- judgements about quality need to be made;
- evaluation should emerge from an open, honest and collaborative dialogue using a shared vocabulary;
- this dialogue should be generated over an extended period of time;
- the dialogue should have a clear, systematic and agreed framework and format;
- the evidence for evaluation is gathered together and questioned together;
- the evaluation process should lead to action plans;
- the action should be followed through, supported and monitored;
- the settings should take ownership of the process and its outcomes;
- all participants in the process should be encouraged to make a contribution which is acknowledged and valued;
- collaboration and participation are more effective than compulsion and hierarchies.

Participatory assessment and evaluation processes adheres to the following principles of operation:

- Evaluation and Improvement are viewed as inseparable.
- The process of Evaluation and Improvement is participatory, democratic and collaborative.
- The process promotes equality of opportunity and acknowledges cultural diversity.
- The process is opted into and not imposed.
- The framework for evaluation is rigorous but flexible.
- The action plans are followed through and supported.
- The process is intended to empower and develop practitioners, parents/carers and children.

The focus of assessment and evaluation

To achieve this deeply transformational agenda, the focus of the assessment and evaluation process has to go beyond assessing and evaluating educational or learning outcomes, and adopt a wider, three-dimensional focus. It has to scrutinise critically and in detail, (1) the pedagogic context, (2) the pedagogic processes and (3) the

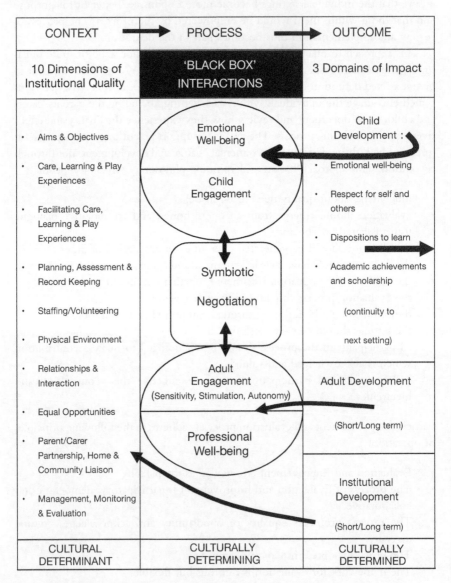

FIGURE 3.1 EEL conceptual framework for evaluating and developing quality in early childhood settings

Source: reproduced from Effective Early Learning Programme, Bertram and Pascal, 2006 pedagogic outcomes, to discern their contribution to the value, power and impact (transformational potential) of the education offered to, and experienced by, the children. This wider evaluative focus has been realised in the Effective Early Learning Programme (Bertram and Pascal, 2006), an established assessment and evaluation strategy in many early childhood contexts in the UK and Portugal Oliveira-Formosinho, 2009; Oliveira-Formosinho, Costa and Azevedo, 2009), which has set out a three-dimensional focus to quality improvement in early childhood settings as set out in Figure 3.1.

In this approach, the focus for assessment and evaluation has three strands:

1. *Pedagogic Context* evidence focuses on aspects of the setting that define the environment in which early learning takes place. This includes such things as:

   - Pedagogic Aims and Objectives
   - Learning Experiences/Curriculum
   - Learning and Teaching Strategies
   - Planning, Assessment & Record Keeping
   - Staffing
   - Relationships and Interactions
   - Inclusion, Equality and Diversity
   - Parent, Family and Community Partnerships
   - Physical Environment
   - Leadership, Monitoring and Evaluation.

2. *Pedagogic Process* evidence focuses on quality and nature of the pedagogic interactions between adults and children within a setting. This will involve evidence gathering about such things as:

   - Child Engagement and Involvement
   - Adult Engagement
   - Child Well-being
   - Professional Well-being.

3. *Pedagogic Outcomes* evidence focuses on the consequent developmental impact of the learning offered by a setting and is assessed at three levels of impact; the children's development, the adults' development and the institutional setting's development. This will involve evidence gathering about:

   - Children's Development – in such areas as communication and language development; attitudes and dispositions to learning; social-emotional competence; physical development
   - Practitioner and Parent Development
   - Setting Development and Improvement.

In this conception of participatory assessment and evaluation, it is fully acknowledged that any measures of Pedagogic Context, Process and Outcomes will be embedded in, and dependent on, the wider socio-cultural environment. Each early childhood setting exists in an environment that is determined by the cultural norms and values of that society or sub group within that society. Evaluation of the quality of a setting will therefore be influenced by how far its values are shared and agreed by all the setting's participants and how far the setting agrees with the values of the wider groups beyond, for example, its local community, the regional authority, the government and other public opinions. This view of individual settings nested in wider circles of influence is called an 'ecological perspective' (Bronfenbrenner, 1979).

This wider, three-dimensional focus for assessment and evaluation in early childhood ensures that the pedagogic quality of a setting is viewed holistically, and that each element of pedagogic practice is assessed and evaluated as a significant constituent part of a dynamic, complex and interrelated system of relationships and interactions.

The process of assessment and evaluation

The process of participatory assessment and evaluation has four distinct phases of cyclical action, which flow into each other and encourage an ongoing process of reflection and action, as exemplified in the EEL programme diagram in Figure 3.2. Each Phase has a set of participatory and ethically agreed methods and strategies that will support settings in implementing the process successfully and democratically. Each stage of the process is also documented rigorously and reflected upon by all those who have participated in the evidence gathering process. The intention is to ensure all feel ownership at each stage of the development process and also a real sense of shared responsibility in the evaluative outcomes and their implications for the further improvement of the quality of practice.

Phase 1: Assessment and evaluation

In this first phase practitioners work together with colleagues, parents/carers and children to document and assess the quality of early learning within the setting. Evidence is gathered collaboratively about all aspects of the setting context and processes. The resultant data are used by practitioners to facilitate a critical assessment of the quality of early learning and care within their setting. All data collected from the quality documentation and assessment are collated into a detailed and carefully structured *Evaluation Report* of the quality of early learning within each setting. The Evaluation Report is then shared with the practitioners in the study setting for validation.

Phase 2: Action planning

The practitioners meet with all participants to identify the priorities for action. This plan will be individual to the needs of each setting. A structured and achievable **action plan** for the development of care, learning and development should emerge which has clearly articulated targets within an identified time scale.

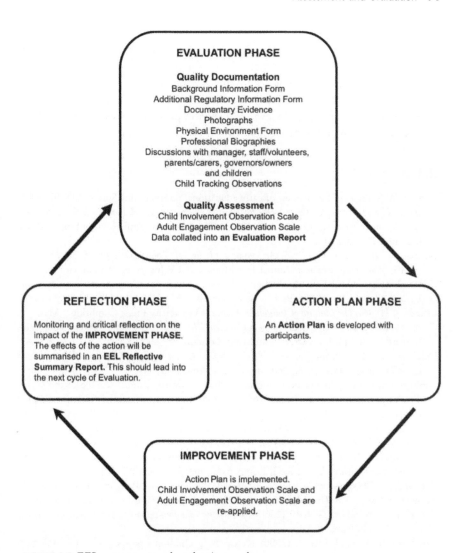

FIGURE 3.2 EEL assessment and evaluation cycle

Phase 3: Improvement

A programme of individual and/or setting development which relates closely to the agreed targets of the action plan is implemented. Throughout this phase, progress should be monitored and the practitioners are encouraged to gather evidence upon the effect of the action on the quality of the children's care, learning and development experiences within the setting (impact measures).

Phase 4: Reflection

Practitioners are encouraged to reflect upon the evaluation and improvement process, and to review the evidence of the impact of their action plan upon the quality of the children's learning within their setting. The practitioners collate their findings in a *Reflective Summary Report* which includes the results of the final data gathering and the participants' views on further improvement, leading into another cycle of evaluation and improvement.

References

Barnett, W.S. (2011) Effectiveness of early educational intervention, *Science*, 333: 975–978.

Bertram, T. and Pascal, C. (2006) *Effective Early Learning (EEL) A Handbook for Evaluating, Assuring and Improving Quality in Early Childhood Settings*. Amber Publishing and TV Junction: Birmingham.

Bertram, T. and Pascal, C. (2008) *Accounting Early for Life Long Learning (AcE), A Handbook for Assessing Young Children*. Amber Publishing and TV Junction: Birmingham.

Bronfenbrenner, U. (1979) *The Ecology of Human Development: Experiments by Nature and Design*. Harvard University Press: Cambridge, MA.

Bruner, J. (1996) *The Culture of Education*. Harvard University Press: Cambridge, Mass.

Clark, A. and Moss, P. (2001) *Listening to Children: The Mosaic Approach*. National Children's Bureau and Joseph Rowntree Foundation: London.

Dahlberg, G., Moss, P. and Pence, A. (2006) *Beyond Quality in Early Childhood Education and Care: Postmodern Perspectives*, 2nd edn. Falmer Press: London.

Formosinho, J. and Oliveira-Formosinho J. (2012) Towards a social science of the social: the contribution of praxeological research. *European Early Childhood Education Research Journal*, 20, 4: 591–606.

Freire, P. (1970) *Pedagogy of the Oppressed*. Herder and Herder: New York.

Gandhi, M.K. (1981) *Young India* Vol. 1: *1919*. Navjivan Publication House: Ahmedabad.

Gibson, J.J. (1977) The theory of affordances. In R.E. Shaw and J. Bransford (eds), *Perceiving, Acting, and Knowing*. Lawrence Erlbaum Associates: Hillsdale, NJ.

Gladwell, M. (2006) *Blink: the Power of Thinking Without Thinking*. Penguin: Harmondsworth.

Knowles, M.S. (1973) *The Adult Learner. A Neglected Species*. Gulf Publishing: Houston.

Lewis, A. and Lindsay, G. (eds) (2000) *Researching Children's Perspectives*. Open University Press: Buckingham.

Lloyd-Smith, M. and Tarr, J. (2000) Researching children's perspectives: a sociological perspective. In A. Lewis and G. Lindsay (eds), *Researching Children's Perspectives*, Open University Press: Buckingham.

Malaguzzi, L. (1998) *The Hundred Languages of Children: The Reggio Emilia Approach*. Ablex Publishing: CA, Greenwich.

Mezirow, J. (2006) An overview of transformative learning. In P. Sutherland and J. Crowther (eds), *Lifelong learning: Concepts and Contexts*, pp. 24–38. Routledge: New York.

McNiff, J. (2010) *Action Research for Professional Development*. September Books: Dorset.

Oliveira-Formosinho, J. (org.) (2009) *Desenvolvendo a qualidade em parcerias: Estudos de caso*. Colecção Aprender em Companhia, da Direcção-Geral de Inovação e de Desenvolvimento Curricular (DGIDC). Lisbon: Ministério da Educação.

Oliveira-Formosinho, J. and Barros Araújo, S. (2006) Listening to children as a way to reconstruct knowledge about children: some methodological implications. *European Early Childhood Education Research Journal*, 14, 1: 21–31.

Oliveira-Formosinho, J., Costa, H. and Azevedo, A. (2009) A minha árvore. In J. Oliveira-Formosinho (org.), *Limoeiros e laranjeiras: Revelando as aprendizagens*, pp. 15–27. Colecção Aprender em Companhia, da Direcção-Geral de Inovação e de Desenvolvimento Curricular (DGIDC). Lisbon: Ministério da Educação.

Pascal, C. and Bertram, T. (2009) Listening to young citizens: the struggle to make real a participatory paradigm in research with young children. *European Early Childhood Education Research Journal*, 17, 2: 249–262(14).

Pascal, C. and Bertram, T. (2012) Praxis, ethics and power: developing praxeology as a participatory paradigm for early childhood research. *European Early Childhood Education Research Journal*, 20, 4: 477–492.

Reason, P. and Bradbury, H. (eds) (2008) *Sage Handbook of Action Research: Participative Inquiry and Practice* (2nd edn). Sage Publications: London.

Rogoff, B. (2003) *The Cultural Nature of Human Development*. Oxford University Press: New York.

Wenger, E. (1998) *Communities of Practice: Learning, Meaning, and Identity*. Cambridge University Press: Cambridge.

Woodhead, M. (1999) Towards a global paradigm for research into early childhood education. *European Early Childhood Education Research Journal*, 7, 1: 5–22.

Vygotsky, L.S. (1978) *Mind in Society*. Harvard University Press: Cambridge, MA.

Zaslow, M., Tout, K. and Martinez-Beck, I. (2010) *Measuring the Quality of Early Care and Education Programs at the Intersection of Research, Policy, and Practice*. OPRE Research-to-Policy, Research-to-Practice Brief OPRE 2011–10a. Office of Planning, Research and Evaluation, Administration: Washington, DC.

4
PARTICIPATORY METHODS FOR ASSESSMENT AND EVALUATION

Christine Pascal and Tony Bertram

Introduction

This chapter builds on the conceptualisations set out in Chapter 3 and aims to offer exemplification of practical and ethically grounded assessment and evaluation methods and processes which may be used to support a participatory pedagogy. As set out in Chapter 3, we are seeking participatory methods for evidence and information gathering (assessment) to enable critical reflection and appraisal (evaluation) of what is working, how it is working and what the impact is. The aim is to establish rigorous, systematically collected, practice based evidence which is based upon daily life in real world, early childhood settings over time. The methods presented are designed to document and assess pedagogic practice and its impact with the intention of reflecting critically on its power to transform learning and development for the children and adults involved.

The methods set out in this chapter meet our ethical code and our belief in adopting rights based, pedagogic practice and so are meaningful, situated and culturally responsive for those involved. They also provide opportunities for the democratic, co-construction of evidence from child, parent and practitioner perspectives, acknowledging the multiple realities of all partners. The assessment evidence gathered through such methods is intended to support critical reflection and evaluative dialogue between children and adults, which will generate knowledge about learning journeys and the quality of the pedagogic environment and can be used to support setting improvement and accountability.

Methodological considerations: observing and listening

In our view, listening to and observing young children and parents is an integral part of understanding what they are feeling and experiencing, and what it is they need from their early education experience. It is important to remember that all children (and parents) are 'experts in their own lives' (Langsted, 1994) and are active 'co-constructors of meaning'. These ideas about childhood, children's rights, democratic participation and voice are central in our consideration of appropriate assessment methodologies. We believe that the process of systematically watching and listening to children and parents and documenting what they see and hear is at the heart of effective evaluation practice.

Observing children and adults

Observation is a way of collecting information about the child, the adult (parent and practitioner) and their individual capacities. When focusing on children it enables practitioners and parents to understand a child's unique approach to the world, the level of their current competencies and skills, to recognise any particular talents and gifts they are developing, any particular needs they have, the state of their emotional well-being and to make sense of how the child's understanding and thinking is evolving. The information gained also allows the practitioner and parent to track children's learning and development over time and in different contexts and to plan for the next steps of learning. Skilled practitioners assess children's progress by analysing and interpreting their regular observations of children engaged in a range of daily experiences and activities. The information gained from observations of the child in the setting is strengthened when the parent's observations of the child at home are added. Observations can be formal (planned and structured) and informal (spontaneous and narrative). Practitioners need both kinds of observation to ensure they capture the child's learning and development profile as a whole. Practitioners plan for learning at an individual and group level on the basis of the information gained by their observations of children. This enables the learning experiences planned to be pitched at the right level of challenge to extend the child's capacities.

When observing adults it is important to do so in the context of settings being viewed as learning organisations in which everyone, children, parents and staff, learn together in 'learning communities' (Pascal and Bertram, 2012; Wenger, 1998). All learning takes place in a social context and we learn best when we have self-esteem, confidence and feel connected. 'Learning communities' create an important climatic and cultural openness to change and development because they are unthreatening. But to avoid being simply self-congratulatory they also need to have systematic and rigorous mechanisms for making judgements and effecting change. Professional 'learning communities' should be a key element of all participatory settings and the use of adult observation instruments in assessment is a useful means of enabling colleagues to focus on their interaction with children by assessing aspects of their interaction such as their Sensitivity, Stimulation and Autonomy (Bertram and Pascal, 2006a, 2006b, 2008). Experienced early childhood practitioners should be able to make and receive informed and critical judgements about the quality of teaching and learning offered. Within this important peer relationship we are aware of the need to foster positive working relations with colleagues. We should stress, however, the equal importance of conducting these observations as honestly and openly as possible to provide an effective means of developing the quality of a setting's practice.

Achieving productive peer review through adult observations requires consideration of the following points:

- staff are trained and understand the purpose of the peer review process and the central importance of their interactions with children, parents and colleagues to effective provision;
- where possible staff should be able to choose with whom they do their peer observations;
- peers should feel they are matched with someone who is credible and who they trust, respect and value;
- the peer review is ongoing rather than one off and part of a continual dialogue about professional development;
- staff receive confidential feedback as a dialogue about their professional interactions as soon as possible after the observation process;
- when giving feedback the emphasis is on encouraging the positives, being explicit about points for development, and prioritising these rather than cataloguing every nuance;
- an individual's feedback should be followed with opportunities for appropriate professional development opportunities;
- personal remarks of any kind should be avoided at all times.

England's *Early Years Foundation Stage Curriculum Guidance* (DCFS, 2008) suggests five generic observation skills:

1. *Looking* – being clear about what aspects of adult or child learning and development the observation is focusing on.
2. *Listening* – paying attention to the adult or child's interactions and narratives as they engage with the world.
3. *Recording* – noting what is significant in an efficient and accurate way.
4. *Thinking* – reflecting on what has been seen and linking this into assessing and planning.
5. *Questioning* – asking questions in dialogue with parents, children and other adults to clarify, confirm or reject judgements about what has been observed.

There are many types of observation. Some observations will be spontaneous and take the form of incidental notes (sticky notes are often used), which capture a child's response to an activity or event as it occurs. Some observations will be more carefully planned. These will be carefully timetabled as the practitioner needs to be able to stand back and watch the child as they are engaged in their day-to-day activity, and in particular, when the child is at play or engaged in a self-chosen activity. The observation is generally focused on certain aspects of the child's development and learning. These observations are often documented in an agreed format, which may map onto defined areas of learning. These planned observations usually last for around two to ten minutes, with some information being recorded as the observation progresses with additional notes added afterwards.

The advantage of these kinds of observations are that, when several of these observations are built up over time and contexts, they can provide more reliable and valid evidence of the child's developmental profile. Some observations are also captured with photographs, audiotapes and video footage. This kind of observational information is useful as it captures a lot more information and contextualises the learning but it can require more time for systematic analysis and interpretation. This type of recorded observations has the advantage of supporting the dialogue with parents and children about the observational evidence. They are a very useful supplement to notes taken and documented in a shortened format.

It is important that observations are carried out regularly and systematically to ensure the evidence gathered is trustworthy, accurate and valid. This requires that the observations should include different times of the day, different activities, different groupings of children and that all key staff should be involved. All children in a setting should be observed over time, and it is important that judgements of a child are not made on the basis of one observation but on a series of observations carried out over time and capturing the child in different contexts and activities.

Ethical and good practice suggests that children from the earliest age and their parents should be involved in the observational and assessment process. All observations should be shared with these partners in the learning process as it provides a wonderful opportunity to celebrate a child's achievements and plan for the next stage of learning. Parents and children also know a lot more about the child's competencies and so can strengthen, validate and extend the observational evidence gathered by practitioners. For example, the AcE assessment process (Bertram, Pascal and Saunders, 2008) not only includes children and parents in the sharing of observations but also encourages the children and parents to carry out their own observations and to record these in the form of a Learning Story in any way they choose. This joint assessment work provides an authentic and positive process of active partnership and involvement of parents and children in learning.

Listening with and to parents and children

Parents come first. They are the child's first educator and the most important influence in the child's life. Children learn from the moment of birth, if not sooner, and their parents and extended family provide both the context in which learning occurs and the continuity between home, nursery and school. As the child progresses into early education and care settings their learning continues to be most strongly influenced by the home, so it follows that the closer the links between parent and the early years setting, the more effective that learning becomes. Parents have a unique knowledge of aspects of their children's development which is central to an effective and accurate assessment process. An essential feature of effective parental involvement is an ongoing, symmetrical dialogue between parents and practitioners. Real partnership with parents in assessment processes demands a shared sense of purpose, mutual respect and a willingness to negotiate. It requires open, regular and reciprocal communication, where achievements are celebrated, problems confronted, solutions sought and policies implemented, jointly and together. It takes time, effort and trust. It implies that parental competence is on a par with professional expertise.

It is important to acknowledge that parents are not a homogeneous group – each family and their lives are different, and practitioners can find communicating with and getting to know parents challenging. There is no one way of engaging parents, what suits one will not suit another, so different ways need to be thought through and tried. Settings must also be prepared to adapt the ways in which they work to suit the changing needs of families and to experiment and innovate where existing practices have not worked well. A starting point for most settings could be the initial visit of the key person or family worker to the family home prior to the child attending the setting. This is an ideal opportunity to begin to build positive relationships with the child and family and to exchange knowledge and information. Often settings offer introductory meetings before a child starts attending, to help parents understand the setting's philosophy and approach to learning and development. This is another way to begin to build up good relationships and mutual respect and understandings.

Developing open and respectful relationships for some parents and practitioners can be challenging for many reasons. Freire (1970, p. 71) says there is a series of steps which have to be taken before participants can begin to develop a symmetrical dialogue with each other. These steps require participants to:

- perceive their own ignorance and give up the idea that they are the exclusive owners of truth and knowledge;
- identify with others and recognise the fact that 'naming the world' is not the task of the elite;
- value the contribution of others and listen to them with humility, respecting the particular view of the world held by different people;
- get in touch with how much we need other people and have no fear of being displaced; and
- be humble; have faith in others and believe in their strengths.

We believe that active listening is one of the most important assessment skills a practitioner can have. How well practitioners listen has a major impact on their job effectiveness, and the quality of their relationship with others. Practitioners listen to obtain information, to understand, for enjoyment and to learn. Effective listening is an active rather than a passive activity. The listener must be an active participant for the cycle of communication to be complete. There are a number of elements in active listening, which include (Pascal and Bertram, 2013):

1. *Pay attention*. Give the speaker undivided attention and acknowledge the message. Recognise that what is not being said also speaks loudly.
2. *Show you are listening*. Use your own body language and gestures to convey your attention, nod occasionally, smile and use other facial expressions, note your posture and make sure it is open and inviting, encourage the speaker to continue with small verbal comments.
3. *Provide feedback*. Our personal filters, assumptions, judgements and beliefs can distort what we hear. As a listener your role is to understand what is being said. This may require you to reflect on what is being said by paraphrasing, 'what I am hearing is' or 'it sounds like you are saying'. Ask questions to clarify certain points, 'what do you mean when you say?', or 'is this what you mean?' Summarise the speaker's comments periodically.
4. *Defer judgement*. Interrupting is a waste of time. It frustrates the speaker and limits full understanding of the message. Allow the speaker to finish and do not interrupt with counter arguments. Respond appropriately. Active listening is a model for respect and understanding. You are gaining information and perspective. You add nothing by attacking the speaker or otherwise putting him or her down.
5. *Be candid, open and honest in your response*. Assert your opinions respectfully. Treat the other person as you would want to be treated.

Just as we are learning to listen more carefully to parents' voices in the education and care of young children, we also have to concern ourselves with listening to children. Much of what has been said above is equally important when listening to young children. Listening to children is an integral part of understanding what they are feeling and what it is they need from their early education experience. It acknowledges their right to be listened to and for their views and experiences to be taken seriously. Listening can make a difference to our understanding of children's priorities, interests and concern and it can make a difference to our understanding of how children feel about themselves. Listening is a vital part of establishing respectful relationships with the children we work with and is central to the learning process. Listening can challenge assumptions and raise expectations. Seeing and hearing children express their interest and priorities can provide unexpected insights into their capabilities (Oliveira-Formosinho and Formosinho, 2012).

We see these perspectives of listening to children and parents as standing together in the construction of dialogues, in which there is mutual respect, active participation and the negotiation and co-construction of meaning. In particular, listening to children and encouraging their participation in assessment and evaluation and consequent decision making and planning is important for many reasons. Educationalists emphasise the importance of participation in empowering children as learners, enabling them to make choices, express their ideas and opinions and develop a positive sense of self (Roberts, 2002; Bruce, 2005). Other writers foreground the benefits of their participation to society as a whole and for development of citizenship. As Miller (1997) points out, children who learn to participate in their early years are more likely to become more capable and involved citizens with respect for the principles and practice of democratic life. Although we might subscribe to this view, we should also be cautious as it looks at children as future adults and therefore frames them in what they are not (yet). However, for us, this perspective has validity only if we see children as active citizens in the here and now, already participating in a democratic life in which they have full rights and responsibilities which they are practising continually in their daily interactions with the world, engaging in what Biesta et al. (2009) call 'learning democracy'. James and Prout (1997) and Dahlberg et al. (2006) allude to this view in the ethical and philosophical stance they adopt which acknowledges children as actors and stakeholders in their own lives, challenging the traditional view of children as empty vessels and vulnerable beings who are incapable of acting with agency and on their own behalf. They see children as powerful, competent individuals who are well able to express preferences and make informed choices. However, Maybin and Woodhead (2003) also warn us against adopting a universal and 'Westernised' notion of children's participation. If the early years setting is truly the first democratic forum where participants learn to understand each other's perspectives, values and histories, then it is an arena of great cultural sensitivity. Nothing can be more culturally sensitive than how families choose to raise their children and how the state's view fits with that perspective. Providers of children's services, particularly those who are state maintained and who deliver programmes and curricula derived from the state, need to balance the values and beliefs of the state with the values and beliefs of individual families. In this sense state early childhood services function as political, as well as educational, civic and economic levers of government.

But our concern in this book is at the micro-level. In our view listening to young children is an integral part of understanding what they are feeling and experiencing, and what it is they need from their early years experience. Giving status to children's voices in our assessment and evaluation work acknowledges children's right to be listened to and for their views and experiences to be taken seriously. We feel that listening well to children can make a difference to our understanding of their priorities, interests and concerns and how children feel about themselves and their lives. Listening is also a vital part of establishing respectful and educative relationships with the children we work with. We have found that listening can challenge assumptions and raise expectations. Seeing and hearing children express their interests and priorities can provide unexpected insights into their capabilities.

For us, listening to young children is an active process of receiving, interpreting and responding to their communications. 'Listening' includes using all the senses and emotions and accessing children's range of communication is clearly not limited to the spoken word. As participatory practitioners, we see it as necessary to ensure the participation of young children and an approach which allows us to tune in to all young children as individuals in their everyday lives. Understanding listening in this way is key to providing an environment in which all young children feel confident, safe and powerful, ensuring they have the time and space to express themselves in whatever form suits them. When listening to babies or children with disabilities it is necessary to look to their body language, different tonal patterns, facial expressions and bodily movements. These signals help build a picture of what life is like in the setting for these children, what their preferences are and how competent and confident they feel.

These ideas about childhood, children's rights, democratic participation and voice have profoundly affected our research and development work and led us to adopt an ethical code which states that children are to be supported as active participants in any assessment and evaluation process and that their voices should always form a central and equally considered part of any evidence base which concerns them. It also acknowledges that we are 'answerable' (Bahktin, 1981) for the way these voices are documented and represented in our evaluation outputs (Formosinho, Chapter 6 of this volume).

Listening is an active process of receiving, interpreting and responding to communication. It includes all the senses and emotions and is not limited to the spoken word. It is a necessary stage in ensuring the participation of all young children and an ongoing part of tuning in to all young children as individuals in their everyday lives. Understanding listening in this way is key to providing an environment in which all young children feel confident, safe and powerful, ensuring they have the time and space to express themselves in whatever form suits them.

Our work has shown us that children are able to express their opinion in ways that are very perceptive and that give a real insight into what their lives are and what meaning they are making of them. These insights provide a profoundly challenging alternative dimension to our knowledge and understanding of early childhood education and care and what shapes the lives of young children. It is clear that supporting and catching children's voices is complex, challenging and multi-layered, involving a profound paradigm shift in the values, actions and thinking of both researchers and practitioners. We are reminded of Woodhead's (1999) perceptive comments:

> Morally, it seems to me that as teachers, students and researchers, we have a responsibility to be attuned to how the tasks of childhood are perceived, felt and understood by those children, their parents and other carers who have to solve the problems of living and growing up, in circumstances that may be vastly different from those that shape our own personal and academic priorities.

and

> The question is about the status we accord the child through the methodologies we adopt and the conclusions we draw; and about whether we allow children the space to alter our agenda of presuppositions.
>
> (Woodhead, 1999, p. 19)

The UN Convention on the Rights of the Child is now part of our thinking and discourse but it is far from being realised in our actions. It is the responsibility of all of us engaged in working with young children to strive to ensure that children's right to active participation maintains a high profile in our assessment practice.

Methodological possibilities

There are a wide range of possible assessment and evaluation methods which are appropriate within a participatory pedagogy. No one method can provide all the evidence, nor support the participation of all interested parties, and so a repertoire of methods is required which allows the collective interrogation and scrutiny of pedagogic contexts, processes and outcomes. A range of possible methods are set out below, but it should be emphasised that those presented are not an exhaustive list and are presented as illustrative possibilities.

Given the ambitions and challenges discussed, this selection of possible methods recognises the need to extend the range of voices and explore different ways of doing, reporting and discussing evaluation evidence. In this way it can enhance its potential to reveal greater complexity and richness in the context by inviting multiple levels of engagement in the evaluation process which are at the same time cognitive, emotional and multi-sensory. Those leading the pedagogic practice need to have the courage to innovate and experiment and go beyond traditional and orthodox assessment and evaluation methods in order to better encourage silenced people to find ways to tell and thus reclaim their own story. So, while early childhood evaluators might use orthodox assessment and evaluation methods such as observations, interviews, case studies, life biographies, questionnaires and so on, there is a clear move among early childhood practitioner researchers and evaluators, including ourselves, to consider storytelling, drawing, painting, song, dance, poetry, photography, film making, socio-drama, mime and plays in their methodological toolbox. It is claimed that this wider range of expressive activity enriches the evaluation and provides complexity and depth, thus allowing a richer vein of knowledge and understandings to be made visible. It also provides a means through which ordinary people may better express, experience and validate the data being generated. We believe that these different forms of expression and representation can provide a more authentic account of the pedagogic practice under investigation and unmask some of the often hidden aspects of understandings and meanings which flow from the evidence. A strong case is being made by people such as Reason and Bradbury (2008) that these alternative and expressive forms of knowing need to be taken more seriously in our assessment and evaluation designs if we are to see more inclusive, democratic, participatory and intense forms of inquiry in the future.

In the rest of this chapter we shall set out a range of participatory assessment methods which could be utilised to evaluate pedagogic quality in the three dimensions outlined previously. These examples are not intended to be an exhaustive list but are provided as exemplars of useful approaches to gathering evidence which meet our ethical principles.

Assessment methods: pedagogic context

Method 1: EEL Child Tracking

The EEL Child Tracking tool is an observational instrument developed by Bertram and Pascal (2006a, 2006b, 2008) in which a sample of children from a setting are tracked throughout their 'normal' session using timed interval Child Tracking techniques. The aim is to provide an overview or snapshot of the child's day. The technique provides statistical and narrative information about the frequency and nature of learning experiences, the amount of choice offered to the children in the setting, the grouping of children, the level of involvement of the children in the activities offered and the dominant interactions between adults and children. The resultant statistical and narrative data are analysed to facilitate an assessment of the nature and breadth of the child's pedagogic and learning experiences within the setting.

Method 2: Documentary analysis

Written documentation from the setting is collected, including latest inspection or quality assurance reports, policy statements, pedagogic and curriculum programme outlines, assessment and record keeping materials, information sheets, prospectus, etc. This narrative and statistical information is critically analysed in relation to each of the dimensions of quality, to determine the stated philosophy, aims, objectives and approach to policy and practice in the setting.

Method 3: Reflective dialogues

Reflective dialogues are convened with children, parents, practitioners, governors/owners. The dialogues are semi-structured but conducted informally, often taking the form of an extended and critical conversation about policy and practice within the setting. Various kinds of information, communication and technology media, social media and web based dialogues are additional forums for facilitating dialogues.

Method 4: Observational instruments

Information is collected using structured proforma or questionnaires regarding an aspect of the provision such as, for example, the physical environment of the setting; the training, qualifications and experience of those who work within the setting and the opportunities staff have for professional development; the nature of interactions in the setting; leadership and management; organisation and grouping; behaviour management. These observations can allow each aspect to be rated according to a numerical scale.

Method 5: Visual/digital images or audio records

Photographs, films or other visual and audio images of practice of reflections, feedback and evaluative comments are encouraged and analysed. Our experimentation and innovations, for example in the Opening Windows Project and the AcE Programme (Bertram, Pascal and Gill, 2008; Bertram, Pascal and Saunders, 2008), stimulated by Freire's (1970) work on cultural circles, and adapting some techniques highlighted in the Mosaic Approach (Clark and Moss, 2001) to listening to children, have led to our experimentation with a number of ways to facilitate and record reflective feedback, including:

- Graffiti walls
- Listening posts
- Comments box
- Cultural Circles
- Critical Incident Analysis
- Story Telling and Naming Your World
- Wishing Trees
- Map Making
- Guided Tours
- Photography and Film Making.

Method 6: Questionnaires/surveys

Structured or semi-structured questionnaires/surveys of parents, children and practitioner perspectives about aspects of policy and practice in the setting are distributed and results are analysed.

Method 7: Journals

Participants (practitioners, parents, children) are encouraged to keep a journal in which they record and critically reflect upon their experiences in the setting. Participants are advised to write down details of what they did, or how they did something and then ask:

- How did it go? Why?
- What were my thoughts and feelings?
- What did I think about and not say? Why?
- What have I learnt?
- What would I do differently another time?
- Have I learnt anything about myself?
- How can I use the experience in the future?

Assessment methods: pedagogic processes

Method 7: BEEL Child Engagement Scale

The BEEL Child Engagement Scale is an observational scale developed by Bertram and Pascal (2006b) for the Baby Effective Early Learning (BEEL) Programme and is aimed at children under the age of three. It provides a means by which the quality of the young child's engagement in the learning and development experiences offered in a setting can be assessed. It has three elements:

- *Connectedness*: this looks at the child's sense of location in the world, and links this to independence, cooperation, openness, alertness, humour, vitality, participation, empathy and friendliness. Research evidence suggests that children who have these qualities have a secure sense of belonging and have strong emotional security and well-being and are more likely to be able to explore confidently and to initiate interactions and learning than those who are uncertain, timid, angry, aggressive, anxious or bewildered.
- *Exploration*: this captures the child's inner motivation to find out about the world, including the strength of the exploratory drive, persistence and the ability to intensify focus. The ability to absorb oneself in reflective activity is at the centre of our development as a species and can be observed even in very young children.
- *Meaning Making*: this looks for evidence of the child's ability to construct hypotheses, to use strategies, try different things and learn from mistakes, to predict what might happen next, to see difference and similarity and to be a purposeful and independent explorer.

Taken together, these three qualities of children's responses to the learning experiences offered will provide an insight into the effectiveness of the setting in stimulating the child's social, emotional and cognitive development (Bertram, Pascal and Saunders, 2008). Children are systematically observed on several occasions and for each observation each of these three key elements of Child Engagement are assessed on a five-point scale. These ratings are collated to generate statistical evidence about the quality of learning processes offered in the setting.

Method 8: Child involvement

The Child Involvement Scale is an observation instrument developed by Laevers (1994) which aims to measure the level of a child's 'involvement' in an activity, focusing on the processes of learning, rather than on outcomes. Involvement is seen as a quality of human activity which can be recognised by a child's concentration and persistence. Involvement is seen as a measure for quality which is applicable to a range of situations and is observable at all ages. It is characterised by motivation, fascination, openness to stimuli and an intensity of experience both at the physical and cognitive level, and a deep satisfaction with a strong flow of energy. Involvement is situated at the edge of a child's capabilities, or in the 'Zone of Proximal Development' (Vygotsky, 1978). There is evidence to suggest that an 'involved' child is gaining a deep, motivated, intense and long term learning experience (Csikszentmihayli, 1979; Laevers, 1994). Children are systematically observed on several occasions and for each observation the level of child involvement is assessed on a five-point scale. These ratings are collated to generate statistical evidence about the quality of learning processes offered in the setting.

Method 9: EEL Adult Engagement

This is an observational scale developed by Bertram and Pascal (2006a, 2006b) for use in the Effective Early Learning (EEL) Programme and which provides a means by which the quality of an adult's pedagogic engagement in the learning and development experiences offered in a setting can be assessed. Engagement may be defined as a set of personal qualities which describe the nature of the educative relationships between the adult and the child. These personal qualities will affect an adult's ability to motivate, extend, enhance and involve children in the learning process. An adult's actions may therefore be categorised as displaying 'engaging' qualities or 'non-engaging' qualities. Drawing on Laevers' (1994) work on Adult Styles this scale assesses three categories of adult behaviour:

- *Sensitivity*: this is the sensitivity of the adult to the feelings and emotional well-being of the child and includes elements of sincerity, empathy, responsiveness and affection.
- *Stimulation:* this is the way in which the adult intervenes in the learning process and the content of such interventions.
- *Autonomy:* this is the degree of freedom which the adult provides for the child to experiment, make judgements, choose activities and express ideas. It also encompasses how the adult handles conflict, rules and behavioural issues.

Practitioners and/or parents are systematically observed on several occasions and for each observation the level of adult engagement is assessed on a five-point scale. These ratings are collated to generate statistical evidence about the style of adult interactions and the quality of learning offered by adults in the setting. Each point on the five-point scale reflects the degree to which the observed actions convey those adult qualities which are supportive of children's learning.

Method 10: Child and adult well-being

Young children's involvement in deep level learning cannot take place unless their emotional well-being is addressed. Adult engagement in learning processes is similarly dependent on the adults' professional sense of well-being. Therefore, we believe it is important to evaluate whether the children and adults in the setting feel valued, encouraged, confident in their abilities and empowered. Well-being focuses on the extent to which children and adults feel at ease, act spontaneously, show vitality and self-confidence. It is a crucial component of emotional intelligence and good mental health. The Leuven Scales for Emotional Well-being (developed by Laevers et al., 2005) are a useful observational tool for assessing this aspect of provision on a five-point scale.

Assessment methods: pedagogic outcomes

Method 11: The AcE Scales

The AcE Scales were developed by Bertram, Pascal and Saunders (2008) and assess the developmental outcomes of children in five learning domains:

- Communication and Language Development
- Attitudes and Dispositions
- Social Competence
- Emotional Well-being
- Physical Development.

Children are systematically observed in their daily activity, with a focus on children's play and self-chosen activities, by both practitioners and parents, at home and in the setting on several occasions. For each observation the capacity of the child in each domain is assessed on a four-point scale. These ratings are collated to generate statistical evidence about the developmental profile of the child in each learning domain, and the progress made by the child or a group of children over time. The assessment information is used to support pedagogic action both in the setting and in the home and is linked to an early support and intervention strategy. The initial assessments using the scale are done after the first few weeks of the child's experience of a programme to allow a child 'settling in' time and then further observations and assessments are carried out periodically to track a child's development and support the planning of learning. The scale will also provide evidence of children's capacity on entry to a programme and show how children have developed during their time in the setting.

Method 12: Practitioner outcomes: professional development

Adults in a setting can also measure their own development. Staff appraisal using self-evaluation and staff/volunteer performance reviews can offer ways of improving effectiveness and identify professional skill progression. Performance indicators should be negotiated. Development may be both short term and long term but all development of adults will feed into their professional well-being and their ability to engage with young children.

Method 13: Parent outcomes

Assessing the development outcomes for parents of an early childhood programme or service will provide valuable evaluation evidence of the quality of a programme to influence the wider social world of the child. Services that actively engage parents in their provision will generate clear development outcomes for parents/carers. This may include such things as increased parenting skills, enhanced parental confidence, improved home learning environments, increased aspirations. These outcomes could be assessed qualitatively through narrative tools such as family case studies, interviews, questionnaires. They might also be assessed using a quantitative scale which invites parents to assess their level of confidence, parenting skills etc.

Method 14: Setting outcomes – quality improvement

Assessment and evaluation processes should generate strong, relevant and robust data about the settings performance in a number of dimensions. An evaluation of this wider body of evidence should feed directly into a setting's development or improvement planning, identifying key action points for improvement. The focus for these quality improvements will depend heavily on the capacity of the staff/volunteers, but short and long term action plans within the cycle of evaluation and improvement should lead to the achievement of self-identified impact measures. Over time, these developmental achievements will improve the setting's context in relation to all three aspects of context, process and outcomes.

Evaluation methods

Method 15: Action planning

The setting leader or an external support worker should act as a change agent and a source of expert knowledge during this process. Their first task is to collate and analyse all the assessment evidence on the context, process and outcomes of the setting in a single summary evaluation document. Working together, the staff, parents and children of the setting then have a series of meetings to discuss the collated evidence and evaluate the practice using the evidence, identifying their priorities for action. This may take the form of expertise, identifying resources, further training, support structures or organisational changes. At the end of this stage a structured and achievable action plan for the development of early learning which has clearly articulated objectives within an identified time scale should emerge.

Method 16: Focused improvement cycles

The evaluation lead should, with team support, identify and mobilise the required resources and support to facilitate the action. This may take the form of expertise, resources, further training, support structures, organisational changes, etc.

In conjunction with the participating staff, the lead worker draws up a timetable for implementation of the action plan and allocates responsibilities. Settings may choose to do the improvement process as a mini-cycle, three or four times in between completing the full evaluation process. The full evaluation phase would then take place every two/three years. The programme of individual and/or setting improvement which relates closely to the agreed targets of the Action Plan is then implemented. Throughout this phase, progress should be monitored and the practitioners are encouraged to gather evidence upon the effect of the action on the quality of the children's care, learning and development experiences within the setting (impact measures). The effectiveness of the action can be established by using the Child Involvement Scale and the Adult Engagement Scale again, and comparing with the previous results.

Establishing rigour

In this account of participatory assessment and evaluation methods, we are seeking to offer robust and practice based evidence which may be used for critical reflection and action (praxis). It is essential that this evidence is perceived as rigorous, trustworthy and of sufficient depth to enable sound and rigorous evaluative judgements to be made. As stated, participatory assessment and evaluation can adopt many different methods but establishing the rigour and trustworthiness in their execution is critically important. McNiff (2010) argues that this is part of a transition from 'traditional scholarship' to what is now called 'new scholarship', and this requires different criteria by which to judge its rigour. In this new scholarship, the old technical criteria which judged the worth or value of data through statistical reliability and validity checks need to be substituted by more qualitative, experiential criteria which should be given equal status and credence. Lincoln and Guba (1985) argue that establishing the trustworthiness or dependability of any evaluative study is important to evaluating its worth. For them trustworthiness involves establishing:

- *Credibility* – confidence in the 'truth' of the findings.
- *Transferability* – showing that the findings have applicability in other contexts.
- *Dependability* – showing that the findings are consistent and could be repeated.
- *Confirmability* – a degree of neutrality or the extent to which the findings of a study emerge from the data and not their own predispositions.

Guba and Lincoln (2005) also describe a series of techniques that can be used to conduct qualitative research that achieves the criteria they outline.

Techniques for establishing credibility

One of the most important factors in establishing trustworthiness in the evidence is that of ensuring credibility. The following provisions within an assessment and evaluation strategy will promote confidence that the evidence has been accurately and authentically documented.

Prolonged engagement: it is important to ensure that those involved in the assessment and evaluation are familiar with the setting, and in this sense are 'attached' not 'detached' and the process emerges from a period of prolonged engagement rather than a 'hit and run' approach.

Persistent observation: the assessments emerge from a process of persistent and regular observations of the practice within a setting.

Peer debriefing: there should be frequent peer debriefing sessions throughout the assessment and evaluation process which is open and allows other experiences and perceptions to be brought into and included in the evaluative process. They also provide a sounding board for the emerging evaluation analysis which may help identify any biases and preferences.

Negative case analysis: this process ensures that all data is included in the evaluation and analysis proceeds until all cases, including negative ones, are accommodated within the evaluation.

Member checking: feedback from participants at all stages provides opportunity for scrutiny of the assessment evidence and the evaluative interpretations being made.

Techniques for establishing transferability

Thick description: detailed description of the various elements of provision in this area can be an important strategy for promoting credibility as it helps to convey the actual situations that have been investigated and the contexts that surround them (Geertz, 1973). This allows for a judgement of whether the findings appear credible and authentic within the wider context and for their wider applicability to be illuminated.

Techniques for establishing dependability

Inquiry audit: this requires an acknowledgement of the subjectivity of the assessment and evaluation process and transparency about any predispositions or preferred way of working. There should be clarity of how the evaluation and interpretation process progressed and an audit showing how this was linked to the data and not to any pre-existing assumptions.

Techniques for establishing confirmability

Audit trail: An 'audit trail' of the evidence clarifies how it was obtained, from whom and when and details the step-by-step decisions made throughout the assessment and evaluation process. This allows any observer to trace the course of the process and critique the analysis and its findings.

Triangulation: this may involve the use of different methods, or obtaining information from different sources or informants, and different documents. This allows a check to be made on the balance of the evidence and the strength of any evaluative judgements made on the basis of the evidence.

Reflexivity: this captures the participant's 'reflective commentary' and requires an internal reflective commentary about emerging patterns, issues arising, possible interpretations. Journaling is a useful tool to facilitate and document this process.

References

Bakhtin, M.M. (1981) *The Dialogic Imagination: Four Essays.* Ed. Michael Holquist. Trans. Caryl Emerson and Michael Holquist. University of Texas Press: Austin and London.

Biesta, G.J.J., Lawy, R.S. and Kelly, N. (2009) Understanding young people's citizenship learning in everyday life: the role of contexts, relationships and dispositions. *Education, Citizenship and Social Justice,* 4(1), 5–24.

Bertram, T. and Pascal, C (2006a) *Baby Effective Early Learning (BEEL), A Handbook for Evaluating, Assuring and Improving Quality in Settings for Birth to Three Year Olds.* Amber Publishing: Birmingham.

Bertram, T. and Pascal, C. (2006b) *Effective Early Learning (EEL) A Handbook For Evaluating, Assuring and Improving Quality in Early Childhood Settings.* Amber Publishing: Birmingham.

Bertram T., Pascal, C. and Gill D. (2008) *Opening Windows: A Handbook for Enhancing Equity and Diversity in Early Childhood Settings.* Amber Publishing, Birmingham.

Bertram, T., Pascal, C. and Saunders M. (2008) *Accounting Early for Life Long Learning (AcE), A Handbook for Assessing Young Children.* Amber Publishing: Birmingham.

Bruce, T. (2004) *Developing Learning in Early Childhood.* Sage Publications: London.

Clark, A. and Moss, P. (2001) *Listening to Young Children: The Mosaic Approach.* NCB: London.

Csikszentmihayli, M. (1979) The concept of flow. In B. Sutton-Smith, *Play and Learning,* pp. 257–273. Gardner: New York.

Dahlberg, G., Moss, P. and Pence, A. (2006) *Beyond Quality in Early Childhood Education and Care: Postmodern Perspectives,* 2nd edn. Falmer Press: London.

DCFS (2008) *Practice Guidance for the Early Years Foundation Stage.* DCFS: Nottingham.

Formosinho, J. (2015) Pedagogic documentation: Uncovering solidary learning. In J. Formosinho and C. Pascal (eds), *Assessment and Evaluation for Transformation,* pp. 107–128. Routledge: London.

Freire, P. (1970) *Pedagogy of the Oppressed.* Herder and Herder: New York.

Geertz, C. (1973) Thick description: toward an interpretive theory of culture. In *The Interpretation of Cultures: Selected Essays,* pp. 3–30. Basic Books: New York.

Guba, E.G. and Lincoln, Y. S. (2005). Paradigmatic controversies, contradictions, and emerging influences. In N.K. Denzin and Y.S. Lincoln (eds), *The Sage Handbook of Qualitative Research,* 3rd edn, pp. 191–215. Sage: Thousand Oaks, CA.

James, A. and Prout, A. (1997) *Constructing and Reconstructing Childhood: Contemporary Issues in the Sociological Study of Childhood.* Psychology Press: London.

Laevers F. (1994) *The Leuven Involvement Scale for Young Children LIS-YC.* Manual and Video Tape, Experiential Education Series, N. 1. Centre for Experiential Education: Leuven.

Laevers, F., Debruyckere G., Silkens, K. and Snoeck, G. (2005). *Observation of Well-being and Involvement in Babies and Toddlers.* A video-training pack with manual. Research Centre for Experiential Education: Leuven.

Langsted, O. (1994) Looking at quality from the child's perspective. In P. Moss and A. Pence (eds), *Valuing Quality in Early Childhood Services: New Approaches to Defining Quality.* Paul Chapman: London.

Lincoln, Y.S. and Guba, E.G. (1985) *Naturalistic Inquiry*. Sage Publications: Newbury Park, CA.

Maybin, J. and Woodhead, M. (2003) Socializing children. In J. Maybin and M. Woodhead (eds), *Childhoods in Context*. Wiley: Chichester.

McNiff, J. (2010) *Action Research for Professional Development*. September Books: Dorset.

Miller, J. (1997) *Never Too Young: How Young Children Can Take Responsibility and Make Decisions*. Save the Children: London.

Oliveira-Formosinho, J. and Formosinho, J. (2012) *Pedagogy-in-Participation: Childhood Association Educational Perspective*. Porto Editora: Porto.

Pascal, C. and Bertram, T. (2012) Praxis, ethics and power: developing praxeology as a participatory paradigm for early childhood research. *European Early Childhood Education Research Journal*, 20, 4: 477–492.

Pascal, C. and Bertram, T. (2013) Small voices, powerful messages: capturing young children's perspectives in practice-led research. In M. Hammersley, R. Flewett, M. Robb and A. Clark, *Issues in Research with Children and Young People*. Sage Publications/Open University Press: Milton Keynes.

Reason, P. and Bradbury, H. (eds) (2008) *Sage Handbook of Action Research: Participative Inquiry and Practice,* 2nd edn. Sage Publications: London.

Roberts, R. (2002) *Self Esteem and Early Learning*. Sage Publications: London.

Vygotsky L.S. (1978) *Mind in Society*. Harvard University Press: Cambridge, MA.

Wenger, E. (1998) *Communities of Practice: Learning, Meaning, and Identity*. Cambridge University Press: Cambridge.

Woodhead, M. (1999) Towards a global paradigm for research into early childhood education, *European Early Childhood Education Research Journal,* 7, 1: 5–22.

5

THE SEARCH FOR A HOLISTIC APPROACH TO EVALUATION

João Formosinho and Júlia Formosinho

This chapter presents our own holistic approach to evaluation which embodies an ethically principled and democratic perspective incorporating the active contribution of children, practitioners and families. This approach is interested in all aspects of children's learning with an intention to see the whole child, rather than fragmented elements of her/his identity, learning processes and progression in learning.

It is known that assessment and evaluation procedures may foster or hinder the full development of the foundational pedagogic approach. This holistic pedagogic approach is congruent with childhood participatory pedagogies and co-constructivist epistemologies.

This holistic pedagogic approach to evaluation sets out to conceptualise and use a standpoint to assessment that is situated in place, time and cultures serving primarily children and families, but also professionals, early childhood centres and the wider community, research and the educational system.

This approach requires from the professionals a conscious engagement of their integrated thinking, doing and feeling to achieve a deeply contextualised understanding of children's learning, thus slowly creating an antidote for resilience to the generalised pressure for using abstract and decontextualised assessment and evaluation instruments.

The epistemological stance – inadequacy of the applicationist view on educational assessment and evaluation

Education has been seen for decades by researchers and policy makers as the application of positivist science, just as technology is seen as a mere application of natural sciences achievements. Scientists like psychologists, sociologists and economists conduct research, develop theory, create knowledge; practitioners and policy makers apply in the field the knowledge thus produced. This sums up this applicationist view of social professional practice.

Thus the identity of the field of education was compartmentalised by the scientific domains that came to be more influential in its development. The very essence of education developed as cumulative processes of the various natures of the central scientific domains: psychology of education (educational psychology and developmental psychology), sociology of education, economy of education and also history of education, anthropology of education and others. But education as a field of action is much more that this accumulation of compartmentalised knowledge. It is a field per se, in its own right (Dewey, 1938; Malaguzzi, 1998). Over the last twenty years, in the field of early years pedagogy, we have also seen a call for attention to pedagogy as a field in its own right (Freire, 1996; Oliveira-Formosinho, 2007; Formosinho and Oliveira-Formosinho, 2012).

The applicationist perspective of the positivist paradigm in educational assessment and evaluation

Rejection of complexity

As Morin (1986) says, classical science rejected complexity in virtue of the *principle of reduction* that consists in knowing any composite from the knowledge of its basic elements. It also embraced the *principle of disjunction* that consists in separating cognitive difficulties, leading to the separation of disciplines. As you isolate the object, the complexity disappears: in a closed discipline this decontextualised object is not a scientific problem.

The rejection of complexity does not serve social sciences nor education and childhood pedagogy. Childhood pedagogy as praxis sits in complexity because it serves multidimensional holistic children in interaction with peers and educators.

Absence of contextualisation

Flyberg (1998, 2010) comments that knowledge mode characteristic of disciplinary science isolates objects one from another and isolates them from their environment. The principle of scientific experimentation allows taking a body in nature, isolating it in a controlled laboratory environment and studying this object in reaction to the variations that one makes it undergo. It is possible to know a certain number of its qualities and properties,[1] but it does not serve either educational action as praxis or educational research as transformation (Oliveira-Formosinho and Formosinho, 2012). According to Formosinho and Oliveira-Formosinho (2012) we need to jointly undertake a search for a *social science of the social* and for an *educational science of praxis*.

Control of subjectivism

The objective knowledge which is the ideal of positivistic science resulted in the need of eliminating subjectivity, i.e. the emotional part inherent to each observer, to each researcher, but it also comprised the elimination of the subject, i.e. the being which conceives and knows.

As Giddens writes:

> The technical language and theoretical propositions of the natural sciences are insulated from the world with which they are concerned because that world does not answer back. But social theory cannot be insulated from its 'object-world,' which is a subject-world.

(Giddens, 1982, p. 13)

The applicationist perspective in early childhood education as reductionism

As early years assessment has been conducted in the psychological tradition within a positivist research paradigm, it is important to elaborate on this to best understand early years evaluation.

Psychological reductionisms

Childhood pedagogy developed in the times where psychology (behavioural psychology and later developmental psychology) was striving to adopt the positivistic research paradigm. The positivistic paradigm of psychological research developed measuring instruments for the purposes of research which were then transferred to early years assessment – we have been seeing the adoption of these research instruments for the pedagogic evaluation of children's learning. The dominance of psychology in the development of childhood pedagogy has been constant throughout the twentieth century – it has been often seen mainly at the level of assessment as mere application either of behavioural psychology or of developmental psychology.[2]

The imperialistic view of psychology over education, as Lawrence Kohlberg (1987) put it, is very clear in what concerns assessment of learning. Childhood pedagogy traditions of assessment mirror practices imported from the field of psychology without the needed contextualisation.

The positivist paradigm of classical science in education transforms childhood pedagogy on a mere applied field for the major disciplines. Education is perceived and conceptualised as a linear and simple application of other major sciences. This is the process of reduction and simplification typical of the positivist paradigm (Morin, 1986).

The *reductionism of behavioural psychology* is the belief that behaviour is the best indicator of capacities and students' learning. Kozulin (1998) says:

Recently a number of attempts have been made to venture beyond both the total rejection and the complete acceptance of the psychometric paradigm. These alternative approaches have been developed in the context of different research and evaluation traditions and in some instances reflected conflicting goals and objectives. Against such a background, it is useful to inquire into those tacit assumptions that constitute the paradigm of standard intellectual testing:

- The manifest level of functioning reveals the child's inner abilities more or less accurately.
- Unaided performance is the best format for assessment.
- The goal of testing is to predict the future functioning and to classify the child according to his or her level of abilities.

(Kozulin, 1998, pp. 88–89)

The belief that the visible functioning is the best way to measure learning and the privileged way to measure capacities is a simplification, which is made untrue by the sheer complexity of human living and learning where cognition and emotion are of paramount importance.

The *reductionism of developmental psychology* that influenced early years curricula (developmental appropriate practices and other similar curricula) gave rise to practices of early childhood education highly centred on psychological stages of different developmental domains. With Malaguzzi (1998) we can say that Piaget presents an image of an interactive child that negotiates with the environment and is a participant in his learning processes; but if his predefined stage sequence is viewed as identical for everyone this may conceal individual processes. This simplification is made fictitious by the fact that the contextual nature of human development and the equal influence of nurture and nature in children's growth generate a diversity of individual paths.

Transmissive pedagogy reductionism

The *reductionism of transmissive pedagogy* is the belief, so well deconstructed by Paulo Freire (1996), that the exact reproduction of learned knowledge is the best indicator to measure learning and to evaluate individual capacities. The devaluing of discovery learning and project work, of creativity and problem solving competences, had been a constant characteristic of transmissive pedagogy. Even when a teacher experiences more participative methods in their classrooms, evaluation is often marked by the transmissive syndrome.

Transmissive pedagogy ignores or minimises the complexity of each child's living experiences, ignores or minimises the complexity of knowledge itself (the interaction between the different scientific disciplines and the inevitable interaction between curricular subjects, the need for interdisciplinary studies and trans-disciplinary topics), ignores or minimises the sheer complexity of the educational act. In short, it ignores or minimises the complexity of human living and learning in a complex world. For this purpose the school creates a closed environment, ignoring all that children learn outside its walls (Dewey, 1938; Freire, 1996).

Education being essentially the preparation of the younger generations for the future, we must recognise the principle of *rational uncertainty* (Morin, 1986, 2008). Education cannot rely solely on the transmission of past knowledge minimising the apprenticeship of the essential competencies of learning how to learn, of searching and organising new information, of problem solving competencies and devaluing educational imagination and human creativity.

Nowadays we experience an acceleration of history (Hargreaves and Fink, 2006) which makes this transmissive emphasis more inadequate. The complexity of learning and knowing and of knowledge development in a complex world cannot be understood only by the reproduction of the different separate disciplinary segments of human knowledge.

Dimensions of the applicationist view of educational assessment and evaluation

As seen in the first chapter, this process of simplification begins in the *organisational dimension*, through the building of an educational assembly line which reduces the complexity of any work to a sequence of very simple mechanical tasks. The shaping of the mass education assembly line makes final assessment and evaluation the equivalent of quality control of the finished product in the industrial world.

This process of simplification pervades the *curricular dimension* through the systematic and sequential explicitation of the prescribed contents for each subject (coupled often with the prescribed didactics), to be transmitted irrespective of the interests, needs and projects of the learning group and independently of the individual progress of each learner. The curriculum is built as an accumulation of the syllabus of the different disciplines. The general curricular aims are to be obtained through the summing up of the specific objectives for each subject. This is the essence of the reductionist simplification process – *uniformity* and *abstractness*.

This process of simplification permeates the *pedagogical dimension*, through standardisation of processes and outcomes in teaching. All this process is based on abstract concepts of schools and classrooms, content and process, teacher and learner. That is, the pedagogical process is designed for abstract schools, abstract teachers and abstract learners in a detached process. This is the essence of the reductionist simplification process – *abstractness and detachedness*.

Finally, this process of simplification ends up in the *evaluative dimension*, through standardisation of processes and outcomes in teaching. Evaluation is nearly reduced to the assessment meaning by the application of measurement instruments. What is valued in this simplistic evaluation process? The exact reproduction of the content transmitted by the teacher that is the devolution of the knowledge deposited by the teacher (Freire, 1996) or presented in textbooks, workbooks, worksheets.

This simplistic mode of evaluation is a consequence of a reductionist process at organisational, curricular and pedagogical levels. It is a consequence of a specific world vision that devalues human agency and rights.

The inadequacy of the applicationist view of educational assessment and evaluation

Education as an application of the positivist science has not been very useful for transforming educational praxis, since it does not generate pertinent knowledge about praxis, about the human condition and the integrated contextual identity of children, or about the processes involved in the transformation processes. These very processes are those which depend fundamentally on the contextual human action and interaction.

The reason why the natural sciences paradigm is not adequate to conduct educational action (or research in social sciences) is that the object of the research is not an inert raw material; it is a subject with cognition, sentiments and will; it is a social actor with agency; it is a person with a specific life story and singular projects. Many of the variables which influence the cause-effect relationship described above are process variables dependent on the agency of the persons involved and their life learning stories (Giddens, 1982; Formosinho and Oliveira-Formosinho, 2012; Pascal and Bertram, 2012).

The predictions and explanations of the context-independent truths of natural sciences do not apply to context dependent action which is a characteristic of human activity as social theory cannot be insulated from its 'object-world', which is a subject-world (Giddens, 1982).

The epistemological stance – a co-constructive view on educational assessment and evaluation

A characterisation of holistic evaluation using comparison

One of the obstacles for learning is our own limited means for learning. In the community of early childhood education, the applicationist view of assessment and evaluation established some fixed ideas about rigour and objectivity. These fixed ideas need to be confronted with other ideas because generation after generation of professionals had been formed in dialogue with them. The only way to challenge the imperialism of some ideas is to counter use other ideas. So, in summary, we are sharing with the readers two tables that helped us in developing an understanding of the aims and the processes of evaluation, Table 5.1 and Table 5.2.[3]

Assessment and evaluation should acknowledge the complexity of children's experience and of the educational act

The first important characteristic of a holistic assessment and evaluation in early years is the *respect towards the complexity* of children's identities and learning

TABLE 5.1 The characteristics of holistic evaluation: the aims of evaluation in early childhood

	Reductionist evaluation	Holistic evaluation
Intentionality of the evaluation	• Seeks just measuring learning	• Seeks to understand learning and contribute to further learning
Main characteristic of the evaluation	• Traditional, compartmentalised, transmissive, selective	• Participatory, holistic, ecological, inclusive
Assessment vs evaluation	• Evaluation is centred on assessment of limited areas thus narrowing the teaching and learning	• Evaluation encompasses integrated learning in all areas
Orientation of the evaluation	• Outcomes oriented	• Oriented towards contexts, processes and outcomes
Actors involved in the evaluation process	• It is a closed non-interactive process, involving only the teachers and/or the evaluators	• It is a participatory process, involving the contribution of the professionals, the children and the families
Orientation of the evaluation	• It is a process in closed circuit, closed in itself	• It is an ecological process open to various contexts
Focus of the evaluation process	• The evaluation process focuses on what the learner does not yet know – deficit approach – to overcome that deficit	• The evaluation process focuses on what the learner knows to enlarge and enrich it
Selection versus inclusiveness	• The selective dimension is strong	• The inclusive dimension is of paramount importance

Source: adapted from Formosinho and Oliveira-Formosinho (1996)

experience of the world and of themselves, the respect of the complexity of knowledge and the respect of the complexity of the educational act. We propose a complex holistic evaluation – holistic is not another concept to reduce and simplify reality, rather it is a concept to uncover the complexity of learning, of knowledge, of knowing about knowledge, and of being. In what concerns this last aspect, neurosciences have made very clear the relationship between cognition and emotion (Damásio, 1994, 1999).

The notion of holism has been developed by many, in different disciplines and methodologies, for instance in Goethe's scientific method. The essence of Goethean science is that of being holistic in two planes: firstly, at the level of process putting forward the engagement of the researcher doing, feeling and thinking and, secondly, at the level of the outcomes by trying to reach a deeply contextualised

TABLE 5.2 The characteristics of holistic evaluation: the processes of evaluation in early childhood

	Reductionist evaluation	*Holistic evaluation*
Mode of evaluation	• Abstract processes	• Concrete and situated processes
Mode of evaluation simple vs complex	• Follows the simplifying logic of the transmissive pedagogy (such as tick box tasks)	• Acknowledges the complexity of the educational act through documentation
Comprehensiveness	• Compartmentalised fragmented	• Holistic and integrated
Time of evaluation	• Periodic	• Continuous and systematic
Type of effects	• Immediate effects	• Immediate, medium and long term effects
Connectedness with learning	• The evaluation is independent from the learning process, is self-sufficient	• The evaluation is connected with the learning process
Rigour in evaluation	• Rigour is obtained by distance	• Rigour is obtained by attachment and triangulation

understanding of phenomena understudy. It is recognised that to fully understand the nature of Goethe's method requires sustained engagement. Bortoft (1996, 1998) and Steiner (1984) are helpful in the elucidation of Goethe's method and assert that throughout the course of life we forget that we learned our way of looking at the world around us. He says that our ordinary way of seeing takes it for granted that everything, including our bodies and minds, can be understood as manipulated objects that can be taken apart and described in terms of their parts to then be artificially put together.

So we learn separateness to see everything separated from us. In Lehrs' (1951, p. 73) terms we become *permanent onlookers*. Everything is separated from everything thus we think of wholes as more or less well-organised collections of separate objects, separate parts. There are many consequences of this, one is a poor understanding of wholes *as wholes* decomposed in parts later recombined into the whole. The whole is nothing in itself, as it is only a collection of parts.

Bortoft (1996, 1998) continues by saying that the merits of this method have proven themselves beyond doubt in science and technology – the 'inorganic' world. He doubts about its merits to understand the living world and uses the example of a plant.

Of course we can see a plant as built up of root, stem and leaf and this may be useful for practical purposes, such as food, or medicine. However, the living and growing plant as it is, is not actually built up from a root, stem and leaf. At no point in the plant's growth and development are these three parts put together to form the whole plant. Root, stem and leaf gradually form the process of growth in which they are continuous with each other and the plant as a whole. The plant as a whole cannot therefore be fully understood by explaining it in terms of its parts only.

(Bortoft, 1996, p. 77)

The problem is our learned way of seeing. The solution is to relearn our way of seeing. Our learned way of seeing taught us to separate things that are not separated, so after separating we recreate an artificial whole. The essential whole is lost. The gap produces a dualistic thinking that then needs bridging and sometimes we discover artificial bridges. Why do we not go upstream and explore another world view and another scientific paradigm? Why not explore complexity?

The whole is larger than the parts, meaning that the whole is not merely the sum of the parts. The whole is more significant than the sum of the parts – any evaluation of a part (a subject, a competence, a performance, etc.) is less revealing than the evaluation of the whole and can only be properly understood in the appreciation of the whole.

The whole does not assimilate the parts and the addition of parts does not substitute the whole. The group of children is not just the sum of the individual children; the classroom is not just the addition of all the children plus the educators. Similarly the professional community of a centre is not just the sum of the individual educators; likewise an early childhood centre is not the mere juxtaposition of the different classrooms.

There is a dynamic character among the different parts that is an intrinsic part of the whole. The relationship between the different parts is characterised by interactivity, bi-directionality and re-cursivity (Morin, 1986, 2008). This means that there is complexity in this dynamic. This holistic perspective does not represent a reductionist simplification of the reality.

This means that a holistic perspective of assessment and evaluation cannot be based on the summative appreciation of the different parts – the individual children, the individual teachers and the individual classes. We have to set up mechanisms to evaluate also the dynamics of the whole, that is, the recursive interaction among the parts as will be seen in Chapter 6 when presenting the documentation of learning.

The child is a holistic entity, a holistic identity. This identity should be characterised as an interactive (and recursive) integration of all the psychological dimensions (cognitive and emotional, social and civic, aesthetic and physical) and also of the social, historic and cultural dimension. Both the whole and the parts should be considered (and evaluated) within their contexts and their interactions (Bronfenbrenner, 1979, 2006). At the level of rigour, a participatory intercultural pedagogy should take into account the interactive and recursive integration of all the constituting dimensions of children's identity. At the level of ethics this is a pre-requisite for equity for all. Indeed it is known that children's capacities and intelligences are plural as well as the cultures they belong to. A participatory intercultural pedagogy cannot ignore either the cultural difference or the individual differences.

Since a paradigm of simplification controls classical science, by imposing a principle of reduction and a principle of disjunction to any knowledge, the paradigm of complexity put forward a principle of distinction and a principle of conjunction (Morin, 1986).

Assessment and evaluation should acknowledge that human action is contextual and culturally situated

Bronfenbrenner (2004, 2006) and other ecological approaches help the under-standing of learning as developing in context. Learning of each individual child and the group develops in their plural, social contexts and its interactions. Learning is then ecological. Contexts are socially constructed, located in time, space and culture. Evaluation is to be referred to children's experiential learning in socio-cultural contexts in specific pedagogic situations. Then assessment and evaluation should follow an ecological approach.

As learning is contextual, there is a methodological[4] (and ethical) stand on the part of the professionals to conduct a reflexive analysis about the context of learning – the educational environment. To assess and evaluate with thoroughness children's learning, professionals have to evaluate beforehand the quality of the learning contexts, of the educational environments, and of the educational opportunities provided for all children and for each individual child.[5]

Assessment and evaluation should acknowledge that human action is not completely predictable

Assessment and evaluation should acknowledge that human action is not completely predictable, meaning children's learning and progress has a degree of uncertainty. A certain degree of (apparent) failure is the price for human freedom. Education is an action of persons with persons through persons. Persons have a will – this mean that one cannot predict exactly the outcome of any given educational process. This non predictability is inherent to human freedom (Formosinho, 2009).

Evaluation has consequences in the educational system since it facilitates or hinders the progress in school, and has consequences for employment since it leads to certification of educational and professional credentials. But evaluation is done against a background of expected behaviour, expectations from society, professionals, parents and the teacher. Hence the evaluative judgement depends not only on compliance with the standards achieved but also on the standards expected. Since evaluation impinges on a current child's self image influencing her current and even later life, it should be conducted within ethical principles as presented in Chapter 7.

Assessment and evaluation should acknowledge that easily observable short term outcomes are not the most important results in education

The easily observable outcomes are not the only important results in education. The most significant and relevant results of the educational action are not easily observed only by the learner's behaviour and/or by scales. The comprehensive outcomes involve a blend of cognition, emotion, morality, social and civic education, affective and empathetic education, values – not easily reachable by measurement instruments.

The most significant and relevant outcomes of the educational processes can only be evaluated in the medium and long term as seen in many longitudinal studies (Araújo, 2015), since they are related with school success, job success and success in personal life and other dimensions like wisdom and happiness.

Assessment and evaluation should acknowledge the isomorphic nature of a co-constructive participatory pedagogy

A co-constructive participatory pedagogy is always embedded in the isomorphic mode. *Pedagogical isomorphism* is a metaphor borrowed from natural sciences[6] to express the same equivalence of mode of development between adult learning mode and children learning mode. Assessment and evaluation should acknowledge the isomorphic nature of a co-constructive participatory pedagogy.

In a co-constructive pedagogy, when professionals promote children's learning journeys they are also encouraging their own learning journeys. Isomorphic pedagogy acknowledges children and adults as persons and implies a pedagogy of involvement which recognises the previous knowledge and experience of participants and actively involves them in the processes of their own change (Formosinho and Oliveira-Formosinho, 2005).

As all human beings (adults and children alike) learn through homologous processes, interpersonal interaction is an important scaffold for the intrapersonal learning of both of them. There is interdependence between the *intrapersonal dimension* of the learning process – the building of individual learning journeys – and the *interpersonal dimension* – this building of individual learning journeys within a learning community.

Assessment and evaluation are also subject to the same isomorphic mode, thus the evaluation of children's learning is always an instance to evaluate the professionals' learning.

There are different levels of isomorphism that are of significance for holistic evaluation. Through the ontological isomorphic level between children and adults we call attention to the parallelism of both deserving respect and the exercise of rights; through the psychological isomorphism level we call attention to the homologous mode of children and adult learning, both deserving involvement and participation; through the pedagogic isomorphism stance we call attention to children and adults having the need of liberating educational situations that grant them voice and answers.

Assessment and evaluation should acknowledge the connectedness in early years' development

Another important characteristic of holistic evaluation is *connectedness* – as all parts of the whole are connected, interrelated, all partial appreciation is incomplete or even misleading.

In opposition to reduction, complexity requires that one tries to comprehend the relations between the whole and the parts. The knowledge of the parts is not enough, the knowledge of the whole as a whole is not enough, if one ignores its parts; one is thus brought to move in loops to gather the knowledge of the whole and its parts. Thus, the principle of reduction is substituted by a principle that conceives the relation of whole-part mutual implication.

The principle of disjunction, of separation (between objects, between disciplines, between notions, between subject and object of knowledge), should be substituted by a principle that maintains the distinction, but that tries to establish the relation.

As Morin (1986) says, since we have been domesticated by our education which taught us much more to separate than to connect, our aptitude for connecting is underdeveloped and our aptitude for separating is overdeveloped. Holistic peda-gogic evaluation of children's learning needs sustained praxis both of deconstructing separateness and of constructing connectedness to honour all children's right to participate in learning with their individual and social idiosyncrasies.

Assessment and evaluation should acknowledge the intersubjectivity in early years assessment and evaluation

All authentic evaluation has a degree of *subjectivity* – the self-proclaimed objective evaluation is necessarily partial and incomplete since it does not include the self-awareness of the subject evaluator. All our appreciation of reality has a degree of subjectivity. In holistic complex evaluation intersubjectivity is the criterion. This means that triangulation of voices (teachers, children, parents) and triangulation of instruments over time are of paramount importance to achieve a more authentic appreciation (Bertram and Pascal, 2004, 2006). All authentic appreciation is obtained not through distance but through reflexive critical close proximity.

Professionals have the civic right and the civic duty to monitor the daily development of childhood pedagogy and to document children's learning. They use daily documentation as a tool for the pedagogic evaluation of learning aiming at the understanding of the holistic learners' identities as dynamic and modifiable through solidary teaching[7] that brings about children's learning possibilities through the creation of cooperation and communication in learning situations and in its narration.

Notes

1. But, as Morin (2008) said, one can also say that this principle of decontextualisation was ill-fated, as soon as it was ported to the living. The observation since 1960 by Jane Goodall of a tribe of chimpanzees in their natural environment showed the supremacy of observation in a natural environment over experimentation in a laboratory for knowledge. The idea of knowing the living in their environment became capital. The autonomy of the living needs to be known in its environment, within context and culture. The identity of the learner should to be developed and assessed in its context.
2. We note that psychology has been and is of paramount importance as one of the dialogues of pedagogy.
3. Reductionist and holistic evaluation are presented as ideal types (pure types) using Max Weber concept – it is a description and interpretation which stresses elements common to most case of the given phenomenon, a synthesis of many diffuse individual phenomena arranged according to a specific viewpoint built into a unified analytical construct. This specific viewpoint is presented in the tables provided.
4. There is also an ethical stand to evaluate the contexts to better evaluate the child's learning.
5. Assessment and evaluation based on documentation needs to make visible the relationship between teaching and learning as has been seen in Chapter 2 and will be seen in Chapter 6.
6. *Isomorphism* means in *chemistry* and *mineralogy* the property of crystallising in the same or closely related forms, as exhibited by substances of analogous composition. In *mathematics* means identity of form and operations between two sets or an exact correspondence as regards the number of constituent elements and the relations between them.
7. To understand the concept of solidary teaching and solidary learning see Chapter 6.

References

Araújo, S.B. In press. Impacto da experiência em contexto de creche: Contributos do estudo de programas longitudinais de intervenção. *RELAdEI (Revista Latinoamericana de Educación Infantil)*.

Bertram, T. and C. Pascal. (2004). *The effective early learning programme*. Birmingham: Centre for Research in Early Childhood.

Bertram, T. and C. Pascal. (2006). *The baby effective early learning programme: Improving quality in early childhood settings for children from birth to three years*. Birmingham: Centre for Research in Early Childhood.

Bortoft, H. (1996) *The wholeness of nature*. Edinburgh: Floris Books.

Bortoft, H. (1998) Conterfeit and authentic wholes. In *Goethe's way of science*, eds D. Seamon and A. Zajons. New York: Suny.

Bronfenbrenner, U. (1979) *The ecology of human development*. Cambridge, MA: Harvard University Press.

Bronfenbrenner, U. (2004) *Making human beings human: bioecological perspectives on human development*. Thousand Oaks, CA: Sage Publications.

Bronfenbrenner, U. (2006) *The ecology of human development: experiments by nature and design*. Englewood Cliffs, NJ: Harvard University Press.

Damásio, A. (1994) *Descartes' error: emotion, reason, and the human brain.* New York: Putnam Publishing.

Damásio, A. (1999) *The feeling of what happens: body and emotion in the making of consciousness.* New York: Harcourt Brace & Company.

Dewey, J. (1938) *Experience and education.* Indiana: Kappa Delta Pi.

Flyvbjerg, B. (1998) *Rationality & power: democracy in practice.* Chicago, IL: The University of Chicago Press.

Flyvbjerg, B. (2010) *Making social science matter: why social inquiry fails and how it can succeed again,* 12th edn. Cambridge: Cambridge University Press.

Formosinho, J. (2009) *Dilemas e tensões da universidade frente à formação de profissionais de desenvolvimento humano.* São Paulo. Cadernos Pedagogia Universitária. Pró-Reitoria de Graduação.

Formosinho, J. and Oliveira-Formosinho, J. (1996) *The search for participatory curricular approaches for early childhood education.* Research Report, Aga Khan Foundation, Lisbon.

Formosinho, J. and Oliveira-Formosinho, J. (2005) *Developing learning communities: the final report on the evaluation of the impact of the National Professional Qualification in Integrated Centre Leadership (NPQICL) leadership programme.* National College for School Leadership.

Formosinho, J. and Oliveira-Formosinho, J. (2012) Towards a social science of the social: The contribution of praxeological research. *European Early Childhood Education Research Journal* 20, 4: 591–606.

Freire, P. (1996) *Pedagogy of the oppressed.* London: Penguin Books.

Giddens, A. (1982) *Hermeneutics and social theory. Profiles and critiques in social theory.* Berkeley, CA: University of California Press.

Hargreaves, A. and Fink, D. (2006) *Sustainable leadership.* San Francisco: Jossey-Bass.

Kohlberg, L. (1987) Democratic moral education. *Psicologia (Revista da Associação Portuguesa de Psicologia* V, 3: 335–341.

Kozulin, A. (1998) *Psychological tools: a sociocultural approach to education.* Cambridge, Mass.: Harvard University Press.

Lehrs, E. (1951) *Man or matter.* London: Rudolf Steiner Press.

Malaguzzi, L. (1998) History, ideas, and basic philosophy: an interview with Lella Gandini. In *The hundred languages of children: the Reggio Emilia approach – advanced reflection,* eds C. Edwards, L. Gandini and G. Forman, pp. 49–97. Greenwich, CT: Ablex.

Morin, E. (1986) *O Método 3 – O Conhecimento do Conhecimento.* Lisbon: Europa América.

Morin, E. (2008) *On complexity.* Cresskill, NJ: Hampton Press, Inc.

Oliveira-Formosinho, J. (2007) Pedagogia(s) da infância: reconstruindo uma práxis de participação. In *Pedagogias(s) da Infância. Dialogando com o passado, construindo o futuro,* eds J. Oliveira-Formosinho, T.M. Kishimoto and M. Pinazza, pp. 13–36. São Paulo: Artmed Editora.

Oliveira-Formosinho, J. and Formosinho, J. (2012) Special issue. Praxeological research in early childhood: a contribution to a social science of the social. *European Early Childhood Education Research Journal* 20, 4.

Pascal, C. and Bertram, T. (2012) Praxis, ethics and power: developing praxeology as a participatory paradigm for early childhood research. *European Early Childhood Education Research Journal* 20, 4: 477–492.

Steiner, R. (1984). *The philosophy of freedom.* London: Rudolf Steiner Press.

6

PEDAGOGIC DOCUMENTATION

Uncovering solidary learning

Júlia Formosinho

Introduction to the chapter

This chapter aims at analysing the role of pedagogic documentation in participative pedagogies and its relationship with assessment and evaluation, using examples
mainly from the Pedagogy-in-Participation approach (Oliveira-Formosinho and
Formosinho, 2012).[1]

The *first section* focuses on the identification of the ethos of participatory
pedagogies and its implication on the new roles and relationships between
children and educators. These new roles and relationships do not wash out teachers'
voice and educational intentionalities but make teaching a much more complex
activity since the flow of the educational process is less predictable. As pedagogic
documentation reveals children's learning in a specific pedagogic context, it sits at
the heart of the enactment of learning-teaching processes.

The *second section* presents the professional journey inside the Pedagogy-in-
Participation approach that has been building a *praxis* of documentation which serves
learning and evaluation. This approach to documentation has evolved through two
sources: theoretical dialogues and the ongoing experiential practices debated in the
Childhood Association learning community through context based professional
learning journeys. In this second part we will reflect on the epistemological
consequences of this journey focused on a new understanding of the complexity
of the educational process and of children's learning.

The *third section* shows pedagogic documentation as a study of children's learning
processes and achievements that give support to evaluation. This section ends with
a brief presentation of Andreia's classroom as an inspiration for how to develop
individual and collective documentation as a basis for assessment and evaluation
that will be continued in Chapter 8.

The *fourth section* develops the pedagogic concept of *solidary learning* which has been gradually built by the Childhood Association professional journey and is now embodied in the Pedagogy-in-Participation approach. *Solidary learning* is presented as the harmonisation of children's voices and teachers' voices, of children's purposes and educational intentionalities to be reflected through pedagogic documentation.

The ethos of participative pedagogies

Observing, listening and answering to children

Traditional childhood pedagogy departs from a well-organised subject matter, if possible presented in a pleasant form. This predefined knowledge commanded the teaching and the methodology would facilitate the learning, meaning the appropriation of the desired knowledge by the students. The deconstruction of this simplistic thinking has been a great inheritance of twentieth century childhood pedagogy (Oliveira-Formosinho et al., 2007). This deconstruction raises new questions about the role of the children in the educational process, about the part of children's voices in the co-construction of knowledge, and about the collaboration between children and educators in daily life and learning in the early childhood classrooms.

A revisitation of *Experience and Education* published by Dewey in 1938 is enlightening to understand this:

> The main purpose or objective [of education] is to prepare the young for future responsibilities and for success in life, by means of acquisition of the organised bodies of information and prepared forms of skill which comprehend the material of instruction. Since the subject matter as well as standards of proper conduct are handed down from the past, the attitude of pupils must, upon the whole, be one of docility, receptivity, and obedience. Books, especially textbooks, are the chief representatives of the lore and wisdom of the past, while teachers are the organs through which pupils are brought into effective connection with the material. Teachers are the agents through which knowledge and skills are communicated and rules of conduct enforced.
>
> [. . .] When the implied criticism is made explicit it reads somewhat as follows: The traditional scheme is, in essence, one of imposition from above and from outside. It imposes adult standards, subject matter, and methods upon those who are only growing slowly towards maturity. The gap is so great that the required subject matter, the methods of learning and of behaving are foreign to the existing capacities of the young. They are beyond the reach of the experience the young learners already possess. Consequently, they must be imposed; even though good teachers will use devices of art to cover up the imposition so as to relieve it of obviously brutal features.

But the gulf between the mature or adult products and the experience and abilities of the young is so wide that the very situation forbids much active participation by pupils in the development of what is taught ... Learning here means acquisition of what already is incorporated in books and in the heads of the elders. Moreover, that which is taught is thought of as essentially static. It is taught as a finished product, with little regard either to the ways in which it was originally built up or to changes that will surely occur in the future. It is to a large extent the cultural product of societies that assumed the future would be much like the past, and yet it is used as educational food in a society where change is the rule, not the exception.

If one attempts to formulate the philosophy of education implicit in the practices of the new education, we may, I think, discover certain common principles amid the variety of progressive schools now existing. To imposition from above is opposed expression and cultivation of individuality; to external discipline is opposed free activity; to learning from texts and teachers, learning through experience; to acquisition of isolated skills and techniques by drill, is opposed acquisition of them as means of attaining ends which make direct vital appeal; to preparation for a more or less remote future is opposed making the most of the opportunities of present life; to static aims and materials is opposed acquaintance with a changing world.

(Dewey, 1997, pp. 18–20)

All this means a Copernican revolution in pedagogy. This 'revolution' did not swap over the child's and the teacher's places and roles, rather it brought together their action for joint thinking, collaborative planning, shared decision making, sustained action and reflection, and integrated evaluation. The interconnected realities of learning and teaching stand on a theory of education that, in turn, stands on a theory of knowledge. Participatory pedagogies assume that knowledge is a co-construction in contextual action and that pedagogical praxis is the co-construction of educational processes and achievements through participative methods. At this level we stand *on the shoulders of giants*, the giants who developed the co-constructivism: Berger and Luckman, 1966; Vygotsky, 1978; Wertsch, 1985, 1991; and Rogoff, 1990. They hold that knowledge is gradually co-constructed through exploration, communication, negotiation and meaning making which calls for a non-traditional epistemology, for a complex epistemology (Morin, 2008).

It is very important that all children, very young children and older children, participate in the 'revolutionary' process of the re-creation of their role as subjects considering the educational reality as a permanent process of humanisation and democratisation. This is the core of the Copernican revolution in early years teaching and learning. The right of children to learning that is seen as a cultural democratic lived experience challenges educators to be deep thinkers about children's identities and minds and about their own identity and roles. Pedagogic documentation helps the professionals to be reflexive and have agency at these levels. The right of children to learning challenges educators also about the type of relationships between these identities, about how to use their knowledge (power) to scaffold children's thinking processes, and about the suspension of the power of their knowledge in order to create for each child and for the group a space for the exercise of their own powers.

Participatory pedagogies create an educational participative ethos that grants interactive space for all actors involved in the learning-teaching situations (Oliveira-Formosinho, 2007). For Paulo Freire, teachers and students are people that became each other's students by listening to each other's voices, to each other's perspectives and so communicating and developing a better understanding to *name the world*. Freire (1970) speaks about helping the student to stop being a silent student and venturing 'to tell the world' and to be active in the learning processes. Freire inspires us to practise an educational approach that challenges the learners to actively think, listen, speak, communicate to *name the world*, to give it meaning.

If traditionally the concern was centred on children's study of facts and their memorisation and reproduction, in participatory pedagogies we are concerned with the study of how to study and how the study of study moves us to understand the modes of meaning making through joint activity. Documentation serves this reflexive journey. Communicative processes can be critically analysed and reflexively negotiated to reconcile the roles of children and teachers in the heart of the learning process. The central *ethos* of participative pedagogies is the daily praxis of observing, listening and answering to children, supported in the critical processes of documenting educational situations and learning.

The image of the child in participatory pedagogies: the search for meaning

We started this chapter in Dewey's company, raising questions – why in traditional pedagogy is subject matter the centre of children learning? Why is the teacher the sole speaker? Why . . .? Why . . .? To answer these questions we need a deep reflection about the nature of the child, which include the expectation we hold for a child either as a person or as a learner. This is related to the adopted theory of education that conceptualises the answers to what is education and what is a school, what is learning and what is teaching, what is documentation and what is assessment and evaluation.

Traditional transmissive pedagogy says chiefly what the child is not; what she does not yet have; what she cannot yet do. That means that right from the beginning it is predefined, in adult terms, what she will be because of what adults will do to her and with her. Participatory pedagogies understand the image of the child through his/her actual identity: what she is, what she feels, what she thinks, what she has, what she does, what she has already learned.

For participatory pedagogies this child is a subject of life and learning, both as an individual subject and a social subject, a person and a citizen, both as user and creator of cultural artefacts. This child is an autonomous and cooperative competent individual with rights and duties, reflexive and critical, active and participative that relates to the world and to persons, things and knowledge. This child thinks, feels and questions, accepts and rejects, says yes and no; she has a relational identity that participates where she belongs with the expectation of respecting and of being respected. This child, using Malaguzzi's concept, expresses herself with one hundred languages (Malaguzzi, 1998).

When societies speak about very young babies they tend to conceptualise them as a non-yet being. Participatory pedagogies like to say that even babies are curious beings, willing to experience and to explore the world, nature, the objects, persons with intelligent senses and sensitive intelligences (Oliveira-Formosinho and Formosinho, 2012) and have the ability to communicate and share their explorations and experiences through communicative processes that create knowledge and meaning right from the beginning. Documentation helps to understand this precocious agency of children.

Is this an easy child for a traditional culture and for transmissive education? This child brings surprises to the process of education, creates emergent situations and poses unpredictable questions, sometimes creates problems . . . This child asks from the educators the ability and will to deal with the novelty, the unknown, the not planned . . . This child has very interesting things to say to us if we want to listen to what she wants to say and not to what we want her to say . . . If we as professionals learn to enjoy being caught by surprise with emergent topics, themes, issues, questions and learn to engage in shared and negotiated learning journeys with children we will contribute for empowered citizens, persons, learners.

In participatory pedagogies education becomes a complex challenge, a rewarding civic enterprise that cannot be accomplished only with pre-designed objectives and activities. The flow of this type of processes is less predictable; this does not mean to say that it is a chaotic process but rather to say it is a non-linear, non-fully programmed process. It encompasses the complexity of bringing together competent children with competent teachers both having the right to express purposes for the educational situations, activities and projects. It encompasses the challenges of communication, negotiation for the set up of compromises for the planning of educational experience and its development in action. It involves shared reflection and evaluation on the basis of documented experiential learning.

The harmonisation of children's purposes and educators' intentionalities

Participatory pedagogies develop a specific understanding of the image of the child as a competent co-constructor with competent peers and competent teachers negotiating through communicative processes her/his participation in learning and learning how to learn. But children's purposes do not wash out the educational intentionalities and teachers' voice. Documentation does not only reveal children's learning, it reveals children's learning in a specific pedagogic context under a specific pedagogy, meaning it also reveals the teaching. Pedagogic documentation sits at the heart of the enactment of learning-teaching processes thus implying a clear understanding of educational aims, curriculum content, and pedagogy (Malaguzzi, 1998; Rinaldi, 2012).

The harmonisation of children's purposes and educators' intentionalities in Pedagogy-in-Participation: the axes of educational intentionalities

Figure 6.1 shows Pedagogy-in-Participation axes of educational intentionalities that challenge professional imagination and creativity to prioritise the need to answer the child, not rendering her silent by asserting the 'truth'.

We conceptualise pedagogy as a process to cultivate humanity through education, to cultivate the relational holistic *being* in context(s) and culture(s), the *competent* learner in communication, dialogue and participation, the *meaning maker* in progress with well-being, the *learner* dealing with the vicissitudes of the narratives about experiential learning as a way to order experience and construct knowing and knowledge, meaning for learning (Bruner, 1990).

Our educational axes constitute anchors to think about education as an important open window for the promotion of humanity and democracy (Dewey, 1916), to create meaning for the educational process integrating being, learning and narrating, so that learning becomes a door to culture, democracy and humanity.

The educational environment created with children and for children encompasses educational intentionalities; these intentionalities are ample enough to be inclusive, clear enough to orient and inspire processes of interactive learning and teaching. These educational intentionalities are to be negotiated between children and educators in an interpersonal social context, since they constitute anchors for the think-do-reflect pedagogic cycle. They are oriented to support:

1. the plural relational identities' development;
2. the feelings of belonging and the participation in life and learning;
3. the learning identities in communicative explorations of the world, nature, persons and knowledge through intelligent senses and sensitive intelligences;
4. the narration of learning with one hundred languages developing meaning for learning;
5. children's awareness and understanding of themselves as persons and learners.

The professional journey inside the Pedagogy-in-Participation approach to build a praxis of documentation

Two sources for the development of a praxis of documentation

Our praxis of pedagogic documentation is located in time, place and culture, is informed by paradigmatic issues (how we see and make sense of the world and of nature and people, relationships and knowledge), by a theory of education that stands on a theory of knowledge, by the specific pedagogic approach adopted and by the official curricular guidelines (Ministério da Educação, 1997).

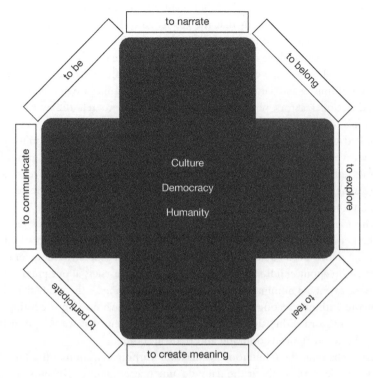

FIGURE 6.1 Axes of educational intentionality

Our own approach (Pedagogy-in-Participation approach to documentation) has evolved through two important sources – the multiple theoretical dialogues developed over time and the ongoing experiential practices debated in the Childhood Association learning community. Since the early 1990s when Pedagogy-in-Participation started to be developed (Formosinho, 1987, 2007; Oliveira-Formosinho, 1987, 1992, 2001) we ventured into experiential learning in the doing of documentation that supported the creation of professional practical knowledge (Bordieu, 1990, 1998; Dunne, 1993).

In regard to the theoretical dialogues, the Childhood Association community has been open to other communities such as Reggio Emilia (Malaguzzi, 1998; Rinaldi, 2012), Pen Green (Whalley, 2001; Mairs and Pen Green Team, 2013), CREC (Pascal and Bertram, 2009), Carr and Lee learning stories (Carr and Lee, 2012), Fleet and colleagues' conversations about documentation (Fleet et al., 2012).

Pre-school professionals have always conducted some kind of documentation – children's books, classroom books, children's learning books. But today's theories and concepts about pedagogic documentation benefit from the dialogues around paradigms of research methodology of the last five decades of the twentieth century (Azevedo, 2009) as well as the end of the nineteenth century and all twentieth century debates around the ethos of participatory pedagogies.[2]

Right from the beginning of our venture in developing pedagogic documentation it became obvious that the challenge of this praxis comes from being affiliated to the family of participatory pedagogies. The child is not a silent child but a person that needs to have space and time to name the world, that needs space and time to show competence in a documentation process where communication is central (Emilson and Samuelson, 2014). Similarly, families are not silent but rather are educational actors with space, time and voice to tell the world of their children's learning.

In Pedagogy-in-Participation we learned that praxis of documentation is a process that weaves together theories, practices and beliefs;[3] it is action grounded in theories, ethics and experimentation. Documentation as a way to uncover children's and teachers' learning needs theoretical and conceptual clarification as well as clarification at the level of *techne,* that is, of the how to do it.

The Childhood Association learning community (which includes pre-school teachers and university teachers, trainers and researchers, supervisors and practitioners) jointly debated how to do documentation as a generative mode of creating information about children's learning and to raise awareness about praxis. We did not want to enter a nominalistic mode of venturing change – the mode that changes the name without creating the substance, often just renaming a pre-existing reality with a new word. Educational change does not happens that way . . . it needs the fusion between rigorous thinking and rigorous doing.

The debates in the Childhood Association learning community tried to answer many questions asked about the daily documentation praxis – *What is in it for the children? What is in it for me? What is in it for the families? Is it so beneficial? It gives me information about the ongoing processes but can it help me in being accountable about outcomes? How can I use techniques to make my doing feasible? How can I interact with children and densely document the interaction? How can I at the same time do and document the doing? How does documentation enable me to evaluate each child's progress in learning?*

The journey through a context based learning

These and other questions were addressed through a specific approach to staff development. We learned long ago that any pedagogic strategy can be generative or degenerative depending on the way we bring it from the world of thinking to the world of doing. One of the challenges for our learning community (Oliveira-Formosinho and Formosinho, 2001) was that of creating participatory learning situations for teachers in a situated mode – contextual staff development – that allows us to recreate new meanings in action (Oliveira-Formosinho, 1998). As experiential learning is important for children and for teachers alike, this process of creating participatory learning situations is an experiential, critical, reflexive approach to professional learning; experiential learning needs to be scaffolded either with children or with adults. These are levels of pedagogic isomorphism that highlight the proximity between children's and teachers' learning modes (Formosinho and Oliveira-Formosinho, 2005).

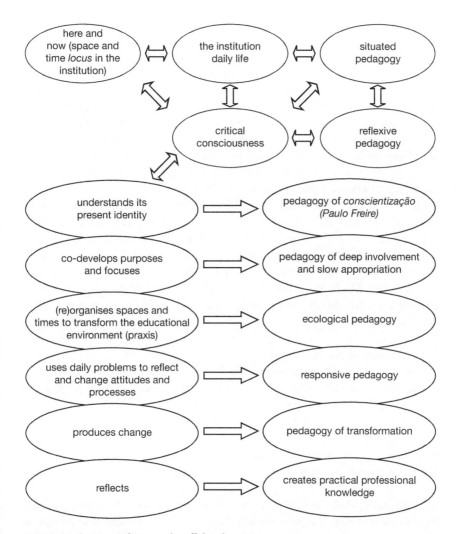

FIGURE 6.2 Contextual/situated staff development

Figure 6.2 presents in an iconic mode our understanding of contextual staff development (Oliveira-Formosinho, 1998) that developed from dialogues with other approaches that search for professional learning in reflexive mode such as the Modern School Movement (Niza, 2012; Folque, 2008), some Italian approaches (Malaguzzi, 1998) and situated learning (Lave and Wenger, 1991).

The specific process of collaboratively scaffolding teachers' learning around documentation allows us a brief look at *contextual professional learning* that is situated in spaces and time, and has resonance for teachers' classrooms and early childhood centres. Contextual professional learning starts with the creation of awareness and critical consciousness about a specific theme – for instance, about what is assessment of children against a measurable set of outcomes in a fixed point in time to check for readiness for the next stage. It supports the understanding of the present professional identity as a step to develop new understandings. So the deconstruction process supports the further experimentation in creating alternative possibilities – the thinking and doing of participatory documentation and evaluation, the creation of meaning about the nature of pedagogic documentation and pedagogic assessment and evaluation. All this calls for new meanings about the human being – the child, the learner, the teacher – supported and sustained in experiential learning around the challenge of how to document daily life in the classroom. This responsive pedagogy produces contextual change, reconstructs praxis and creates professional knowledge (Oliveira-Formosinho, 1998, 2014).

The collective professional learning journey that Childhood Association has undertaken using its approach of contextual staff development has been developed over the last two decades and researched, mostly, in the format of case studies (Oliveira-Formosinho, 1998; Azevedo, 2009; Araújo, 2011; Parente, 2004; Lino, 2005; Craveiro, 2007; Vieira, 2010; Novo, 2010; Pires, 2013, Azevedo and Sousa, 2010; Machado, 2014). Each of these case studies has idiosyncratic characteristics but also shared saliencies. Both allow us to create awareness about key issues such as:

1. the nature of persons and knowledge;
2. the psychological nature of children;
3. the need of childhood pedagogy to be conceptualised as appropriate to children's nature and identity;
4. the relationships between teaching and learning;
5. relationships between documentation and assessment;
6. the support to experiential learning in the doing of documentation;
7. the importance of sharing documentation with families.

We enter now, until the end of the chapter, into the details identified by praxeo-logical case studies that sustain our actual approach to pedagogic documentation. At first our learning community created awareness about the fact that, as all knowledge is provisional, knowledge about documentation and evaluation is also provisional. We assumed that the knowledge we were creating about pedagogic documentation would not be definitive, rather it would be subject to error and would undergo developmental processes (as it did). We consider it work-in-progress that benefits from being shared and submitted to our professional peers because for us that is the way to reconstruct praxis that seeks to better serve children and families.

This set of case studies contributes to our search for pertinent pedagogic knowledge about assessment and evaluation that acknowledge the complexity of the child. Our learning community created awareness about the need of research, teaching and evaluation of children to acknowledge and celebrate complexity. This requires departing from an integrated vision of education and of creating integrated liberating educational questions, answers and situations. Accepting error in these processes is a pedagogy that knows that we do not own the truth, we only search for it.

We debated the relationship of the children with their contexts (Bronfenbrenner, 2004, 2006), since psychological processes are interdependent with their contexts. Relationships between people and contexts are bidirectional, transitional and interactive (Valsiner and Winegar, 2000); multidimensional human beings, holistic, psychological beings live in contexts. Any relevant pedagogic knowledge knows that context is the scenario.

Pedagogic documentation as a study of children's learning processes and achievements to support assessment and evaluation

As seen, our current approach to documentation comes from a long journey. In the search for novel integrated ways of pedagogic evaluation, we confronted the complexity of assessing and evaluating multidimensional holistic learners in specific pedagogic situations.

Assessment and evaluation are based on documentation of the learning

Assessment and evaluation is an integrated process interwoven with teaching and learning through pedagogic documentation (see Figure 6.3). Pedagogic documentation should be able to:

- reveal teaching and learning processes;
- see the learning-in-the-making;
- see the teaching-in-the-making;
- create information for learning about situated learning (of children and teachers);
- reveal outcomes connected with the learning processes.

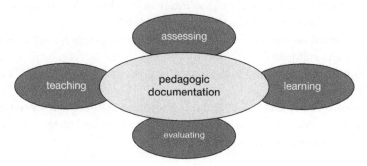

FIGURE 6.3 Pedagogic documentation

axis one: learning through living democratic participatory processes

axis two: learning through experimenting respect for one's own identity

axis three: learning through a solidary encounter of children and teachers

axis four: melody of voices that contribute to information gathering and ethical evaluative judgments

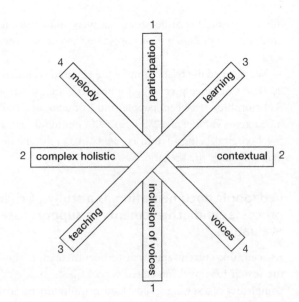

FIGURE 6.4 Pedagogy-in-Participation anchors for evaluation

As explained our approach to documentation has evolved through learning journeys around theoretical dialogues and ongoing experiential praxis. So Pedagogy-in-Participation anchors for evaluation (see Figure 6.4) come upstream from our world vision and epistemological approach (see axes 1 and 2) and downstream from our theory of education in action (see axes 3 and 4).

These anchors helped us to clarify that the Pedagogy-in-Participation holistic approach to assessment and evaluation is:

- **participatory** because it includes a melody of voices that contribute to information gathering about learning that give raise to evaluative judgments;
- **multidimensional** because human beings are multidimensional (physical, biological, psychological, cultural, social, historical);
- **holistic** because the psychological nature of the child is holistic and children are the subject and not the object of evaluation;[4]
- **contextual** because the historical nature of human beings is situated in time, space and cultures;
- **connected to teaching** because teaching processes are the pedagogic context for learning;
- **intersubjective** and **local** because it is sustained in multiple voices (children, parents, teachers) and in the learning context where the teacher is the choir-master harmonising the voices.

FIGURE 6.5 Attunement in the revisitation of documentation

Pedagogic documentation in Pedagogy-in-Participation journey: the voice of Tiago

I have experienced and thus learned that giving voice to children to explain their pedagogic experience is more illuminating that all other possible discourses. So we are going to listen to Tiago speaking with Andreia (the teacher) about his educational context: the pedagogic spaces (workshops, areas), the pedagogic times (the daily routine as a succession of rhythms) and his overview about life and learning in the classroom as well as about documentation (see Figure 6.5).

> We sing songs . . . Look at our portfolios . . . Read stories and play music. We build houses, savannahs, farms . . . We travel to many places: the beach, the savannah, the zoological park . . . We make puzzles, separate objects, count and write. . . I observe small things with a magnifying glass.
>
> We draw with many materials . . . We paint . . . We build objects with clay and other materials.

Tiago's description of pedagogical times of Andreia's classroom:

> *Welcome time*: We sing the good morning song . . . Talk about what we'll do throughout the day.
>
> *Planning time*: We plan for the workshop we want to go to finish and start works and to continue working in the project work.

Activities and/or projects: We go to the workshops . . . We work together or alone.

Reflection time: We say to colleagues and to Andreia and Maria [*assistant*] what we've been doing and they write what we say.

Playground time: I go outside and play with my friends . . . Catch seeds and leaves . . . See animals climbing trees . . . I also talk to my girlfriend.

Intercultural time: We tell stories, do games, dramatise stories . . . Parents come to help us in the project works.

Moment of small group work: We work on what we planned to research . . . Each group working in different things.

Council: We talk together about what we've been doing . . . Andreia shows us the documentation she did and we plan with her what to do next.

Tiago's overview about life and learning in the classroom when revisiting his learning portfolio:

These are my classmates. Some of them are my colleagues since we were babies . . . Others joined our school later . . . Others were already here at school but in other rooms.

Andreia chats with us, listens to us and writes what we're doing and what we want to do and to research. She also researches the things that she doesn't know. Sometimes also learns with us.

Andreia makes our portfolios with us: puts the photos of what we're doing. But we select the most important things. She also puts in our families.

She documents . . . Puts in the walls what we're learning and what we want to learn.

In order to plan the week's activities, Andreia projects on the wall documentation of what we were doing throughout the week, we talk and we decide what we want to learn next.

Families also help us to research the things we want to learn.

According to Tiago, 'Andreia shows us the documentation she did and we plan with her what to do next . . . puts in the walls (through documentation) what we're learning and what we want to learn'.

There is a *'we-ness'*, in Christine Pascal's non-standard English terminology. It is not 'you and me', nor 'us' and 'them', but a pronoun which says we are together, jointly and individually, in the first person plural. That 'we-ness' is visible in this classroom, which is a social *niche* for the development of individual plural identities. Tiago refers specifically to how this learning community plans: 'In order to plan the week's activities, Andreia projects on the wall documentation of what we were doing throughout the week, we talk and we decide what we want to learn next.'

How does this learning community achieve this 'we-ness' in planning? Andreia documents and edits the documentation. The sharing of edited documentation (in council time) allows conversations between Andreia and her children as a revisitation of learning and as negotiations for further learning that allow *compromises* and shared decisions for the next week's educational planning that will sustain another cycle of activity development that in turn will allow us to see again children in action and documentation-in-the-making. We are at the heart of what we call lived *solidary planning*.

Building the concept of solidary learning: from solidary planning to solidary learning

Solidary planning

Figure 6.6 represents our imagistic mode of giving meaning to the concept of *solidary planning* since participative pedagogies need to promote joint planning of educational activities and shared intentions for the development of action. The novel

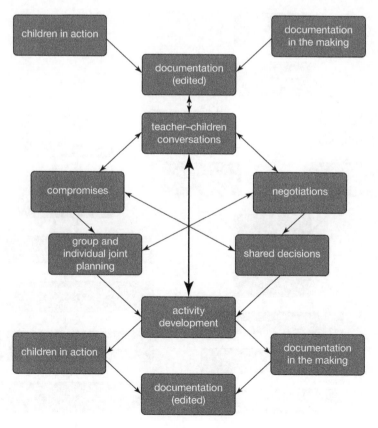

FIGURE 6.6 Solidary planning

ways for documentation and evaluation should be connected with the decision making processes of negotiated educational planning.

Monitoring solidary learning

Andreia's civic duty towards her children and families challenges her to discover multiple forms of uncovering learning, to monitor the progress of learning. She starts a companionable professional journey of triangulation of instruments, times and voices to see, understand and show her children's learning. She is challenged by children and parents to make these processes of uncovering solidary learning visible, shared and public. For that purpose she develops the individual learning journeys of each child organised in a portfolio and at the same time develops her professional portfolio. These portfolios support her in the acknowledgement and celebration of learning and in the visibility of individual and collective progress in learning. In this classroom the first purpose that assessment of learning serves is the contribution for further learning through systematic critical reflections about solidary learning as shown in Figure 6.7.

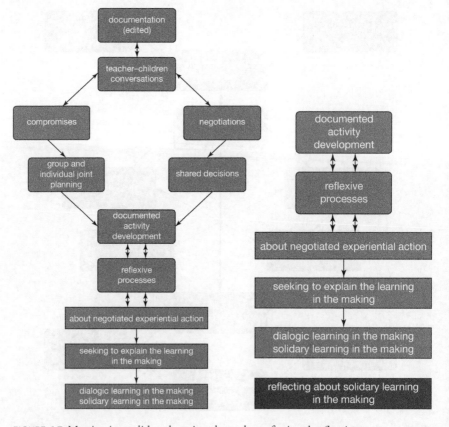

FIGURE 6.7 Monitoring solidary learning through professional reflection

Uncovering learning: documenting, assessing and evaluating solidary learning

Documentation of learning developed over time concerning each child (individual portfolio) and concerning the group constitutes information amenable to various analyses through the use of plural modes in order to uncover learning (see Figure 6.8):

1. Pedagogy-in-Participation pedagogic axes and learning areas;
2. the official curricular areas;
3. narratives of children, parents and teachers;
4. different types of symbolisations;
5. pedagogic instruments of observation.

Documentation of learning developed overtime is an open resource that can be questioned through various means to assess and evaluate learning. In our experiential learning journey on documentation we often questioned: How to

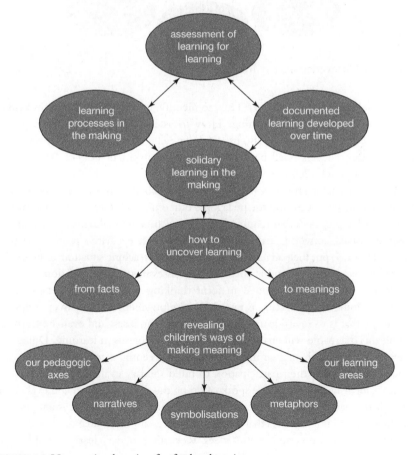

FIGURE 6.8 Uncovering learning for further learning

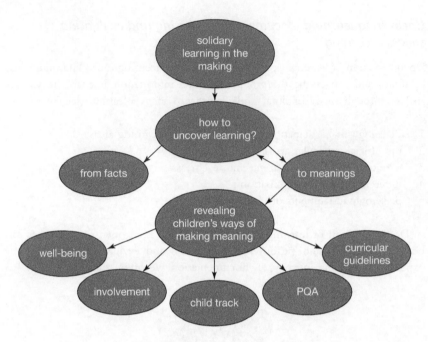

FIGURE 6.9 Uncovering solidary learning

uncover learning (see Figure 6.9)? How to identify, understand and show individual and collective progress in learning? How to assess learning to promote further learning? For that purpose we also use what we call *pedagogic instruments of observation* such as Ferre Laevers' well-being (2005) and involvement (1994), Bertram and Pascal's child track (2004, 2006).

These evaluative processes involve people attached to the pedagogic context, the pedagogic processes, and the pedagogic outcomes – children, teachers, parents. They involve processes that require from these actors the willingness to see, listen, observe, discuss, converse, analyse and interpret. These evaluative processes require that professionals put their attachment to the learning-teaching situation at the service of children and families, and at the service of assessment and evaluation.

Documented action sustained in joint thinking through processes of shared planning, doing and reflecting is pregnant with possibilities to uncover children's learning – that is to reveal learning and to document, assess and evaluate learning. Doing this over time will enable us to understand progress in learning. Doing this over time requires the active involvement of the central actors in the evaluative process and through their participation to build solidary evaluation.

In an inclusive approach, we speak of doing the documentation and evaluation with all the participants and not to them. Evaluation, through documentation, is conducted by multiple voices that undertake conversations; evaluation is scrutinised by plural voices in diverse circumstances. Revealing solidary learning implies the triangulation of all voices that have the democratic right to participate, thus enabling them to feel that they belong to a process of evaluation traditionally seen as an arena of power only for externals and/or professionals.

Solidary learning strives to create space for children's competence and participation

We want to finish this chapter with the exploration of the concept of solidary learning. The brief illustration that we gave about Andreia's classroom (to be followed in Chapter 8), through Tiago's voice, speaks about the lived 'we-ness' of the connected pedagogic processes: planning, acting, documenting and reflecting, assessing, evaluating. This implies a solidary authorship of pedagogic praxis. We are looking at various layers that interactively contribute to what we call solidary learning.

We revisited conceptions of learning hoping to clarify our understanding of children's learning. We came to the understanding of children's learning as dialogic learning, meaning that two apparently independent people (child and teacher) with two apparently independent roles (learning and teaching) enter in interdependency through communication, interaction and negotiation and grant together the essential role of co-construction of knowledge, knowing, meaning and learning. It is the encounter of children and teachers in their common learning purpose (once looked at as separated and even opposite) that produces a new positive order and a productive role in the universe of childhood pedagogy. It produces a kind of union, simultaneously complex and simple, between two previously opposing logics – the logic of the teacher (once the owner of knowledge) and the logic of the child (once the mere depository of that knowledge).

It hopes for a complementary association between different stances for the existence, development and functioning of learning. Instead of separation and isolation of the different contributions of children and teachers, we undertake a search for relationships, communication, cooperation and respect of differences at the levels of knowledge, feelings and intents. This requires the creation of a new understanding of differences and a new praxis of bringing them together for the sake of children's rights to be participants and of teachers' civic duties of promoting that participation. It requires a deep understanding of – using Dewey's (1897) terminology – *children's powers* that show teachers' democratic powers and processes.

The previously presented example of solidary planning reveals that this professional's know-how is sustained by an ethical stance – the intentional suspension of the teacher's voice, power and knowledge for the creation of children's rights to participate in educational planning, for the creation of a balanced power space for two voices. Solidary learning strives to create space for children's competence and participation because awareness has been created about their hundred languages and multiple intelligences as well as about their rights to play an active part in the learning-teaching process. The knowing about how to do this is a constant challenge that pedagogic documentation has the power to reveal. Developing solidary learning is liberating for children and educators and promising for democratic societies.

Notes

1. Chapter 2 of this book makes a detailed presentation of Pedagogy-in-Participation.
2. See Chapter 1 of this book.
3. See the concept of *pedagogical praxis* (Formosinho and Oliveira-Formosinho, 2012).
4. Inspired in Morin and Giddens we can say that pedagogy must be appropriate to its subject.

References

Araújo, S.B. (2011) *Pedagogia em creche: Da avaliação da qualidade à transformação praxiológica.* Tese de Doutoramento em Estudos da Criança – Especialização em Metodologia e Supervisão da Educação de Infância. Braga: Universidade do Minho.
Azevedo, A. (2009) *Revelando a aprendizagem das crianças: a documentação pedagógica.* Tese de Mestrado em Educação de Infância. Braga: Instituto de Estudos da Criança, Universidade do Minho.
Azevedo, A. and Sousa, J. (2010) A documentação pedagógica em contexto de creche: a partilha de poder. *Cadernos de Educação de Infância (Revista da Associação de Profissionais de Educação de Infância)* 91: 34–39.
Berger, P.L. and Luckmann, T. (1966) *The Social Construction of Reality: A Treatise in the Sociology of Knowledge.* Garden City, NY: Anchor Books.
Bertram, T. and Pascal, C. (2004) *The Effective Early Learning Programme.* Birmingham: Centre for Research in Early Childhood.
Bertram, T. and Pascal, C. (2006) *The Baby Effective Early Learning Programme: Improving Quality in Early Childhood Settings for Children from Birth to Three Years.* Birmingham: Centre for Research in Early Childhood.
Bordieu, P. (1990) *The Logic of Practice.* Cambridge: Polity Press.
Bordieu, P. (1998) *Practical Reason: On the Theory of Action.* Cambridge: Polity Press.
Bronfenbrenner, U. (2004) *Making Human Beings Human: Bioecological Perspectives on Human Development.* Thousand Oaks, CA: Sage Publications.
Bronfenbrenner, U. (2006) *The Ecology of Human Development: Experiments by Nature and Design.* Englewood Cliffs, NJ: Harvard University Press.
Bruner, J. (1990) *Acts of Meaning.* Cambridge, Mass.: Harvard University Press.
Carr, M. and Lee, W. (2012) *Learning Stories: Constructing Learner Identities in Early Education.* London: Sage Publications.
Craveiro, M.C. (2007) *Formação em contexto: Um estudo de caso no âmbito da pedagogia da infância.* Dissertação de doutoramento em Estudos da Criança. Braga: Universidade do Minho.
Dewey, J. (1897) My pedagogic creed. *School Journal* 54: 77–80.
Dewey, J. (1916) *Democracy and Education: An Introduction to the Philosophy of Education.* New York: Macmillan.
Dewey, J. (1997) *Experience and Education.* The Kappa Delta Pi Lecture Series. New York: Touchstone.
Dunne, J. (1993) *Back to The Rough Ground: Phronesis and Techne in Modern Philosophy and in Aristotle.* Notre Dame: University of Notre Dame Press.
Emilson, A. and Samuelson, P. (2014) Documentation and communication in Swedish preschools. *Early Years: An International Research Journal* 34, 2: 75–187.
Fleet, A., Patterson, C. and Robertson, J. (eds) (2012) *Conversations: Behind Early Childhood Pedagogical Documentation.* New South Wales: Pademelon Press.
Folque, M.A. (2008). *An investigation of the Movimento da Escola Moderna (MEM) pedagogy and its contribution to learning to learn in Portuguese Pre-schools.* London: Institute of Education, University of London. PhD dissertation.

Formosinho, J. (1987) *Educating for passivity – a study of Portuguese education*. PhD Dissertation. London: University of London, Institute of Education.

Formosinho, J. (2007) *O currículo uniforme pronto-a-vestir de tamanho único*. Cadernos de Políticas Educativas e Curriculares. Mangualde: Edições Pedago. First edition in J. Formosinho (ed.), *O Insucesso Escolar em Questão, Cadernos de Análise Social da Educação*. Braga: Universidade do Minho, 1987.

Formosinho, J. and Oliveira-Formosinho, J. (2005) *Developing Learning Communities: The Final Report on the Evaluation of the Impact of the National Professional Qualification in Integrated Centre Leadership (NPQICL) Leadership Programme*. National College for School Leadership.

Formosinho, J. and Oliveira-Formosinho, J. (2012) Towards a social science of the social: the contribution of praxeological research. *European Early Childhood Education Research Journal* 20, 4: 591–606.

Freire, P. (1970) *Pedagogy of the Oppressed*. New York: Continuum.

Laevers, F. (1994) *The Leuven Involvement Scale for Young Children LIS-YC. Manual and Video Tape, Experiential Education Series, nº1*. Leuven, Belgium: Centre for Experiencial Education.

Laevers, F. (ed.) (2005) *Well-being and Involvement in Care. A Process-oriented Self-Evaluation Instrument*. Belgium: Kind en Cezin and Research Centre for Experiential Education, Leuven University.

Lave, J. and Wenger. E. (1991) *Situated Learning: Legitimate Peripheral Participation*. New York: Cambridge University Press.

Lino, D. (2005) *Da formação escolar à formação em contexto: Um percurso de inovação para a reconstrução da pedagogia*. Dissertação de Doutoramento. Braga: Universidade do Minho, Instituto de Estudos da Criança.

Machado, I. (2014) *Avaliação da qualidade em creche: um estudo de caso sobre o bem-estar das crianças*. Tese de Mestrado em Educação de Infância, Instituto de Educação da Universidade do Minho, Braga, Portugal.

Mairs, K. and the Pen Green Team (2013) *Young Children Learning Through Schemas: Deepening the Dialogue about Learning in the Home and in the Nursery*. Oxon: Routledge.

Malaguzzi, L. (1998) History, ideas, and basic philosophy: an interview with Lella Gandini. In C. Edwards, L. Gandini and G. Forman (eds), *The Hundred Languages of Children: The Reggio Emilia Approach – Advanced Reflection*, pp. 49–97. Greenwich, CT: Ablex.

Ministério de Educação (1997) *Orientações curriculares para a educação pré-escolar*, Lisbon: Ministério de Educação.

Morin, E. (2008) *On Complexity*. Cresskill, NJ: Hampton Press, Inc.

Niza, S. (2012) *Escritos sobre educação*. Eds António Nóvoa, Francisco Marcelino and Jorge Ramos do Ó. Lisbon: Edições Tinta-da-China.

Novo, R. (2010) *A aprendizagem profissional da interacção adulto-criança: Um estudo de caso*. Dissertação de Doutoramento. Braga: Instituto de Estudos da Criança, Universidade do Minho.

Oliveira-Formosinho, J. (1987) Fundamentos psicológicos para um modelo desenvolvimentista de formação de professores. *Psicologia (Revista da Associação Portuguesa de Psicologia V*, 3: 247–257.

Oliveira-Formosinho, J. (1992) A formação de professores para a formação pessoal e social: relato de uma experiência de ensino. In Sociedade Portuguesa de Ciências de Educação, *Formação pessoal e social*, pp. 151–163. Porto: Sociedade Portuguesa de Ciências de Educação.

Oliveira-Formosinho, J. (1998) O desenvolvimento profissional das educadoras de infância: Um estudo de caso. Dissertação de Doutoramento em Estudos da Criança. Braga: Universidade do Minho.

Oliveira-Formosinho, J. (2001) The specific professional nature of early years education and styles of adult/child interaction. *European Early Childhood Education Research Journal* 9, 1: 57–72.

Oliveira-Formosinho, J. (2007) Pedagogia(s) da infância: Reconstruindo uma práxis de participação. In J. Oliveira-Formosinho, T.M. Kishimoto and M. Pinazza (eds), *Pedagogias(s) da Infância. Dialogando com o passado, construindo o futuro*, pp. 13–36. São Paulo: Artmed Editora.

Oliveira-Formosinho, J. (2014) A avaliação holística: A proposta da Pedagogia-em-Participação. *Revista Interacções* 10, 32: 27–39.

Oliveira-Formosinho, J. and Formosinho, J. (eds) (2001) *Associação Criança: Um contexto de formação em contexto*. Braga: Livraria Minho.

Oliveira-Formosinho, J. and Formosinho, J. (2012) *Pedagogy-in-Participation: Childhood Association Pedagogical Approach*. Porto: Porto Editora.

Oliveira-Formosinho, J., Kishimoto, T.M. and Pinazza, M. (eds) (2007) *Pedagogias(s) da Infância. Dialogando com o passado, construindo o futuro*. São Paulo: Artmed Editora.

Parente, C. (2004) *A construção de práticas alternativas de avaliação na Pedagogia da Infância: Sete jornadas de aprendizagem*. Dissertação de Doutoramento. Braga: Universidade do Minho, Instituto de Estudos da Criança.

Pascal, C. and Bertram, T. (2009) Listening to young citizens: the struggle to make real a participatory paradigm in research with young children. *European Early Childhood Education Research Journal* 17, 2: 249–262.

Pires, C. (2013) *A voz da criança sobre a inovação pedagógica*. Tese de doutoramento em Estudos da Criança, área de especialização de Metodologia de Supervisão em Educação de Infância. Braga: Universidade do Minho.

Rinaldi, C. (2012) *Diálogos com Reggio Emilia: escutar, investigar e aprender*. São Paulo: Paz e Terra.

Rogoff, B. (1990) *Apprenticeship in Thinking: Cognitive Development in Social Context*. New York: Oxford University Press.

Valsiner, J., and van der Veer, R. (2000) *The Social Mind: Construction of the Idea*. New York: Cambridge University Press.

Vieira, F. (2010) *A aprendizagem da profissão: Um estudo de caso de portefólios reflexivos de educadores de infância*. Dissertação de Doutoramento. Braga: Universidade do Minho, Instituto de Estudos da Criança.

Vygotsky, L.S. (1978) *Mind in Society: The Development of Higher Psychological Processes*. Cambridge, Mass.: Harvard University Press.

Whalley, M. (ed.) (2001) *Involving Parents In Their Children's Learning*. London: Paul Chapman Publishing.

Wertsch, J.V. (1985) *Vygotsky and the Social Formation of Mind*. Cambridge, Mass.: Harvard University Press.

Wertsch, J.V. (1991) *Voices of the Mind: A Sociocultural Approach to Mediated Action*. Cambridge, Mass.: Harvard University Press.

PART III

Portraits of practice

Case studies

7

ETHICAL PRINCIPLES FOR HOLISTIC PEDAGOGIC EVALUATION

Júlia Formosinho, João Formosinho,
Christine Pascal and Tony Bertram

We jointly developed a Pedagogic Creed for Assessment and Evaluation sustained in our images of children and educators, in our understanding of the nature of school and education, of childhood pedagogy and pedagogic evaluation. We put forward twelve principles that can inspire an ethically oriented assessment and evaluation. Our Pedagogic Creed has been presented in the introduction and we will proceed now to make an enlarged presentation of it.

Three stances for the organisation of the principles

In order to think about the pedagogic principles for a holistic assessment and evaluation perspective we created three stances: the paradigmatic stance; the theoretical stance; the praxeological stance. Indeed most of the principles we assumed can be framed within more than one of these stances.

The *paradigmatic stance* is built upon the *beliefs, values and principles*. Beliefs are mental representations, fusions of thinking and feeling, of cognitions and emotions, which do not pretend to be empirically supported. Beliefs about life – the world view, the respect for persons, the respect for voices, the relationships between people and knowledge. These beliefs generate priorities for action: first priority being the respect for all persons involved in the evaluation processes: children, parents, teachers and researchers. This means that all have voice in the evaluation process; this means as well that all have the right to be answered.

The *theoretical stance* is built upon a theory of education. Our theory of education sits in the crossroads of participatory pedagogies (Formosinho and Oliveira-Formosinho, 2008; Oliveira-Formosinho and Formosinho, 2012) and the socio-cultural approach to human development (Wertsch, 1985). The educational vision we are referring considers education as situated in time(s), space(s) and culture(s) and developed through layers of participation aiming at children's integrated learning of skills, knowledge and thinking in processes that allow metacognition.

Our theory of education at the evaluation level grew out of a very specific dialogue between Pedagogy-in-Participation (Oliveira-Formosinho, 1998; Oliveira-Formosinho and Formosinho, 2001; Formosinho and Oliveira-Formosinho, 2008) and the EEL Project (Bertram and Pascal, 2004, 2006).

This vision of education speaks about images: the image of the learner – the oneness of the child/learner; the image of the educator – the oneness of the teacher. It speaks about concepts: the concept of education, the school, teaching-learning situation modes, content, evaluation. It clarifies evaluation as a dimension which needs to be congruent with the other pedagogic dimensions.

The *praxeological stance* says that it is indispensable to think around the answer to the how to do evaluation. Having gone through a reflexive journey about principles and theories we need to promote congruent action. It is indispensable to develop coherent praxis for assessment and evaluation; otherwise assessment and evaluation will pervert the ethos of the overall pedagogy. Documented listening, observation and negotiation are central tools that can be used with the support of videos, cameras, audio tape recorders, narratives, among others. The organisation of the information gathered is central to its open use in the learning community. Professional action in the area of assessment and evaluation comes from the fusion of heart and mind. Professional action in the area of assessment and evaluation requires beliefs, supported in knowledge, experienced in daily life teaching and learning, shared in the learning community.

The twelve principles for holistic assessment and evaluation when used in integration should safeguard ethical thinking and promote the coherence of pedagogic thinking with daily praxis. They invite professionals to think about ethics, theoretical foundations and praxis of assessment and evaluation.

Table of ethical principles for a holistic pedagogic evaluation

We will proceed now to present Table 7.1. which synthesises our ethical principles for the praxis of pedagogic evaluation.

Principles for a holistic assessment and evaluation in early childhood education

Assessment and evaluation should better serve children and families following a philosophical principle of the greater good for all

The history of early childhood education slowly developed three core rationales for its services (Lloyd and Penn, 2014; Bennett, 2014) that we interpret as such:

1. to contribute to children's learning and development;
2. to support families, mainly working mothers, in their need and right to access paid employment by providing daycare for young children;

TABLE 7.1 Ethical principles for pedagogic evaluation

Any assessment and evaluation in early childhood education should:

1	better serve children and families following a philosophical principle of the greater good for all
2	be democratic and participatory
3	actively involve children
4	take into account children's holistic learning
5	seek participation of parents and of other primary carers of the children
6	be ecological, that is, referred to contexts, processes and outcomes
7	support individual learning journeys
8	support the learning journeys for children and professionals
9	be (inter)culturally relevant
10	be documented, that is, informed by the documented learning of each child
11	provide useful and usable information for children and families, professionals and schools, teacher educators and policy makers
12	contribute to a civic spirit of accountability

3.   to contribute to the development of social justice and equity and to the reduction of poverty by providing for all children and families, especially the more vulnerable, an empowering quality early education, thus facilitating their access to cultural capital that highly increases their life chances.

The *first rationale* has been stated since the very beginnings of the services and says that early childhood education and care has as its central goal the promotion of children's learning and development. This goal has been subjected to multiple interpretations depending on what is expected from children and what is the societal image of childhood and children. Each society creates its image of the child and the learner which is influenced by its expectations about children; in turn, that image has a sustained influence over time on expectations.

We sustain an image of a competent child with rights that should be supported with learning journeys that favour their integrated learner identities. So in our understanding of this rationale, early childhood education should contribute to integrated holistic learning and development at various levels such as: care and education, play and learning, autonomy and cooperation, feelings and reasoning as well as to an integrated approach to the appropriation of plural languages and multiple intelligences. Assessment and evaluation, as a pedagogic dimension, is to be congruent with the overall pedagogic approach to integrated learning that answers to the holistic plural learner's identity in presence.

The *second rationale* is historically situated in the times of the industrial revolution and women's liberation movements with the connected need of industry to employ more labour and the right of women to have a working professional life.

In our understanding early childhood education should support children and families, mainly working mothers, in their need and right to have a job and go to work with well-being feelings because they know that their children are well cared for and educated. Families' perceptions and understandings of their children's well-being and learning are key to their own well-being and represent a contribution to the quality of their own work. We assert that children and societies need childhood education services that look interactively at children's and families' rights and duties.

During the last ten years, research has been emphasising a *third rationale* (Bennett, 2014) based on the evidence that only quality education opens doors and gives access to cultural capital for children and families. In our understanding this rationale is of great relevance since we are aware that access to the knowledge society through education and culture is central for children's actual learning and for their later access to good jobs and identity development. Educational systems and educational centres have the duty not only to provide quality but to make it available, affordable, and accessible to all children. As João Formosinho says: equity and quality are two sides of the same coin.

Children's rights and competence will be better served by this view of respect for the interconnectedness of children's and families' well-being and the ethical stand of challenging educational systems to develop competent support for teachers, centres and children and to expect from professionals civic accountability of the services they provide.

Assessment and evaluation of children's learning cannot be conducted in a vacuum, as if looking at isolated, separated, independent processes. It is to be conducted and understood with an open mind of a bigger picture.

Assessment and evaluation should be democratic and participatory

The first service to children and their families, and indeed to the wider society, is the willingness to pursue the civic goal of helping each child to become a participative learner. This requires a democratic worldview as well as technical, professional, reflexive, critical competences in tune with the underlying educational philosophy.

Faundez and Freire (1992) in *Learning to Question: A Pedagogy of Liberation* inspire us to think that raising critical questions and working at them in a reflexive and dialogic mode constitutes a liberation because it brings dynamism, new understandings, new possibilities to the reality we are facing. Learning to question deeply around assessment and evaluation may eventually free us from ready-made answers to questions such as: why evaluate?, what to evaluate?, how to evaluate? what to evaluate for?

The answers to these questions should be inspiring of pedagogic methods that give children's voices in all stances of life in school and learning situations. Children have the right to be given voice in the pedagogic sphere of assessment. How to do this calls for a professional learning journey that should be travelled in companionable action and thinking within an organisation that supports ethical professionalism.

The very first answer to the very first question – *why* to evaluate – leads our thinking about assessment to start with beliefs and principles. The answer to the *what* question is connected with the image of the child that we want to assess and evaluate in an ethical decision of monitoring the quality of professional practices. Assessment needs to help us to better see the learning action and the learner-in-action in order to make evaluation a stance of crediting the child with competence, agency and participation and also to support further learning.

An early education centre that develops participative pedagogy in daily life needs to create the ethos of a democratic, pluralistic worldview that develops care for all and defines principles for action that search for the greater good for all. This ethos should pervade both the centre as an organisation and each of its learning spaces. The central principle of the greater good for all children will be better sustained by congruence of a democratic and participatory ethos between the educational system, the educational organisation and the pedagogic approach.

Assessment and evaluation should actively involve children

The concept of democracy develops in a context of respect for human rights (including obviously the rights of children, namely the right to learn) and of identity development for children and professionals which is also a process of learners' identity development. Assessment and evaluation should be congruent with a rights based approach. The very first concern is that of making sure that assessment and evaluation does not introduce a harmful approach in the assessment of learning, that is, should not cause harm to children. It should not concentrate on the so-called deficits of the children thus harming their well-being. It should respect their right to protect their own image as capable persons and respected competent learners. It needs to avoid the harm of early 'labelling' of children, and subsequent early diagnosis and intervention. It should avoid the observation of children in artificial learning situations induced by distant and decontextualised assessment and evaluation scales, tasks and tests.

We are speaking about very young children whose rights we are supposed to protect: the right to a positive image, the right to well-being, the right to a respected identity, the right of developing a learner identity. This means that ethically it is indispensable to start with the evaluation of the educational contexts along with the evaluation of the educational processes. Learning does not happen in a vacuum. The quality of the educational contexts and processes impacts on the quality of learning. Professionals, researchers and politicians do not have the right to create abstract outcomes that are evaluated through decontextualised procedures that will harm children's pathway to a positive learner identity.

Assessment and evaluation should take into account children's holistic learning

One of the critical questions about evaluation is that of asking what we want to evaluate. The answer to this question depends on the image of the child and the concept of education. In what can be called the *family of participatory pedagogies* the child is competent, an agent with rights to participation and to the integrative use of senses, cognitions and emotions. Early childhood education is to safeguard the education of the holistic human beings that children are and the holistic learners that we, professionals, have the duty to help them to be.

Evaluation needs to inform us about:

*   *what the child does* – making visible the learner-in-action: developing the agreed upon learning compromises between the child, the children, the professionals;
*   *what the child feels* – making visible the child-in-feeling: enjoying physical and psychological well-being, integrating action, cognition and feelings;
*   *what the child learns* – making visible the child-in-learning: learning how to learn, learning about herself/himself as a learner, learning about the world, nature, the social world. Developing an inquisitive, provocative mind that explores the world with energy and pleasure.

Assessment and evaluation is to be concerned with the study of children's ways of making meaning of learning experiences, creating narratives of their learning through communicative processes.

Assessment and evaluation should actively seek the participation of parents and of others involved in the primary care of the children

Parents and primary carers should be involved, in our perspective, in their children's learning. They should be involved in the documentation of their children's learning journeys and thus, in coherence, they should also be involved in shared critical reflection about their children's pathways to learning and to their co-construction as learners.

In our research (Azevedo, 2009) the process of making learning visible through documentation of the processes involved in learning situations has revealed a space for well-being of children, families and educators. It demands firm beliefs on the rights of all the actors involved as well as empathic openness. Last but not least, it demands rigorous professional practical knowledge.

All this in place, it can be said that educators' learning journeys are enriched and parents' learning about their children's learning becomes rigorous and enjoyable. The involvement of parents and primary carers in the evaluation of their children promotes their cooperation in daily life educational processes and facilitates the support they can offer to their children in the transition processes, mainly the transition to primary school.

Assessment and evaluation should be ecological (contextualised and situated), that is, referred to contexts, processes and outcomes

Assessment and evaluation is to be contextualised both in the specific pedagogic praxis and in the children's circumstances and identities, contexts and cultures. A holistic evaluation is *ecological*, meaning it is contextual, culturally referenced and situated in time. The evaluation encompasses the appreciation of all ecological dimensions (elements) – contexts, processes and outcomes. As evaluation is to be referred to children's experiential learning in sociocultural contexts in specific pedagogic situations, assessment and evaluation should be referred also to these contexts and pedagogic processes. A rigorous approach to evaluation recognises the interactivity between contexts, processes and outcomes at all levels of learning.

It is very common to see professionals who claim a progressive educational theory but make incongruent statements and develop inconsistent practices when it comes to evaluation. This can be explained by lack of available knowledge and support in thinking and action, at this level, as well as because of external pressures that favour traditional systems of evaluation exclusively oriented to outcomes. This is a question of principles, an ethical question that cannot be forgotten but it is also a technical question that demands professional practical knowledge for the evaluation of the educational environment.

Assessment and evaluation should support children's individual learning journeys

The importance of early education for the co-construction of the learner-in-action means to help each child to develop her/his possibilities as a competent learner that: identifies learning situations; develops awareness about his/her interest in the situations; decides to join (or not); creates purposes; uses her skills to participate (alone and in cooperation); persists in the dynamics of the learning situation; identifies and overcomes difficulties; accepts mistakes without feelings of debilitation; reflects and celebrates achievements; and narrates learning.

The sociocultural constructivist theories of learning used in different pedagogical participative approaches for early years education call attention to the fact that once learning is acquired through processes of learning how to learn and how to analyse learning, childhood pedagogy needs to engage with the challenge of supporting the learner in their situated learning processes – the child in action, the learner in the making.

The social and interpersonal humanistic, democratic climate that is an aim of childhood centres and activity rooms should create the texture for the expression of each learner and guarantee he/she is respected, listened to and answered both at the level of learning and assessment of learning.

Assessment and evaluation should support the interdependent learning journeys of children and professionals

Assessment and evaluation of learning should help the child, the educator, the family to understand and enjoy their interactive learning journeys and facilitate the development of further learning. The first aim of assessment and evaluation is that of serving children's learning journeys through processes of reflection on daily life and activity in order to enhance further learning.

Listening to children, looking at them, entering in conversation and dialogue, coming to compromises between their purposes and professional purposes, planning for the accomplishment of the compromises, documenting the whole process, reflecting on the documentation that makes visible the learning journey of each child and of the collective; all this sets the stage for looking at assessment and evaluation as a support of learning journeys. Professionals looking at children's learning-in-process through documentation-in-progress create the conditions for the more meaningful development and reflection of their own professional learning journeys. Children's and professionals' learning journeys are deeply interdependent.

The noble desideratum is that the respect of children's intents, motivations and purposes will be negotiated with professionals' intentionalities and purposes creating productive encounters of voices and cultures. Thus assessment and evaluation should be respectful of professionals' identities, intentionality and purposes in connectedness with children's purposes.

When assessment and evaluation are conducted within a psychological approach (either psychometric or developmental), educators lose power and identity because pedagogy (not psychology) is their professional domain. If they are to be accountable they should be asked to develop monitoring, assessment and evaluation within childhood pedagogic frameworks once that is their professional knowledge base and their sphere of action. Professionals have the right to the respect of their professional identity; they have the duty to live up to it and to show what they deliver with their respected professional identity. The sustainability of a pedagogic evaluation of daily learning allows them to make children's learning visible and public and to create awareness of the deep relationship between teaching and learning in the desired context of a democratic organisation.

Only an empowering quality early education opens doors to culture and to the power of the knowledge society. To develop quality education it is neececessary to support educators in the thinking and doing (praxis) of an ethical participatory pedagogy that looks at evaluation as a value for all and conducts it as assessment of learning for further learning. We need to remember that competent teachers need competent educational organisations and all of them need competent educational systems.

Assessment and evaluation should be (inter)culturally relevant

A democratic educational theory departs from the awareness of psychological, social, cultural differences between people, places and cultures and calls for a pluralistic, integrated approach to life, learning and evaluation in the children's centre.

When speaking of children's learning we are speaking about plural identities. In congruence with speaking about children's assessment and evaluation we should be speaking about the evaluation of plural processes and plural outcomes developed by plural identities through plural learning journeys.

The challenge to follow this principle in action is that of the need of an intercultural pedagogy to be systematically developed and monitored. Indeed for childhood pedagogy to be relevant in today's schools it needs to be one that deals systematically with similarities and differences and support social cohesion.

Assessment and evaluation need to uncover the consequences of an explicit pedagogic approach that claims to be intercultural; they need to show that childhood pedagogy is necessarily intercultural because the diversity of actors, contexts and cultures calls for plural learning journeys. This in turn calls for flexible, complex approaches to assessment and evaluation that tune with present diversities.

Assessment and evaluation should be informed by the documented learning of each child

The development of participative assessment and evaluation benefits from being considered in the framework of a holistic pedagogy that requires coherence among the thinking for all the dimensions of the educational environment. The overall theory of education is to be present in all facets of the educational environment and should inform the specific stance of evaluation.

A pedagogical approach to assessment and evaluation is conducted by reference to learning-teaching processes and search for congruence with them. An explicit pedagogic approach to assessment emerges from pedagogical knowledge. Traditionally assessment of learning has been conducted with psychological techniques either psychometric or developmental.

The introduction of documentation by Malaguzzi (1998) contributed highly to a Copernican revolution in childhood pedagogy. The children entering in the Early Childhood Centre hoping for constant conversation with their teachers (and other carers) develop sustained dialogues, action and reflection, and sustained co-construction of knowledge. The interactive documentation of learning allows the educator to see (and revisit) children's learning processes and to see children as co-constructors of knowledge and ethics. We are in the realm of a very favourable space for knowing about knowledge of the child, the learner, the teacher, of relationships and interactions, and of advances and mistakes in children's and professionals' learning journeys.

In this complex view of teaching and learning, professionals search for methods of evaluation with trustworthiness which implies credibility (confidence in the truth of things) and neutrality (suspension of themselves) to create space for children. This allows evaluation to be shaped by children's motivations, interests, actions and learning in relation with teachers' actions and not merely by pre-determined decontextualised agendas. The individual child's knowledge and the knowledge acquired by the group of children should be documented to create information about children's learning journeys thus allowing research about the connectedness of teaching and learning.

Assessment and evaluation should provide useful and usable information for children and families, professionals and schools, teacher educators and policy makers

What is assessment and evaluation for? What does it serve? In our understanding, the first use of assessment and evaluation is the child and family, it is to help children and families to look, to see and to understand children's learning journeys and their development as learners.

Another use of assessment and learning is the service to professionals in order to sustain reflection on the quality of the educational environment, its learning opportunities and children's responses to these learning opportunities. Assessment and evaluation are to support professionals' awareness about their strategies, competences and motivations to serve each child's individual learning journey as well as the collective learning journey. Another use of the assessment and evaluation procedure is the service to the children's centre leaders in order to analyse and reflect on the services that are being provided. Last but not least, policy makers are to be served by the vast information that can be collected through rigorous and valid processes of assessment and evaluation throughout the system. It can constitute a solid basis for decision making and innovation. Indeed this is the only way for policy makers to have access to authentic pedagogic evaluation as opposed to abstract, decontextualised evaluation. This is a gift that teachers and schools can offer to the system. Indeed praxeological research (Formosinho and Oliveira-Formosinho, 2012; Pascal and Bertram, 2012) clearly shows that the only way to create change and better services is through systematically analysed and interpreted action that creates meaning and knowledge for further reconstructed action.

Assessment and evaluation should contribute to a civic spirit of accountability

When assessment and evaluation are conducted, within the perspective that is present in the above stated principles, professionals assume it to be an integrant part of their praxis. Being empowered in one's own knowledge base, being acknowledged and respected in one's own professional praxis brings about, simultaneously rights and duties. The right to be in charge of evaluation means the duty to share it with the key actors involved in learning: children, parents, professionals, organisational actors, local communities and society.

The experience of sharing the complex processes of documenting and monitoring, assessing and evaluating proves to be professionally rewarding and engrosses the civic spirit of accountability.

As professionals we need to find ways of assessment and evaluation that are compatible with our central principles of democracy and participation, and with children's rights and motivations, interests and purposes. Assessment and evaluation should contribute to the enhancement of learning. Its processes and outcomes should be shared with a democratic spirit of collaboration and the awareness about a professional, civic spirit of accountability.

References

Azevedo, A. (2009) Revelando a aprendizagem das crianças: A documentação pedagógica. Tese de Mestrado em Educação de Infância. Braga: Instituto de Estudos da Criança, Universidade do Minho.

Bennett, J. (2014) Special Issue: Disadvantage and Social Justice. *European Early Childhood Education Research Journal* 22, 3.

Bertram, T. and Pascal, C. (2004) *The Effective Early Learning Programme*. Birmingham: Centre for Research in Early Childhood.

Bertram, T. and Pascal, C. (2006) *The Baby Effective Early Learning Programme: Improving Quality in Early Childhood Settings for Children from Birth to Three Years*. Birmingham: Centre for Research in Early Childhood.

Faundez, A. and Freire, P. (1992) *Learning to Question: A Pedagogy of Liberation*. Trans. Tony Coates. New York: Continuum.

Formosinho, J. and Oliveira-Formosinho, J. (2008) *Pedagogy-in-Participation: Childhood Association's Approach*. Research Report, Aga Khan Foundation, Lisbon.

Formosinho, J. and Oliveira-Formosinho, J. (2012) Towards a social science of the social: the contribution of praxeological research. *European Early Childhood Education Research Journal* 20, 4: 591–606.

Lloyd, E. and Penn, H. (2014) Childcare markets in an age of austerity. *European Early Childhood Education Research Journal* 22, 3: 386–396.

Malaguzzi, L. (1998) History, ideas, and basic philosophy: an interview with Lella Gandini. In C. Edwards, L. Gandini and G. Forman (eds), *The Hundred Languages of Children: The Reggio Emilia Approach – Advanced Reflection*, pp. 49–97. Greenwich, CT: Ablex.

Oliveira-Formosinho, J. (1998) O desenvolvimento profissional das educadoras de infância: Um estudo de caso. Dissertação de Doutoramento em Estudos da Criança. Braga: Universidade do Minho.

Oliveira-Formosinho, J. and Formosinho, J. (eds) (2001) *Associação Criança: Um contexto de formação em contexto*. Braga: Livraria Minho.

Oliveira-Formosinho, J. and Formosinho, J. (2012) *Pedagogy-in-Participation: Childhood Association Educational Perspective*. Porto: Porto Editora.

Pascal, C. and Bertram, T. (2012) Praxis, ethics and power: developing praxeology as a participatory paradigm for early childhood research. *European Early Childhood Education Research Journal* 20, 4: 477–492.

Wertsch, J.V. (1985) *Vygotsky and the Social Formation of Mind*. Cambridge, Mass.: Harvard University Press.

8

CASE STUDY 1

Why do the Omo River children paint themselves? A pedagogic evaluation

Júlia Formosinho, Andreia Lima and
Joana Sousa

Introduction

The contextualisation of this case study starts in a classroom (Andreia's classroom), in a centre (Olivais Sul Children's Centre), in a programme (Early Childhood Development – ECD Programme). We present the partnership between the Aga Khan Foundation and the Childhood Association for the development of childhood pedagogy, staff development and research. We proceed to a praxeological case study that highlights the journey of a project work which makes visible the relationship between children's and teachers' learning, documentation and assessment. We finish with a demonstration about how documentation is sustained in solidary planning and action that, in turn, will allow solidary learning to be revealed.

Contextualising the case

The ECD Olivais Sul Children's Centre is part of a larger programme (the ECD Programme) that encompasses a network of centres, a research approach, an approach to childhood pedagogy (Pedagogy-in-Participation), an approach to staff development (situated/contextual staff development) and Master and PhD programmes (in collaboration with Lisbon Catholic University).

In 2009, the Aga Khan Foundation Portugal signed an agreement with the Ministry of Social Security for the management of this ECD Centre. The Aga Khan Foundation and the Childhood Association have a partnership that allows that pedagogic support and research, in this centre, is provided by the Childhood Association. Here and in affiliate centres, the pedagogical approach used is Pedagogy-in-Participation, developed over the years by the Childhood Association with AKF support.

It is known that childhood education can sustain beneficial effects. It is known that it can alleviate effects of poverty at an early age. Several reports and studies show that low-income families and minority groups have unequal access to preschool education and when they have access, they often enrol in poor quality services (Bennett, 2014).

João Formosinho has been calling attention to the fact that quality and equity are two sides of the same coin (Formosinho and Figueiredo, 2014) meaning that if early childhood education wants to truthfully fight against poverty it has to make available accessible and affordable quality preschool for all children. Quality makes a difference in learning and equity requires that quality learning that impacts on later life chances will be made available to all children not only to a few (Formosinho and Figueiredo, 2014).

Privatisation and marketisation practices are widening inequality in access and poor enrolment. There is a need for civic/public policies to address these issues. In the Olivais Centre we tried to reverse the trend making services available, accessible and affordable to minority groups (15 per cent) and low-income families (48 per cent) and integrating them with majority families and higher-income families.

Services are available, accessible and affordable, but also useful for children and families. They include services such as: extended hours before and after sessions; integration of 0–3 and 3–6 and *crèche familiar* (childminder services); services for special needs; and a transition programme to primary school.

Further contextualisation of this case is the explicit pedagogical approach used in this centre and in Andreia's classroom, an approach that has been developed throughout the last 25 years (Oliveira-Formosinho, 1998; Oliveira-Formosinho and Formosinho, 2001; Formosinho and Oliveira-Formosinho, 2008). The first challenge of this development has been the one of integrating a worldview, a theory of education, an epistemology and a methodology (see Figure 8.1). This challenge has been answered by a process-in-progress through the integration of experiential praxis development and theory reconstruction.

So it is clear that we faced another challenge, that of weaving the foundational theories with daily life practices aiming at the development of praxis.

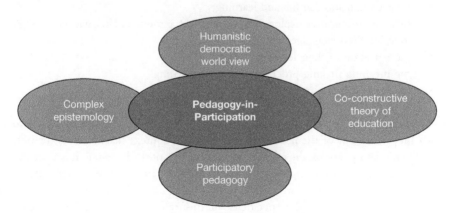

FIGURE 8.1 Pedagogy-in-Participation

The conceptualisation of pedagogy as praxis challenges our traditional understandings of teaching and learning because it speaks about action grounded in ethics and theories, and developed through daily cooperative experiential situations (Oliveira-Formosinho, 2007).

Pedagogic knowledge is developed through situated action and infused with theories and beliefs (beliefs, values and principles). Pedagogy is an 'ambiguous' space between action, theories and beliefs in a solidary integration of the contributions of all these stances.

It challenges us to deconstruct the delivering situations where content is passed to students through a banking system (Freire, 1970) and reconstruct children's and teachers' creation of educational environments and situations, where children and teachers together develop experiential participatory learning and evaluation.

Pedagogical action that aims at the development of children's learning and learning how to learn in interaction and communication is complex; it involves cognitions, feelings and motivations and it needs regulation, especially, social regulation aiming at self-regulation.

Assessment and evaluation are integrative parts of the process of social and self-regulation once they aim at monitoring and understanding the processes and the outcomes of the pedagogical action. Pedagogical action oriented to learning demands from professionals the development of self-regulation strategies that help to understand if the learning processes are being civic, integrated and effective. Documentation that allows assessment and evaluation is a means to develop professional regulation strategies of children's learning.

Within Pedagogy-in-Participation we evaluate learning having in mind the pedagogic anchors for the development of learning. For us assessment and evaluation should be able to tell us how children are progressing in our intentionality axes:

- their relational identities development;
- their feelings of belonging;
- their participation in life and learning;
- their communicative exploration of the world, persons and knowledge through 'one hundred languages';
- the narration of their learning;
- the meaning making processes about the learning;
- the understanding of themselves as learners.

Teaching, learning and assessment are developed in context. Learning relates to teaching and both of them develop in pedagogic context that nurtures (or not) children's nature. For us, the quality of educational contexts is central (it is a 'second educator') one reason being that it is (or not) the first mediator of the educational intentionalities we opted for.[1]

We enter now into the specificity of this case study that makes a dense presentation of a project work through the systematic documentation of its development, where the fusion between teaching and learning, documentation and evaluation is made visible. The literature in the area shows the need to develop novel ways of assessment and evaluation of learning (Carr, 2001; Bradbury, 2013; Dubiel, 2014).

Pedagogic documentation is the space where professional action is made visible and understood in relation with children's learning (Malaguzzi, 1998; Rinaldi, 2012). This being the case, pedagogic documentation should reveal pedagogic processes as well as creating information about their consequences for children's and educators' learning. A central contribution of this case study is making evident the respect for the complexity of the relationship of the learning situations with the evaluating situations.

The methodological nature of this case study is praxeological (Formosinho and Oliveira-Formosinho, 2012; Pascal and Bertram, 2012) meaning that it is a vivid thinking (logos) about the evolving nature of praxis densely documented in order to create novel ways of conducting holistic evaluation. Dense documentation of the change processes in action allows not only the understanding of transformation but also the creation of knowledge about transformation in view of pedagogic assessment and research.

The key criteria for a praxeological study are those of allowing the entrance in a vivid transformational situation, densely studied through documentation so allowing the entrance in research, involving the central actors so allowing the entrance in participation. Uncovering, simultaneously, the phenomenology of the lived experience, the study processes and the participation of the people involved allows us by that means to create praxeological knowledge (Oliveira-Formosinho and Formosinho, 2012).

Let us now enter Andreia's classroom (a central actor and author of this case study, the teacher of the classroom where the case is being developed),[2] going through the study of a project work called *Why do the Omo River's children paint themselves?*

The group's motivation to study the Omo River's children comes from the contribution of an empowered mother. The mother comes forward to Andreia (the teacher) with a suggestion of an activity resulting from her daughter's interest:

Andreia, Ana likes much the paintings of Omo River's children. May she bring and share some of the images with her peers?

This mother is used to the welcoming attitude of Andreia in what concerns families' contributions and involvement. The mother and Andreia enter in a conversation and think how to use this motivation to make it an educational opportunity for all. So it is time to jointly enter in the process of the educational planning. This mother's suggestion and her daughter's interest set up the creation of a learning situation that was reflected on as having the potential for the development of our educational intentionalities. So the pedagogic axes and learning areas of Pedagogy-in-Participation are considered (as well as the opportunities within the daily routine)

FIGURE 8.2 Group sharing

and specific intentionalities for this situation are defined: to be responsive to cultures and diversities present among the group and to learn about distant cultures and diversities; to share information, images, videos gathered by families; to share interests, ideas, thoughts, motivations and experiences, to integrate different languages.

Although the mother can't be present to share images of Omo River's children with her daughter, Ana (the daughter) willingly and assertively does it, confident in a responsive educational environment that respects children and provokes their participation. Ana, as an assumed competent child, sets out the learning situation presenting with enthusiasm her interests and ideas around the images that are so telling to her (after the images have been prepared by Andreia in a format big enough to be shared in a group) (see Figure 8.2).

FIGURE 8.3 Natural fashion: tribal decoration from Africa/Ethiopia: people of the Omo Valley (© Hans Silvester)

Inspired by the aesthetic appeal of these images (see Figure 8.3), Ana's peers grow in curiosity and interest giving their own insights about the images of Omo River's children:

- These children of Omo River have their face painted, have leaves and flowers on their head.
- They paint themselves because it's Carnival.
- No. It's not Carnival. They paint themselves because they are from Africa.
- They paint themselves to be more colourful.
- They go to a wedding.
- The paintings on the face of Omo River's children are marvellous. The family is very beautiful. They look like statues.

This welcoming and competent educator feels the need to search for new information (see Figure 8.4) not only to widen the range of information available to children, but also, as very well put by Tiago before (Chapter 6), *to research the things she doesn't know.* These children are aware that the teacher does not own knowledge, this teacher facilitates that awareness to develop . . .

Children enter in plural conversations (they are used to the conversation style of Andreia's pedagogy) with one another, with the educational team and with parents. Conversations deepen ideas, provoke dialogues, raise questions and possible focuses they might want to pursue (see Figure 8.5).

FIGURE 8.4 The decorated faces of children of the Omo Valley (© Hans Silvester)

FIGURE 8.5 Children studying the faces of the Omo River children

- Look at the boys and girls with their face painted. They look so beautiful. They have white stripes.
- Why is it that they paint the face?
- To look more cute.
- To go to weddings.
- It's because they are from Africa and have different figures.
- I don't know. We'll have to research.

By expressing their own ideas, confronting them, questioning them, children look for meaning making assuming openly that they don't know and have to research. They assume themselves to be, children and teacher, learners in the making.

Andreia documented these learning situations, edited the documentation and returned it to the children during one of the moments of daily routine, the council time (see Figure 8.6). This learning community reflects on past learning for future learning (supported by the edited documentation). Together they create questions for research:

- We want to know where the children of Omo River live.
- Why do the Omo River's children paint themselves?

Andreia and children together plan for the next week negotiating purposes and actions and creating compromises. In Pedagogy-in-Participation, a pedagogy of

FIGURE 8.6 Documenting children in action

conversation and communication exists between children and their educators, where they develop dialogic encounters and where their mutual intents and purposes are made solidary. The creation of solidary planning is our first lived answer to our conceptualisation of participatory children. The intentional suspension of the adult's power creates space for the exercise of, in Dewey's terms, *children's powers*.

Group and individual joint planning is followed by a new cycle of children's activity in cooperation with Andreia's professional activity, that of documenting the children in action. Again Andreia lives an ethical stance of suspension – she steps back, looks, listens to each child and the group. Her doing is not doing . . . but allowing the children to do and allowing herself to see. Creating for herself space and time to see, to listen, to hear. Encountering for herself another task – documenting children's learning-in-action. Andreia attends to individual experiential learning seeking to describe, interpret and understand each child's ideas, hypothesis and knowing through aesthetic and artistic narratives. Children represent their ideas through paintings, combining visual narratives with oral narratives (see Figure 8.7).

FIGURE 8.7
Children's representations of
their ideas

Then, Andreia recreates her voice and asks:

– What are our sources of information to answer to our research questions?

Children are prompted to present their suggestions and come to compromises:

– We'll search in books, in the internet and will ask our fathers and mothers.

Group experiential learning is supported by parents' and families' involvement in the development of this project work contributing with diverse sources of information: internet research, video and image browsing, book and atlas research and cultural artefacts. Parents and families support learning situations with the group of children participating in the daily routine with materials and dialogues that sustain the progress in learning. Here, parents and families, children and teacher exercise their powers of cooperation facilitated by this democratic educational environment and constitute themselves as a learning community (Wenger, 1998) within a broader educational community (Formosinho, 1989) and exercise their competence assuming themselves as learners.

Figures 8.8–8.12 show groups of children working with a father who brought in an atlas, with another one that brings a cultural artefact, a mother that brings masks made by her from printed images. The educational dynamism is made out of these plural contributions that children deeply appreciate.

– This is a world atlas. It has many countries. Omo River goes through Ethiopia which is a country in the African continent. [*A father's sharing*]
– Look, I know that image! Those are Omo River's children.
– Omo River's children paint themselves to distinguish themselves from one another. [*A mother's sharing*]
– They don't use clothes like we do. They live close to the river and eat fish. They also paint themselves to talk to each other. [*A brother's sharing*]
– That's because they are friends.

*

– They use less clothes. [. . .] They paint their body because they don't have clothes as we do. Painting is also important to protect themselves from insects and not be bitten. [*A mother's sharing*]
– We made masks looking like the ones from the children of Omo River. [*A daughter's sharing*]

*

FIGURE 8.8 Family participation

FIGURE 8.9 Sharing knowledge and participating

The children of Omo River that live in Ethiopia

Africa is beautiful and is even more beautiful
with the amazing makeup of Omo River's children.
Men and women use their body as a space of artistic
and cultural expression, in many cases working as a
communication code between them.
People of this region not only create their own fashion,
their paintings serve many purposes.
The paintings may also serve practical purposes
such as natural insect repellent when mixing
specific elements of nature, like ash and cow's urine.

FIGURE 8.10 A mother's contribution to children's research

– Men and women use their body as a space for artistic expression. In many cases it works as a vocabulary between them. Paintings have also a useful utility when mixed with cow's urine becoming a powerful natural repellent. [*Research and drawing of a mother*]

FIGURE 8.11 A child's representation

– I drew children of Ethiopia. I didn't research on the internet but I already discovered that they paint themselves to talk to each other. Rita told me so. I draw their painted faces and some of them have the same colour because they are friends and talk to each other. We should put my drawing in my learning portfolio. [*The voice of a child that not only did the drawing but expresses the desire to see it in the learning portfolio.*]

*

– We brought this wooden statue from a friend who bought it during a trip to Africa. It looks like a child of Omo River but from another tribe. Body and face are also painted. [*A father's sharing*]

Routines are part of this pedagogic culture. Throughout the day children go through a succession of rhythms. Different rhythms that allow them the constitution of different types of groups, a diversity of learning experiences, a wealth of communicative situations in search for action and meaning. Again meeting in council time,

FIGURE 8.12 A painted wooden statue

children and their teacher go through a reflexive process supported by pedagogic documentation that has been thoroughly edited by Andreia allowing children to engage in conversations about experiences, processes, discoveries, achievements.

Processes and achievements are considered creating a reflection that sets the pathway to new negotiated experiential action. Negotiated and shared decisions come up to redefine and make new compromises creating further group and individual planning. We are immersed in *solidary planning* where the teacher suspends her power of creating the educational planning and allows space for children's and parents' contributions making the preparation of learning situations an occasion of empowerment:

> We want to know what paints children of Omo River use to paint their face and body.

Edited pedagogic documentation becomes a means to facilitate authentic solidary planning as the starting point of solidary action. As Iram Blatchford says, *sustained shared thinking* is powerful for learning but our research (Oliveira-Formosinho, 1998; Azevedo, 2009; Araújo, 2011) allows us to think that the power lies in the relation of shared thinking and shared doing. Reflexive processes referred to experiential learning situations that followed this joint planning are pregnant with possibilities for meaningful learning. Sustained joint thinking connected with sustained joint action has a high power for meaningful learning that can easily be remembered by children and allows meta-cognition.

In a new cycle of documented activities, the cooperation with a father is of most relevance in response to the group's shared decisions and joint planning: *to know what paints children of Omo River use to paint their face and body.*

Through father–teacher conversations the cooperation is agreed, compromises are assumed and a joint planning of the learning situation is reached (see Figure 8.13). The father gathers the natural materials to produce paints and the teacher organises the educational environment to respond to the agreed planning as well as to any educational requirements of the national curricular guidelines and development of Pedagogy-in-Participation intentionality axes.

- Children of Ethiopia use stones, river mud, fruits, leaves and flowers to paint themselves.
- They are very beautiful and magic. They make such nice colours.
- It takes a lot of strength to be able to break the clay and put into little grains. Molly's father has a lot of strength.
- The raspberry is very sweet and very red. The colour gets very nice.
- The blueberry and blackberry are very little and dark. I collect them in the hills just like the children of Omo River. They are sweet and smell good. But these are sour.

FIGURE 8.13 A father–teacher collaboration

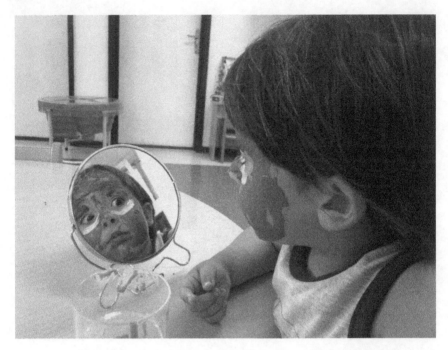

FIGURE 8.14 Bringing nature and imagination together

- I like to paint myself as do the children of Omo River. These paints are perfumed and smell good. Ours (acrylic and gouache paints) smell bad.
- They also use cow's pee to keep away insects. We use Fenistil.

Enthusiastically involved in the discovery of the transformation of materials to create natural paints, children are motivated to use the natural paints and to transform themselves and become other selves (see Figure 8.14). They are given the opportunity to seize the intercultural reality and open themselves to other possible worlds. They bring nature and imagination together.

- (Putting clay on her face) Look, I'm looking like Mary (of African heritage).
- My friends won't know that is me, I want to leave it this way.
- It looks so beautiful.
- I look so cute, I look like a boy of Omo River.
- His mask looks so beautiful.
- I look very nice. I look like a giraffe and then like a girl from Omo River.
- I really like to paint myself. I'd like to do it every day.
- Sandra has three dots on her forehead like I do.

The project work is coming to an end. It is time to understand what we have learnt. It is time to see if we have answered the research questions. This will be done through a triangulation of evaluative methods and actors' voices. First, we listen to the group of children explaining their learning in travelling along the project work journey.

Children start identifying the emergence of the experiential learning journey:

- Ana brought pictures of children from Omo River.
- We liked the pictures very much. Children were different. They have straw on their heads, fruits and flowers.
- We wanted to know why they painted themselves and where they lived.

Continue ascertaining the sources of information and the information collected:

- They live very, very far away. We did research on maps. Their country is called Ethiopia and Africa. Our mothers and fathers researched on the internet and came to the classroom.
- They actually paint themselves to talk to each other and because they are friends.
- They don't use paints like the ones we do. Molly's father came to the classroom to show what they discovered: they use fruits, leaves, river mud, stones to make the paints.

And finally, children explain the learning and meaning they co-constructed:

– It takes time to make the paints. We need to have many leaves.
– They don't use almost any clothes. They use necklaces, paint themselves in many ways: big and small dots, stripes, with many or few colours.
– They don't use elastic hair ties like we do. They do hair braids and adorn them with fruits, sticks and straw. I like it, they are very beautiful.
– The children of Omo River look like me. They have my colour and a little bit like Lucas's colour.
– We are white and Omo River's children are browner, a little more like black.

Then, it is time for Andreia to exercise her civic duty to the group and to be accountable in the light of the curricular guidelines of her country. Andreia shows that children developed experiential learning in the key learning areas of Pedagogy-in-Participation (compatible with the national curricular guidelines for preschool education):

• *Identities* – developed the notion of personal identity and relational identity.
• *Relationships* – developed awareness of learning processes in company with peers and adults.
• *Languages* – *Oral language* (they read images and made narratives about events related to the same images; they communicated their ideas to peers and adults); *Artistic language* (they enjoyed the aesthetic of images and paintings); *Scientific language* (they researched different sources of information; reflected upon experiences they lived and used these reflections to understand the world around them; they raised questions and created hypothesis); *Mathematical language* (they created symbols; coordinated elements with coherence in specific spaces).
• *Meanings* – they created meaning making from these experiences and the world. They related knowledge constructed in previous experiences to the present reality.

Now we want to listen to the individual voice of a child; we are going to listen to Tiago's voice.[3] He is given time to present his individual explanation on the development of the project work. He sits with Andreia and together they revisit the pedagogic documentation on the project work *Why do Omo River's children paint themselves?*
He remembers:

I remember the project work about Omo River's children. I remember that Ana's mother brought some pictures of children from Omo River. I remember we researched on where they lived. We saw on the map it was in Ethiopia. It is very far away from our school. Then, we went on researching

on why they painted themselves. We found out that they painted themselves
to keep away the bugs; to belong to the same family; to talk to each other
and to look cute. I remember they would go to collect things from nature:
flowers, straw, leaves. I drew a child from Omo River. Then, Molly's father
came to help us make paints with stones, clay, avocado, blackberries,
raspberries, leaves. After that, we painted our own face. I remember that the
painting on my face looked like dragons, close to the eye and the hair. We
were together in a small group and we had a mirror and we were looking at
each other. I learned that children from Omo River paint themselves and are
different from us. They paint their body and their face and we use a lot of
clothes. Of course, in Ethiopia it is very hot, that's why they don't use many
clothes. What I enjoyed the most was to paint myself because we looked
cute. I would like to be a child from Omo River because I would like to paint
myself every day. I would like to know more about why we don't put things
from nature on our head like they do. I think we could be the way they are.
I would like that!

This may be redundant . . . We all know Tiago is learning but Andreia wants to
collect evidence that allows her to present arguments about his learning journey.
She needs to do this for herself as a responsible professional but she wants to do
this as well because she feels it is her civic duty to be accountable for each child's
individual learning journey.

Andreia's repertoire of practices around pedagogic documentation encompasses
portfolios of activities and projects as well as children's individual portfolios that
narrate children's learning journeys. She includes in these learning journeys a
selection of sequences of documentation – fusing images, the child's voice and the
teacher's written narrative (see Figure 8.15).

Tiago represents his understanding about Omo River's children through a
dialogue with an image he wants to represent.

> He selects the image and selects the same colours present in the image as
> well as colours of his own choice. He is completely focused for a long time
> in the development of his task, absorbed by the production of pictorial details.
> He doesn't pay attention to the lively environment around him and pursues
> calmly and actively the creation of his painting.

Finally, he describes the result of his action: *I did a man from Ethiopia. He painted
his face to go to Carnival and dance. He put dry leaves on his face to look beautiful.*

Andreia analyses and interprets Tiago's experience with *The Child Tracking
Observation Schedule* (Pascal and Bertram, 1997) following the norms for the use of
this instrument for pedagogic observation:

* *Zone of initiative*: Level 4 (Tiago has total freedom of choice).
* *Group situation*: Moment of small group work.

FIGURE 8.15 Peer review and evaluation

- *Child's involvement*: Maintained intense activity (during the observation period Tiago shows clear signals of involvement in his task: precision, energy, motivation, creativity, persistence and satisfaction).
- *Interaction*: TC – A (balanced interaction between Tiago (the Target Child, TC) and the adult, A).
- *Learning experiences* (OCEPE – the Portuguese Preschool Guidelines):

  - *Personal and social development*: Tiago selects materials and decides what to do with them; develops awareness of himself as being competent and creative; shares with his peers his achievements.
  - *Expression and communication*: Tiago organises pictorial details in a space (mathematics development); represents his ideas through painting (creative/aesthetic development); communicates verbally his observations (language development).

The richness of a case study dense with information about learning and evaluation is tested through its openness to various forms of evaluation. Indeed, Tiago's learning journey in this case study is revealed by Andreia through various and interactive means: different pedagogic instruments for observation, narratives, artefacts, the pedagogical intentionality axes, the learning areas . . . However we want to follow another procedure: to look back to the case in the light of our own principles for evaluation (presented earlier in Chapter 7). We want to see their presence or absence in the case we have under study.

This procedure as well as seeing children's learning allows us to see teachers' teaching. In the present case study, it is very visible that Andreia actively involves children in teaching, learning and evaluation as indicated in Principle Eight (*be democratic and participatory and actively involve children*), and involves parents as indicated in Principle Ten (*seek participation of parents and of others involved in the primary care of the children*); that she *takes into account children's holistic learning* (as said in Principle Four); searching for *(inter) culturally relevant* knowledge (as said in Principle Seven); and she *provides highly useful and usable information for children and families, professionals and schools, teacher educators and policy makers* (as said in Principle Eleven).

Pedagogic documentation as a source for assessment and evaluation gives us a strong sense of authenticity; a wealth of information; evidence to show the learning and argument in favour of children's competence to learn and to learn how to learn; a contextual, dialogic, integrated and holistic solidary assessment and evaluation of learning and of progress in learning, and an antidote to maintain resilience against the pressure to use other types of assessment and evaluation, instruments which are abstract and decontextualised.

Notes

1. See Chapters 2 and 6 of this book.
2. The other author, Júlia Formosinho, decided to do a praxeological study around this project work and invited Joana de Sousa to join both at the level of praxis development

and its study. This is an ethically important clarification because it means that the first author has a particular interest in the case because she is one of the creators of Pedagogy-in-Participation, the approach that informs praxis in this case.

3. In Chapter 6 we started following his presentation of the educational environment of Andreia's classroom and its learning culture and he was very enthusiastic about the idea of his colleague Ana to share the Omo River's children paintings.

References

Araújo, S.B. (2011) *Pedagogia em creche: Da avaliação da qualidade à transformação praxiológica*. Tese de Doutoramento em Estudos da Criança – Especialização em Metodologia e Supervisão da Educação de Infância. Braga: Universidade do Minho.

Azevedo, A. (2009) *Revelando a aprendizagem das crianças: a documentação pedagógica*. Tese de Mestrado em Educação de Infância. Braga: Instituto de Estudos da Criança, Universidade do Minho.

Bennet, J. (2014) Special Issue: Disadvantage and Social Justice. *European Early Childhood Education Research Journal* 22, 3.

Bradbury, A. (2013) *Understanding early years inequality: policy, assessment and young children's identities*. London: Routledge.

Carr, M. (2001) *Assessment in early childhood settings: learning stories*. London: Paul Chapman Publishing.

Dubiel, J. (2014) *Effective assessment in early years foundation stage*. London: Sage Publications.

Formosinho, J. (1989) De serviço de estado a comunidade educativa: uma nova concepção para a escola portuguesa. *Revista Portuguesa de Educação (Universidade do Minho, Braga)* 2, 1: 53–86.

Formosinho, J. and Figueiredo, I. (2014) Promoting equity in an early years context: the role of participatory educational teams. *European Early Childhood Education Research Journal* 22, 3: 397–411.

Formosinho, J. and Oliveira-Formosinho, J. (2008) *Pedagogy-in-Participation: Childhood Association's approach*. Research Report, Aga Khan Foundation, Lisbon.

Formosinho, J. and Oliveira-Formosinho, J. (2012) Towards a social science of the social: the contribution of praxeological research. *European Early Childhood Education Research Journal* 20, 4: 591–606.

Freire, P. (1970) *Pedagogy of the oppressed*. New York: Continuum.

Malaguzzi, L. (1998) History, ideas, and basic philosophy: an interview with Lella Gandini. In C. Edwards, L. Gandini and G. Forman (eds), *The hundred languages of children: the Reggio Emilia approach – Advanced Reflection*, pp. 49–97. Greenwich, CT: Ablex.

Oliveira-Formosinho, J. (1998) *O desenvolvimento profissional das educadoras de infância: Um estudo de caso*. Dissertação de Doutoramento em Estudos da Criança. Braga: Universidade do Minho.

Oliveira-Formosinho, J. (2007) Pedagogia(s) da infância: Reconstruindo uma praxis de participação. In J. Oliveira-Formosinho, T. Kishimoto and M. Pinazza (eds), *Pedagogia(s) da Infância: Dialogando com o passado construindo o futuro*, pp. 13–36. São Paulo: Artmed.

Oliveira-Formosinho, J. and Formosinho, J. (eds) (2001) *Associação Criança: Um contexto de formação em contexto*. Braga: Livraria Minho.

Oliveira-Formosinho, J. and Formosinho, J. (2012) Special issue. Praxeological research in early childhood: a contribution to a social science of the social. *European Early Childhood Education Research Journal* 20, 4.

Pascal, C. and Bertram, T. (1997) *Effective early learning: case studies in improvement*. London: Sage Publications.

Pascal, C. and Bertram, T. (2012) Praxis, ethics and power: developing praxeology as a participatory paradigm for early childhood research. *European Early Childhood Education Research Journal* 20, 4: 477–492.

Rinaldi, C. (2012) *Diálogos com Reggio Emilia: escutar, investigar e aprender.* São Paulo: Paz e Terra.

Wenger, E. (1998) *Communities of practice: learning, meaning and identity.* Cambridge: Cambridge University Press.

9

CASE STUDY 2

Pedagogical attunement: documenting toddlers' learning

Júlia Formosinho, Sara Barros Araújo and Hélia Costa

Pedagogical and cultural contextualisation

This case study was carried out in Crèche and Preschool Albano Coelho Lima, an institution from the private sector located in the North West of Portugal, in Pevidém, in the municipality of Guimarães (Figure 9.1).

Pevidém is a town in the centre of one of the major industrial spots of the country, with a predominance of the textile industry. Nowadays, this region is particularly affected by the economic crises that Portugal has been facing in recent years that led to the closure of many factories and a contingent rise in the unemployment rates and degradation of socio-economic conditions of several families.

Crèche and Preschool Albano Coelho Lima is an institution that from the early 1990s onwards enrolled with Childhood Association and Institute of Child Studies (University of Minho) in a continuous process of staff development. All six teachers completed a Diploma Course in Early Childhood Education and enrolled in Master degree courses. The pedagogic director is highly supportive of the teachers' learning journeys. One of the consequences of this motivation to learn, highly centred in early childhood pedagogic approaches, was the decision to contextualise Pedagogy-in-Participation (presented in Chapter 2 of this book) in all the classrooms of the centre.

This case study was carried out in the realm of Pedagogy-in-Participation, the pedagogical perspective of Childhood Association. This perspective considers that childhood pedagogy is organised around knowledge constructed in situated action, articulated with theory and with beliefs and values, in an interactive triangulation. Childhood pedagogy tries to answer to different levels of complexity, directly or indirectly implicated in educational action, through this interactive process of dialogue and confrontation among theory, practices and beliefs. So, childhood

FIGURE 9.1 Preschool, Pevidém, Portugal

pedagogy has a profoundly holistic and integrated nature, centred in a praxis of participation (Oliveira-Formosinho, 2007).

In Pedagogy-in-Participation, experiential learning is transversal (Formosinho and Oliveira-Formosinho, 2008). Pedagogy-in-Participation proposes the creation of experiential situations for the development of identities and relationships (relational identities), belonging and participation (participatory belongings), languages and communication (communicative experiential learning), narratives and meaning (the creation of meaning through narratives for daily learning). Pedagogy-in-Participation organises the educational environment in order to create opportunities that are rich in experiential possibilities for manipulation, exploration, representation, communication and creation of meaning. In this perspective, pedagogical spaces are plural, which means that children shouldn't be confined to a single monolithic, didactic space, but need to have access to plural spaces, such as spaces in nature, in the community, in the centre, as well as connection between centre and home contexts.

Pedagogical materials need to be responsive to all kinds of difference: age, gender, social class, race and ethnic background, religion, temperament and personality. So, books, toys, music, games and songs need to be carefully chosen in order to be responsive to all these differences (Oliveira-Formosinho and Araújo, 2011).

The crossed understanding of psychological, pedagogical and neuroscience studies clearly asserts the need of an early education for diversity starting from birth.

One central reason for this is that social processes of creation of all kinds of bias are established early in children's lives, around age three (Oliveira-Formosinho and Araújo, 2011). In a review of the literature concerning the knowledge base on respect for diversity, MacNaughton (2006) points out that there is evidence that children between 9 and 14 months can distinguish racial cues in adult faces. The author stresses that there is relative certainty that children are racially aware by three years of age, that their own race influences their racial understanding and the racial markers they use to identify racial differences and that children from a tender age can display positive and negative attitudes towards racial diversity. Indeed, Aboud (1988) suggests that from three years old onwards children are capable of developing negative attitudes and prejudices concerning racial differences. In the review undertaken by MacNaughton (2006), the author also states that children's gender awareness and identity are established by three years old. By three or four years of age, children not only know their gender, but they are also aware of the play preferences, behaviours and expectations that adults favour for this gender. Thus, it is reasonable to assume that conceptions and attitudes towards diversity are built from birth and that the ecological systems in which the child lives have a very important influence on the formation of those conceptions and attitudes, including early childhood education and care contexts.

This case study was conducted in one classroom, that of one of the authors of the study, Hélia, and her children.

The methodological nature of this case study is praxeological (Formosinho and Oliveira-Formosinho, 2012; Pascal and Bertram, 2012) meaning that it is a vivid thinking (logos) about the evolving nature of praxis densely documented in order to create novel ways of conducting holistic evaluation. Dense documentation of change processes in action allow not only the understanding of transformation but also the creation of knowledge about transformation in view of pedagogic assessment.

The key criteria for a praxeological study are that of allowing the entrance in a vivid transformational situation densely studied through documentation, so allowing the entrance in research, involving the central actors, so allowing the entrance in participation, uncovering simultaneously the phenomenology of the lived experience, the study processes and the participation of the people involved and by that means creating praxeological knowledge (Oliveira-Formosinho and Formosinho, 2012).

Music baskets: documenting attunement and learning

The activity room where this pedagogical situation took place was attended by two-year-old children. The pedagogical situation that we intend to present and analyse starts from a visible interest of children for musical instruments. After several experiments with musical instruments, the group of children likes to explore them, manipulate them, produce sounds. Children show satisfaction and self-confidence during these experiments. In order to value this interest, the early childhood teacher suggests an activity: a music basket. Six toddlers were involved in this proposal, five boys and one girl. The activity was developed around several musical instruments: rain sticks, tambourine, wooden guiro, bamboo xylophone, metal xylophone, African drum, castanets, maracas, pan flute, wooden whistles, harmonica, rattles.

Besides the visible interest of children in musical instruments, the early childhood teacher took into consideration other criteria for choosing these specific instruments namely the multisensory appeal and the cultural diversity that they represent. Besides this, the professional had in mind Pedagogy-in-Participation's pedagogical axes in order to guarantee nurturing, integrated and meaningful opportunities for learning, development and well-being. Hélia's intentionality was also expressed in other pedagogical decisions:

- Organisation of space: the early childhood teacher carefully made an option for a pedagogical space that was safe, comfortable, guaranteeing opportunities for large movements, full of natural light.
- Organisation of the group: a small group of children, which facilitates exchanges, social play, communication.

This creates, before action, conditions and opportunities for each child and the group to experiment, communicate, represent and give meaning to her/his experience. These pedagogical options were guided by Pedagogy-in-Participation pedagogical axes. Indeed, the early childhood teacher departs from an explicit pedagogy that allows intentionality in what concerns several pedagogical dimensions, including evaluation.

This pedagogical organisation of the situation creates a climate of expectation and motivation, intensely shown by children, as Hélia's written notes show:

> Pedro[1] says to another child: 'João, silence! Hélia is going to bring the baskets. She is! She is . . .' João replies: 'The baskets! Eiiii' (claps hands and shouts) 'Hélia! Come!' Ricardo says: 'The baskets! Cool! Hélia, quickly!'

The group welcomes the music baskets, looking, touching, grasping, reaching. . . Children express, from the beginning, intense signs of well-being and involvement. The created pedagogical situation provokes intense aesthetic feelings – it is dynamic, beautiful, colorful, engaging.

The pedagogical properties of materials (see Figures 9.2 and 9.3) created a deep initial engagement with/in the situation. Indeed, there is an indisputable pedagogicity in the materiality of space, said Paulo Freire regarding his visit to schools in São Paulo, Brazil's municipal schooling system, as São Paulo State Secretary of Education. He wrote:

> I drew attention to this fact . . . How is it possible to ask of the children the minimum of respect for their material surroundings when the authorities

FIGURE 9.2 Music baskets

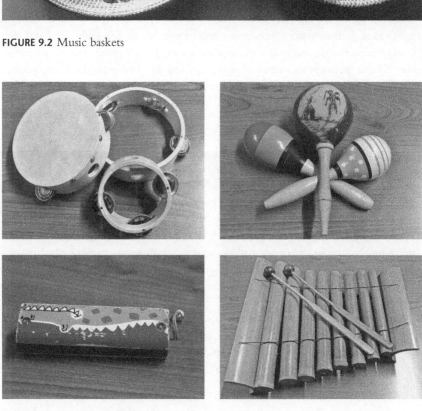

FIGURE 9.3 Musical instruments

FIGURE 9.4 Children's experiential reactions

demonstrated such absolute neglect of and indifference to the public institutions under their care? It's really unbelievable that we are unable to include all these elements in our 'rhetoric' about education. Why does such 'rhetoric' not include hygiene, cleanliness, beauty? Why does it neglect the indisputable pedagogical value of the 'materiality' of the school environment?

(Freire, 1998, p. 48)

Hélia created a climate of enthusiasm and then sat back and observed children's different experiential reactions: observation of the musical instruments, touching, grabbing and starting to experiment (see Figure 9.4). The power of the pedagogical objects is so dense that the children react instantaneously. They are drawn to the objects. She pulls back her body to create space for them. She remains attentive to them – they know that she is there but she is not interfering. She's attached but not imposing. She believes in children's exploratory powers.

Children share the motivation but show different interests and exploration styles (see Figure 9.5). Hélia knows when to pass to another phase – an instrumental phase of exploration of different properties of each music instrument: their sounds, textures, colors, their placement in space . . .

This is a long process that challenges the teachers' professional understanding of allowing children's rhythms while actively waiting. The 'kairos' of each child is respected. The teacher follows. The learner 'speaks' with intelligent senses, the teacher listens (see Figure 9.6). Attunement is created and it will allow attached

FIGURE 9.5 Exploring different properties of musical instruments

FIGURE 9.6 Teachers' professional understanding of actively waiting

documentation of learning-teaching processes that it is the basis for pedagogic evaluation.

Let's us take a closer look to Hélia's edited documentation that unravels the learning situation (see Figure 9.7).

> João puts the harmonica in his mouth, it produces no sound. Takes the harmonica from his mouth and observes it attentively . . .
>
> He goes near the teacher and says: 'Hélia, does not! Play!'
>
> He puts the harmonica in the teacher's mouth. The teacher blows the harmonica and produces sound. João again puts the harmonica in his mouth. The teacher observes and says: 'João, you have to blow!' And gently blows into his face. João closes his eyes, blows, but doesn't produce any sound.
>
> The teacher persists: 'Blow! Tightly!' and blows vigorously into his face. Finally, João is able to blow in the right way and to produce sound. When he is able to do it, he opens his eyes. Looks at the teacher who puts her thumbs up to celebrate his success. It is not easy for João to find the necessary energy to play the harmonica. The teacher accompanies his movements with little puffs of air into his face and, slowly, João catches his breath. João produces different tones. João is playing the harmonica.

FIGURE 9.7 João and the harmonica sequence

Departing from a descriptive stance, Hélia proceeds to an interpretative practice, using a rigorous set of pedagogical observation instruments that allows the analysis of the child's experience at the level of well-being and involvement (Laevers et al., 2005), as well as learning experiences with the pedagogical axes of Pedagogy-in-Participation.

Observation of well-being: João showed very intense signs of well-being. It was possible to observe clear signs of comfort, satisfaction, relaxation, vitality, openness and self-confidence. João was tuned in with himself.

Observation of involvement: João showed very intense signs of involvement, visible in his concentration, energy, persistence, precision, in his facial expression and verbal commentaries. João's involvement was more than an initial reaction; he reacted to new challenges as they emerged throughout the action.

Observation of learning experiences:

1. *Axis of identities and relationships:* João expressed initiative, made choices and organised his actions in order to solve problems and fulfil intentions that he defined for himself; João interacted with the teacher, learned to respect times for intervention and for listening, enjoyed discoveries and sensations provoked by the exploration of objects.
2. *Axis of languages and meanings:* João described his observations and explorations through verbal language, used gestures and facial expressions to communicate his interests (emergence of oral language); developed the capacity to observe and analyse objects, and related action upon materials with the production of effects (emergence of scientific language); João learned about physical and sound characteristics of music instruments (emergence of music language).

We could only have had the privilege of seeing this situation because of many interrelated facts. Firstly, because of a very special selfhood, that of Hélia's professional identity in action. By this we mean her sense and sensibility, empathy, respect that helps her to create a very deep attunement with the group and each child. A long journey together allows her to create and live joint experiential situations with children and, through them, create intersubjectivity (Trevarthen, 2011, 2012) with each child. Coming to know what they see, what they feel, what they think, what they expect and tuning her answers to their motivations, desires and expectations. In this trusting relationship, João comes to Hélia to ask for help. He trusts that she will be responsive. She shows how to do. He tries again. No success. But they persevere. Hélia's inventiveness creates new answers adapted to children's modes of learning. She started with a visual and verbal answer and then gives a tactile answer. She knows that from very early on children establish themselves (or not) as successful learners and she creates the answer that helps them to succeed.

Assessment and evaluation practice: principles into practice

In this pedagogical situation, we chose three principles intrinsic to assessment and evaluation practice that allow us to analyse the way principles and practices work together in a coherent synergy, creating opportunities for well-being, involvement and learning.

Firstly, it is clear in this situation that 'assessment and evaluation should be referred to contexts, processes and outcomes within daily life learning' (Principle 6). Assessment is centred on a specific situation, without neglecting previous experience and background. It does not constitute an artificial or application-oriented procedure. It is centred on authentic daily life. The intentionality before, in and on action considers several pedagogical dimensions of context, such as the organisation of space, materials and group. Assessment is also centred on core processes, children's well-being and involvement, that the early childhood teacher used in order to document, interpret and construct meaning on children's experiences, on the educational environment and on her own practices. Finally, there's a focus on outcomes. Hélia used Pedagogy-in-Participation's pedagogical axes to interpret and create meaning around children's learning. As stated in Chapter 7, this constitutes an important basis for the enhancement of learning, in a civic spirit of accountability.

Secondly, this pedagogical situation allows us to reflect on the way assessment and evaluation can 'support individual learning journeys' (Principle 7). The fact that Hélia documented the pedagogical situation presented in this chapter allows us to observe, through a vivid narrative, the process experienced by João and Hélia in order for João to learn how to play the harmonica. We think that, in this particular situation, João is fully acknowledged as a competent learner. In fact, and taking closely this principle (see Chapter 7), João was aware of his interest in the learning situation; decided to join in a very motivated way, created a purpose (he wanted to learn to play the harmonica); used his skills to participate in cooperation (approached Hélia, trusting that she could help him to learn); persisted in the learning situation (experimented again and again, always attentive to Hélia's suggestions and support); identified and overcame difficulties; accepted the difficulties without feelings of debilitation, celebrated his achievement with Hélia.

Finally, the case study recognises the need for 'assessment and evaluation to be (inter) culturally relevant' (Principle 9). Pedagogical documentation clearly reveals the respect for children's plural identities: their idiosyncratic modes to approach the world, explore, communicate and create meaning. Mediation that tunes with those idiosyncratic modes is paramount. In fact, the way Hélia used tactile sensations in order for João to learn how to play the harmonica is the vivid expression of the respect for plural learning journeys.

Documentation allows us access to other processes that are central for intercultural pedagogy, namely the adult's role in introducing the child to cultural instruments, where similarities and differences coexist.

Some final reflections

This case study allows for some reflections on the centrality of documentation for pedagogical assessment. Indeed, pedagogical documentation allows us to describe and interpret, through text and image, experiences of children and adults around observation, play, experimentation and mediation. Pedagogical documentation reveals the learning-in-process of children, turning also visible the teacher's intentional action. So, this is an interwoven process of multiple encounters that turns visible, irreducible rights: the right to learn for both children and adults. In this particular case, we are addressing the right of João, and all children, to have their interests and motivations answered to and sustained by an attentive, intentional and stimulating adult; we are also referring to the right of Hélia, and all professionals, to be supported in learning journeys that will certainly influence children's learning journeys.

Ultimately, we are also talking about the opportunity that this documented learning situation created for all of us to learn and be inspired by these fascinating joint journeys.

Notes

1. The names of children in this case study were changed in order to protect their privacy.

References

Aboud, F. (1988) *Children and prejudice*. Oxford: Basil Blackwell.

Formosinho, J. and Oliveira-Formosinho, J. (2008) *Pedagogy-in-Participation: Childhood Association's approach*. Research Report. Lisbon: Aga Khan Foundation.

Formosinho, J. and Oliveira-Formosinho, J. (2012) Towards a social science of the social: the contribution of praxeological research. *European Early Childhood Education Research Journal* 20, 4: 591–606.

Freire, P. (1998) *Pedagogy of freedom: ethics, democracy, and civic courage*. Maryland: Rowman & Littlefield Publisher, Inc.

Laevers, F., Daems, M., Debruyckere, G., Declercq, B., Moons, J., Silkens, K., Snoeck, G. and Van Kessel, M. (2005). *SiCs [ZiCo] – Well-being and involvement in care: a process-oriented self-evaluation instrument for care settings – Manual*. Brussels/Leuven: Kind & Gezin and Research Centre for Experiential Education, University of Leuven.

MacNaughton, G. (2006) *Respect for diversity: an international perspective*. The Hague: Bernard Van Leer Foundation.

Oliveira-Formosinho, J. (2007) Pedagogia(s) da infância: Reconstruindo uma praxis de participação. In J. Oliveira-Formosinho, T.M. Kishimoto and M.A. Pinazza (eds), *Pedagogias(s) da Infância: Dialogando com o passado, construindo o futuro*, pp. 13–36. Porto Alegre: Artmed Editora.

Oliveira-Formosinho, J. and Araújo, S.B. (2011) Early education for diversity: starting from birth. *European Early Childhood Education Research Journal* 19, 2: 221–233.

Oliveira-Formosinho, J. and Formosinho, J. (2012) Praxeological research in early childhood: a contribution to a social science of the social. *European Early Childhood Education Research Journal* 20, 4: 471–476.

Pascal, C. and Bertram, T. (2012) Praxis, ethics and power: developing praxeology as a participatory paradigm for early childhood research. *European Early Childhood Education Research Journal* 20, 4: 477–492.

Trevarthen, C. (2011) What young children give to their learning, making education work to sustain a community and its culture. *European Early Childhood Education Research Journal* 19, 2: 173–193.

Trevarthen, C. (2012) Finding a place with meaning in a busy human world: how does the story begin, and who helps? *European Early Childhood Education Research Journal* 20, 3: 303–312.

10

CASE STUDY 3

A case study on quality evaluation: a comparison between a traditional and a participatory pedagogic environment

Inês Machado and Júlia Formosinho

The context of this study is a Master's thesis in Early Childhood Education called *Quality evaluation in crèche: a case study on children's well-being* and presented in the University of Minho, Institute of Education, Braga, Portugal.[1]

The objectives defined by Machado (2014) for the study were:

- to construct knowledge about Pedagogy-in-Participation in the classroom;
- to understand the importance that assessment and evaluation of the educational environment has for the future assessment and evaluation of children's learning;
- to contextualise the use of the theory of children's well-being in crèche and its research methodology (Laevers, 2005; Laevers et al., 2005);
- to check and compare the levels of well-being that children experience in contexts with different kind of pedagogical proposals;
- to find out what is the context and the pedagogical proposal that registers higher levels of well-being and understand why;
- to understand the benefits of evaluating the quality of children's learning that can bring improvement to the quality of contexts and to the educators' practices in crèche.

The starting questions that guided the research were: What are the levels of well-being of children who experience a context where Pedagogy-in-Participation is practised? What are the levels of well-being of children who experience a context where a transmissive pedagogy is practised?

From the total material of this thesis the present case study will focus on three aspects:

i)   the necessity of praxeological studies that take into account the specificity of pedagogies used in classrooms as a central variable to understand differences in the children's learning;
ii) the necessity of assessment and evaluation of children's learning be preceded by assessment and evaluation of the educational environment;
iii) the necessity of the pedagogy (with children and with adults) to be monitored by research.

Among the paths Pedagogy-in-Participation has roamed in research sits praxeological research (Formosinho and Oliveira-Formosinho, 2012) as a form of action research's re-visitation responding to the challenges presented by researchers (Reason and Bradbury, 2001; Noffke and Somekh, 2010). The vital importance of action research for educational innovation has been recognised (Máximo-Esteves, 2008) and the need for reconstructed rigour in the research of such innovation processes and its reporting has also been highlighted. Praxeological research presents itself as a possibility of developing rigour in research processes of transformation of action and its dissemination without losing its character of action (Formosinho and Oliveira-Formosinho, 2012; Pascal and Bertram, 2012). Recently the European Early Childhood Education Research Journal published a special issue about this theme (Oliveira-Formosinho and Formosinho, 2012a) that demonstrates the huge potential that praxeological research has for understanding the reality of educational transformation and for the correlative construction of knowledge.

In this special issue, as well as a rich theorisation (Formosinho and Oliveira-Formosinho, 2012; Pascal and Bertram, 2012), case studies are presented that show the utility of researching educational intervention at different levels: children's well-being in crèche (Pinazza, 2012), the circularity of professionals' learning and children's learning (Araújo, 2011), the assertiveness of an organisation and its team of professionals supported by the University of São Paulo working on quality development in care services for children in crèche (Kishimoto, 2012).

Praxeological research defines itself as a way of searching for a 'social science of the social', for an 'educational science of the educational' (Formosinho and Oliveira-Formosinho, 2012, p. 591) that allows us to monitor the processes of transformation and through dense, organised, analysed documentation of the action sustain the construction of knowledge. This may be the answer to the necessity of pedagogy (with children and with adults) to be monitored by research. Praxeological research is a means to monitor transformation but also to compare results of transformational processes. The present study is located in praxeological research.

One of the absences that research in the context of early childhood education presents is that of not taking into account one central variable: the specific pedagogic approaches that are practised in the classroom, in order to understand children's thinking and learning and professional activity of educators. There are very few studies that examine children's perspectives about educators' roles and analyse the nature of the pedagogy that children are experiencing (Oliveira-Formosinho and Lino, 2008) or children's perspectives about educational interaction styles and the contrast of this with the educators' perspectives in the context of differentiated pedagogic environments (Oliveira-Formosinho and Araújo, 2004).

In the research developed in the context of this study, the impact that two different pedagogies had on children's well-being were observed and evaluated (Machado, 2014). One of the pedagogies practised was Pedagogy-in-Participation[2] (Oliveira-Formosinho and Formosinho, 2012b) and the other was a pedagogy with a transmissive tendency. Both reflect a choice from the educators.

Classroom A contextualises the Childhood Association pedagogic approach – Pedagogy-in-Participation. This pedagogy belongs to the family of participatory pedagogies and its theoretical framework is common both for pre-school (3- to 6-year old children) and crèche (0- to 3-year old children). The educational objectives and the images of children have a common theoretic foundation for the education of 0- to 6-years old children, with a democratic and participatory *ethos* (Oliveira-Formosinho, 2014).

Within this perspective early childhood education centres and their educational teams have a role of *conscientisation* (Freire, 1970). Through analysis, dialogue and transformation, they can make a journey of growth in the respect for children and adults, in the acknowledgment of differences (whether they are ethnic, linguistic, cultural, race, gender, social condition or personality), in the inclusion of differences (integrating the difference and fighting against discrimination and inequalities) and encouraging democratic principles and values in the experience of everyday life (Formosinho and Machado, 2007). These democratic processes aim to cultivate an image of the human person with rights and duties that develops from a child that experiences rights and duties. Indeed this educational perspective 'advocates the participatory agency and competence of all children, without reservations created by any idiosyncratic condition' (Araújo and Costa, 2010, p. 8). Adults who work with children are also considered people with participatory rights.

Pedagogy-in-Participation considers that pedagogy can only make the integration of all diversities when it looks and listens to the child, documents his/her action and uses that documentation in order to develop praxis.[3] It has been demonstrated that this is an achievable project if we reconstruct pedagogic thinking in action through situated context based staff development (Oliveira-Formosinho, 1998; Oliveira-Formosinho and Kishimoto, 2002).[4]

Pedagogy-in-Participation developed its own conceptualisation of the educational environment, its pedagogic dimensions and their interfaces:

> to develop Pedagogy-in-Participation as a responsive listening process it is necessary to think of several dimensions of pedagogy – the pedagogical spaces, materials and times; the organisation of groups; the quality of relationships and interactions; the observation, planning and evaluation of learning; the

activities and projects that bring to life co-construction of learning; the pedagogical documentation that creates memory, learning and meta-learning and allows pedagogic evaluation; the involvement of parents, families, communities.

(Oliveira-Formosinho and Formosinho, 2012b, pp. 24–25)

Children's learning is contextual and part of the context is created by the quality of the educational environment. Thus it constitutes an ethical challenge to evaluate the educational environment before evaluating children's learning. This is an ethical requisite expressed in the Third Principle for Assessment and Evaluation in Early Childhood Education, one of the twelve principles that are put forward in Chapter 7 of this book.

The pedagogy used in classroom B is oriented by a transmissive perspective, which will be briefly presented.

The transmissive pedagogy holds up a *ready-to-wear, one size curriculum* sustained in traditional school thinking that has as fundamental organisational assumption the centralisation: 'The conception of curriculum rests with the central services and schools and teachers just execute it' (Formosinho, 2007, p. 19).

This curriculum advocates that pre-organised knowledge through pre-organised materials should be taught to all uniformly without taking into account differentiated learners' identities and learning rhythms. The uniform curriculum leads to a uniform pedagogy. This pedagogy does not consider the effective differences that exist among different children and different educators (Formosinho, 2007).

Oliveira-Formosinho (2007) shows us through a comparative frame that this transmissive pedagogy focuses on acquisition of pre-academic skills, on acceleration of learning and on a deficits compensation model. Teachers prescribe objectives and tasks, give information through structured materials, shape behaviours and assess only results. It is expected from the children that they will correct their mistakes (after feedback) and make changes in behaviour through the teacher's instruction. The learners have a respondent function. Through a passive inculcated attitude, the child receives information, memorises and performs. This is the beginning of the inculcation of cultural and civic passivity through pedagogic passivity (Formosinho, 1987).

The images of child, education and teacher that come from transmissive pedagogy reflect an orientation 'more for obedience than for freedom, for submission than for participation' (Formosinho and Machado, 2007, p. 314).

We will now present the data collected and its interpretation in order to be able to answer if different pedagogic approaches have differentiated impact on children's well-being.

The context that uses Pedagogy-in-Participation is composed of one educator, one auxiliary and eight children, of which six were observed. The context that uses a transmissive pedagogy is composed of one educator, one auxiliary and ten children, of which six were observed.

The observations of children were made with the consent in writing of their parents. The anonymity of the children, teachers and the institution was assured. The criteria for the ethics of research comes from the EECERA Ethical Code for Early Childhood Researchers (2014) available on the EECERA website and were very useful for the design of this study.

Within the objectives defined for this study, the research paradigm that supported the methodology of this research was qualitative (Lessard-Hébert et al., 2012; Lincoln and Guba, 1985) and the method was a case study with an observational nature.

Documents available in the institution were collected to help its general characterisation but the pedagogic instruments of observation and the field notes were the main instruments used to collect the data.

Observation was the central technique of the study: besides the naturalistic observation that gave rise to field notes, semi-structured observation was used, guided by pedagogic instruments of observation. Two semi-structured formats of observation were used: the HighScope Program Quality Assessment (HighScope Educational Research Foundation 2000), an observational instrument that provides information on the quality of the educational environment, and an instrument for observation and assessment of child's well-being (Laevers et al., 2005) that provides information about levels of children's well-being. Photographic documentation was a very rich complement to the observation.

Descriptive statistics were used in order to process the data collected. This provided for the creation of graphics that helped a deeper understanding of the two educational contexts.

The triangulation of data was obtained by different techniques – the field notes, the observational data and the photographic documentation.

To study the classroom environment it was decided to focus on some specific dimensions of the environment that are very important for little children. Besides observing the spatial organisation of classrooms through their respective plans and observing the educational routine, the PQA – Program Quality Assessment (HighScope Educational Research Foundation, 2000) was used. This is an observation format for quality assessment developed for assessing the educational environment, helping the training of educational teams and so ensuring the quality of educational centres that provide care and education in crèche. This instrument allows educators, supervisors, directors, researchers, trainees and other professionals to monitor the quality of educational environments. It also allows them to plan daily activities and to effectively communicate with children's families.

In the educational context, there were attributed levels for each indicator in the categories *physical environment* and *plans and routines* which resulted in an average mean for organisation of the pedagogic space, of pedagogic materials and of pedagogic time in both contexts. The findings are as follows.

In classroom A, which practises Pedagogy-in-Participation, the average notation found in relation to the organisation of space and materials was 4.25 and regarding the daily routine (educational time) was 4.78, revealing very high quality of educational services that are being provided to children in regard to the educational environment.

In classroom B, which sits in the transmissive educational tradition, the average notation found in relation to the organisation of space and materials was 2.38 and regarding the educational time was 2.0 revealing a low quality of educational services that are being provided to children through this central dimension of the educational environment.

In the analysed categories, the educational context that practises Pedagogy-in-Participation presented a significantly higher quality than the educational context which practises a transmissive pedagogy.

These data make us think of a relationship between the pedagogy used (and the access it gives to staff development) and quality of educational environment in regard to the quality of pedagogic space, materials and time.

Considering children's well-being, the semi-structured observation format used was the pedagogical instrument of observation of child's well-being (Laevers et al., 2005), developed by Ferré Laevers' team in the University of Leuven, in Belgium. The use of this pedagogic instrument in different contexts offers the possibility of data comparison under diverse perspectives and offers the assessment and evaluation of quality of the classrooms. Well-being is an excellent measurement for quality.

This instrument has six indicators for well-being: enjoyment; relaxing and inner peace; vitality; openness; self-confidence and being in touch with oneself.

In this study, this pedagogic observation instrument allowed us to observe, analyse, evaluate and compare the well-being levels of children in the two different pedagogic contexts that opted for different approaches to teaching and learning and to daily practices.

In classroom A, which practices Pedagogy-in-Participation, the use of the pedagogic instrument for observation revealed that well-being levels of the six children observed are very high (Figure 10.1).

In classroom B, which practises a transmissive pedagogy, the use of the *pedagogic instrument for observation* of child's well-being revealed that the well-being levels of the six children observed are low (Figure 10.2).

Given the levels of well-being found in both observed educational contexts we can draw the following conclusions.

Regarding the total of well-being levels observed, in the context that uses a transmissive pedagogy, the notations revealed an average of 2.22 and in the context that uses Pedagogy-in-Participation the notations revealed an average of 4.61. The average notations observed in the Pedagogy-in-Participation context are therefore much higher than the average notation found in the transmissive context.

Average notations found in transmissive context are lower than the 3.63 suggested by Laevers (2011) as the midpoint of the child's well-being in a study which incorporated 12,000 episodes of observation.

In the Pedagogy-in-Participation context the notations observed revealed themselves much above the threshold point defined by Laevers (2011).

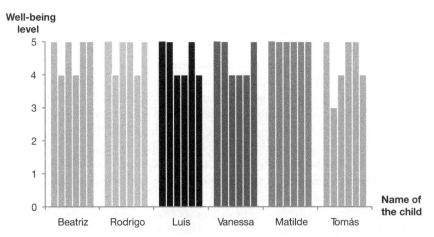

FIGURE 10.1 Well-being levels observed in each child integrated in the context that practises Pedagogy-in-Participation

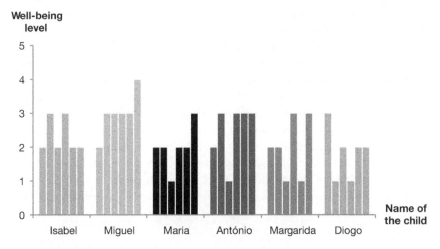

FIGURE 10.2 Well-being levels observed in each child integrated in the context that practises a transmissive pedagogy

Data interpretation

High levels of well-being of children were recorded by those who experienced a participatory pedagogy, as opposed to children who experienced a transmissive pedagogy. The data collected seems to show us that a child's well-being may vary depending on the specific pedagogy that is practised in the context where the child is integrated (evaluated through the PQA).

We consider it important to reflect on the reasons why a child has a lower well-being in the educational environment where a transmissive pedagogy is practised and higher well-being in a participatory educational environment. Laevers (2011) considers that children's well-being is one of the ways of measuring whether children's experiences are creating meaning for them and if the learning environment is responding to the needs and interests of each child.

Studies in the aegis of Pedagogy-in-Participation clearly show that pedagogic dimensions of the educational environment such as space, time, materials, inter-actions, planning, documentation and evaluation have an interactive impact on children's learning (Oliveira-Formosinho, 1998; Azevedo, 2009; Araújo, 2011). The data from this study confirm the previous data. Each context observed (class-room A and classroom B) have different impacts on children's well-being; each context observed (classroom A and classroom B) shows differences in the quality of the educational environment.

Using Júlia Formosinho's concept we can say that well-being is a 'state and not a trait' meaning that it is highly dependent on the nurture of the educational context and not just on children's nature. This represents a challenge to professionals and to their teacher educator as well as to research. More research is needed that compares children's feelings, cognitions and actions in differentiated educational environments and on contexts that differ on the specific pedagogic approach to life and learning in the classroom.

A review of research conducted by Araújo (2011) shows that this variable (the specificity of the pedagogy in the classroom) is highly likely to have a great impact on children's well-being and yet has been neglected in research studies.

The Childhood Association educational interventions through context based staff development (Oliveira-Formosinho, 1998; Oliveira-Formosinho and Formosinho, 2001) have been focused on the central idea that the provision of quality that serves children and families needs to create a dynamic praxis open to transformation that needs pedagogic mediation through situated staff development and the monitoring of change through praxeological research.

The lived educational experience of children in crèche is dependent on daily life professional praxis.

Conclusions

Participatory pedagogies put, at the centre of their work, respect for the child, from birth (Oliveira-Formosinho and Araújo, 2011) and requires the promotion of the child's well-being.

The data collected in both contexts of this research are very different and reveal the impact that the practice of different kinds of pedagogies has on children's well-being development, encouraging us to think that well-being is a contextual variable, influenced by general quality and by the specific pedagogy practised.

According to Laevers (2011, p. 2) 'high levels of well-being lead to high levels of child development', so it is very important that practitioners are aware of the need to provide each child with an educational environment quality where the child can grow and learn with well-being.

Among the principles presented in Chapter 7 of this book, the second principle for assessment and evaluation in early childhood education says that 'assessment and evaluation should be contextualised and situated, that is, should be ecological', and the third principle says that 'as learning is contextual there is an ethical stand on the part of the professionals to conduct a reflexive analysis about the context of learning'. So before assessing and evaluating children's learning, professionals should evaluate the quality of the learning contexts, of the educational environments and of the educational opportunities provided for all children and for each individual child. It is known that self-evaluation is a central contribution to educational quality.

This principle affirms that rigorous practical knowledge is indispensable to carry out the monitoring of the educational environment, of the opportunities that are being created (or not) and of the children's learning.

Here arises the problem of teachers' training: what is the access that training provides to professionals about the thinking and practising of participatory pedagogies? What is the access it gives them about developing ways of monitoring and assessing learning contexts? What is the role of first degrees and further training in this domain? What kind of training can be more effective?

In order to respond to the challenge of a participatory early childhood pedagogy we have to respond to the challenge of an adult pedagogy with a participatory nature (Oliveira-Formosinho, 1998). Research has to sustain both of these processes and provide information about transformational practices.

Notes

1. This research was presented by Inês Machado who is a context based teacher educator working for Aga Khan Foundation and was supervised by Júlia Formosinho.
2. For more information please see Chapter 2 of this book.
3. For more detailed information about pedagogical documentation on Pedagogy-in-Participation please see Chapters 2 and 6 of this book.
4. For more information please see Chapter 6 of this book.

References

Araújo, S.B. (2011) *Pedagogia em creche: Da avaliação da qualidade à transformação praxiológica.* Tese de Doutoramento em Estudos da Criança – Especialização em Metodologia e Supervisão da Educação de Infância. Braga: Universidade do Minho.

Araújo, S.B. and Costa, H. (2010) Pedagogia-em-Participação em creche: Concretizando o respeito pela competência da criança. *Cadernos de Educação de Infância -Revista da Associação de Profissionais de Educação de Infância* 91: 8–10.

Azevedo, A. (2009) *Revelando as aprendizagens das crianças: A documentação pedagógica.* Tese de Mestrado em Educação de Infância. Braga: Universidade do Minho.

European Early Childhood Education Research Association (2014) *Ethical Code for Early Childhood Researchers.* Available at: www.eecera.org/documents/pdf/organisation/EECERA-Ethical-code.pdf (accessed 5 March 2015).

Formosinho, J. (1987) Educating for passivity – a study of Portuguese education, 1926–68. PhD dissertation. London: University of London, Institute of Education.

Formosinho, J. (2007) *O currículo uniforme pronto-a-vestir de tamanho único.* Mangualde: Edições Pedago.

Formosinho, J. and Machado, J. (2007) Anónimo do século XX: A construção da pedagogia burocrática. In J. Oliveira-Formosinho, T.M. Kishimoto and M.A. Pinazza (eds), *Pedagogia(s) da Infância: Dialogando com o Passado, construindo o futuro,* pp. 292–328. Porto Alegre: Artmed.

Formosinho, J. and Oliveira-Formosinho, J. (2012) Towards a social science of the social: the contribution of praxeological research. *European Early Childhood Education Research Journal* 20, 4: 591–606.

Freire, P. (1970) *Pedagogia do oprimido.* São Paulo: Paz e Terra.

HighScope Educational Research Foundation (2000) *HighScope Program Quality Assessment: Infant/Toddler Version.* Ypsilanti, MI: HighScope Educational Research Foundation.

Kishimoto, T. (2012) The integration of care and education: a case study concerning the problem of noise. *European Early Childhood Education Research Journal* 20, 4: 493–503.

Laevers, F. (2005) Experiential education: making care and education more effective through well-being and involvement. In F. Laevers and L. Heylen (eds), *Involvement of Children and Teacher Style, Insights from an International Study on Experiential Education,* Studia Paedagogica 35, pp. 13–24. Leuven: University Press.

Laevers, F. (2011) Experiential education: making care and education more effective through well-being and involvement. In R.E. Tremblay, M. Boivin, R. DeV. Peters, R. G. Barr, *Encyclopedia on Early Childhood Development,* pp. 1–5. Montreal, Quebec: Centre of Excellence for Early Childhood Development. Available at: www.child-encyclopedia. com/documents/LaeversANGxp1.pdf (accessed 5 March 2015).

Laevers, F., Daems, M. Debruyckere, G., Declercq, B., Moons, J., Silkens, K., Snoeck, G. and Van Kessel, M. (2005) *SICs [ZICo] Well-Being and Involvement in Care. A process-oriented self-evaluation instrument for care settings [Manual].* Brussels/Leuven: Research Centre for Experiential Education, Leuven University.

Lessard-Hébert, M., Goyette, G. and Boutin, G. (2012) *Investigação Qualitativa: Fundamentos e Práticas.* Coleção Epistemologia e Sociedade. Lisboa: Instituto Piaget.

Lincoln, Y.S. and Guba, E.G. (1985) *Naturalistic Inquiry.* Beverly Hills, CA: Sage Publications.

Machado, I. (2014) *Avaliação da qualidade em creche: um estudo de caso sobre o bem-estar das crianças.* Tese de Mestrado em Educação de Infância. Braga: Instituto de Educação da Universidade do Minho, Portugal.

Máximo-Esteves, L. (2008) *Visão panorâmica da investigação-acção.* Colecção Infância no. 13. Porto: Porto Editora.

Noffke, S. and Somekh, B. (eds) (2010) *The Sage Handbook of Educational Action Research.* London: Sage Publications Ltd.

Oliveira-Formosinho, J. (1998) *O desenvolvimento profissional das educadoras de infância: Um estudo de caso.* Tese de Doutoramento em Estudos da Criança. Braga: Universidade do Minho, Braga, Portugal.

Oliveira-Formosinho, J. (2007) Pedagogia(s) da Infância: Reconstruindo uma praxis de participação. In J. Oliveira-Formosinho, T. Kishimoto and M. Pinazza (eds), *Pedagogia(s) da Infância: Dialogando com o passado, construindo o futuro,* pp. 13–36. Porto Alegre: Artmed.

Oliveira-Formosinho, J. (2014) A avaliação holística: A proposta da Pedagogia-em-Participação. *Revista Interacções* 10, 32: 27–39.

Oliveira-Formosinho, J. and Araújo, S.B. (2004) Children's perspectives about pedagogical interactions. *European Early Childhood Education Research Journal* 12, 1: 103–114.

Oliveira-Formosinho, J. and Araújo, S.B. (2011) Early education for diversity: starting from birth. *European Early Childhood Education Research Journal* 19, 2: 223–235.

Oliveira-Formosinho, J. and Formosinho, J. (2001) *Associação Criança: Um contexto de formação em contexto*. Braga: Livraria Minho.

Oliveira-Formosinho, J. and Formosinho, J. (2012a) Special Issue. Praxeological research in early childhood: a contribution to a social science of the social. *European Early Childhood Education Research Journal* 20, 4.

Oliveira-Formosinho, J. and Formosinho, J. (2012b) *Pedagogy-in-Participation: Childhood Association Educational Perspective*. Porto: Porto Editora.

Oliveira-Formosinho, J. and Kishimoto, T. (eds) (2002) *Formação em contexto: Uma estratégia de integração*. São Paulo: Editora Thompson Learning.

Oliveira-Formosinho, J. and Lino, D. (2008) Os papéis das educadoras: As perspetivas das crianças. *Educ. foco*, Juiz de Fora 13, 2: 9–29.

Pascal, C. and Bertram, T. (2012) Praxis, ethics and power: developing praxeology as a participatory paradigm for early childhood research. *European Early Childhood Education Research Journal* 20, 4: 477–492.

Pinazza, M.A. (2012) The right of young children to well-being: a case study of a crèche in Portugal. *European Early Childhood Education Research Journal* 20, 4: 577–590.

Reason, P. and Bradbury, H. (2001) *Handbook of Action Research: Participative Inquiry & Practice*. London: Sage Publications Ltd.

11

CASE STUDY 4

How to bring children's voices
into assessment reports: working
with teachers in two São Paulo
public preschools

Maria Malta Campos and
Cristina Aparecida Colasanto

This case study is based on data from an action research developed at two public preschools in the city of São Paulo, Brazil, in the years 2011/2012.[1] This chapter describes how the focus of the research had to be changed, evolving from a more ambitious initial question based on how children participate in their own assessment to more simple ones, as the reality of the two schools became more concrete. Some of these later questions were about how to change teachers' practices at the classroom level, in order to make it possible for children to be heard and how to make their voices visible in the assessment reports. In this process, successive layers of these routine practices, and of what they meant for teachers, had to be explored and transformed.

The action research followed a methodology based on the work of Thiollent (2004). It was a pedagogic intervention conducted by the researcher, with the voluntary participation of two groups of educators (teachers and the pedagogic advisors) from both preschools. The two groups introduced changes in their practices, documented them and developed a collective process of reflection with the researcher. They took part in all decisions, helped with the data collection and discussed the results together along the process.

São Paulo educational and social contexts

In order to understand this particular portrait of practice, it is necessary to deal with two different aspects of this reality: firstly, the urban scenario of one of the third world's biggest metropolises; secondly, the state of art of the ideas and arguments that are part of the present debate about assessment in early childhood education in the country.

São Paulo is the capital of the state of São Paulo and has a population of 11 million people; the metropolitan area has a population of 19 million. It is the richest municipality in the country, but it also reproduces in its area the extreme social inequalities of Brazil. The two preschools where the research was conducted are located in a district where the percentage of households with a monthly per capita income higher than five minimum salaries is 1.5 per cent and where half of the households have a per capita monthly income of less than one minimum salary (approximately 280 US $) (Ação Educativa, 2013, p. 33).

The teachers of the municipal preschools (for four- and five-year-old children) have the same status and work regime of the fundamental (primary) schools' teachers and they can either work at preschools or at the first grades of fundamental schools. Since 2006, according to a federal law, six-year-old children were transferred from preschools to the first grade of the fundamental schools. The number of children per adult in the São Paulo preschools is very large: up to 35 children per teacher. The majority of teachers work four hours a day, so if a child stays all day, he or she will have two or three different teachers every day; children who stay six hours at the preschools have their own teacher for four hours and at the other two hours are cared for by different adults.

As a background to this particular municipal system, it is important to describe some of the ideas about assessment in early childhood education that prevail in the country today. In the last ten or fifteen years, a new, seductive pedagogic discourse has emerged from academic and specialised professionals, under the influence of the Italian experiences with early childhood education at Reggio Emilia and other northern communes in that country. At the same time, the sociology of childhood literature was translated by Brazilian publishers and adopted at the universities' education departments. These influences reinforced a belief that most decisions about curriculum and assessment methodologies have to be left to each school team and to teachers at the classroom level.

The *National Curriculum Guidelines for Early Childhood Education*[2] (Brazil Ministry of Education, 2010) defines the general guidelines for assessment of children at crèches and preschools: assessment results cannot lead to grade repetition; they should be based on observation of children at daily activities; information can be registered in a variety of forms; assessment results must be communicated to families. Curriculum and assessment may have changed in the official documents and orientations, but have not changed that much in the real practices at schools since most teachers get their degrees at private low quality higher education institutions, where they learn very little about how to work with small children at crèches and preschools. Most schools and teachers continue to reproduce old traditional practices in their daily work with small children (Campos et al., 2006, 2011).

At the São Paulo municipal network, new work schedules were offered to teachers in order to include planning and meeting time in their work journeys and salaries. The action research described in the next section benefited from this planning time, allowing groups of teachers and the pedagogic advisors[3] to work with the researcher, discussing their assessment practices and the changes introduced in them during the period of the intervention at each school.

Promoting changes in documentation and assessment practices

At first, the main interest that guided the research project was to investigate the participation of children in their own assessment. The author worked as a pedagogic advisor at a municipal preschool and wanted to develop her doctoral research at other preschools. With the help from a municipal pedagogic supervisor, two preschools were selected in the regional area number 10; they were known as good schools that promoted the participation of children in their pedagogical practices.

After the first contacts with the two teams, a group of teachers at each school decided to take part in the intervention. They were two very distinct groups: at school 1, they worked in the midday period, caring for children from the morning period for the first two hours and for children from the afternoon period for the last two hours. They followed a special programme designed to foster literacy, with telling stories time and a selection of books for children to take home and have their parents reading to them. At school 2, they worked with classrooms in the morning or afternoon period, using the other period for planning time.

Both schools were known in the area for their 'children's assemblies', where representatives chosen in each classroom discussed and decided many issues. So, one of the first observed events at each school was an assembly. At school 1, children discussed what they liked to do in the playground and which new equipment they wished the school could provide for it. At school 2, they discussed the programme chosen for the 'children's week'[4] in the school. Parts of the dialogues observed in each school are reproduced below. The moderators at both schools were the pedagogic advisors (PA).

Assembly, school 1

> *PA*:   What did you have to ask your schoolmates about?
> Many children speaking together: About the park.
> *Carlos*:   What we like at the park.
> Many children mention toys and places in the park: swings, slides, the sand pit.
> (. . .)
> *PA*:   How do you play in the swings?
> *Mirian*: We can't, the swing is broken.
> (Follows a discussion about how it got broken; the children describe how they play at swings and slides and why some of them fall on the ground)
> *PA*:   How do you feel when you play at the park?

Mirian: I stay at the slide and my friends play around, but a boy keeps running trying to catch us.

Janaina: He is the monster.

PA: I can see that the park is great not only because of the toys that are there but also because playmates are important.

Mirian: That's because they make our play even better!

Janaina: They invent new plays! (. . .) Monster's kind of play! You have to run and ask him if he wants to be the monster, then he gets you, takes you to prison and you have to run to escape.

PA: So boys and girls can play together?

Mirian: Just one boy, who is the monster, the others are the monster assistants.

(Colasanto, 2014, pp. 96–97)

Assembly, school 2

PA: What would you like to have in the children's week? (. . .)

João: I asked my father to give me a cell phone.

(Many children speak at the same time)

PA: We have to plan together what we will do at the children's week and you have the responsibility to tell our decisions to your schoolmates. It's better not to speak all at the same time.

Lucas: This weekend I went to a barbecue at my aunt's home . . .

PA: It is fine to tell about what happened in the weekend, but now we have to discuss the children's week.

Many children mention different things: a pool full of small plastic balls; a slide; a special equipment to jump on and another to make wall escalations; soap bubbles; tattoos; paintings . . .

Carlos: A different slide.

Sara: One that goes to the sky.

(The PA makes no comments about that)

PA: And what to eat?

Many children: hotdogs, chocolate sweets, hamburgers, sodas, cakes, apples, lollipops . . .

PA: I have taken notes about what you asked for and we are going to see what we can buy, but if something turns out to be impossible, we will tell you.

(Colasanto, 2014, p. 109)

The researcher analysis about these two assemblies pointed out how in school 1, the moderator was attentive to what the children were telling her and could make questions that motivated the children to further explore their memories about the kinds of play activities they enjoyed most at the park. The provision of new equipment does not seem to have the same importance for children as the peer interactions. The second example revealed many shortcomings: at first, the proposed questions seemed more limited than what the children themselves wanted to talk about; in the following dialogues, matters appear to be very consumer oriented. The only exceptions – a different slide, one that goes to the sky – get lost between other suggestions.

The researcher expectations about the pedagogical practices adopted at these schools were at first very positive. But, after the first contacts, she had to change her focus: instead of looking at children's participation at their own assessment, she acknowledged that it was necessary to investigate how teachers registered the children's participation in the daily activities at the classroom. She started to discuss with the two groups of teachers the kinds of assessment reports that were used in each school.

In school 1, the teachers that worked in the midday period adopted a questionnaire provided by the literacy programme. It was composed of a few simple questions such as 'Does the child retell the story?' which could be answered by 'yes' and 'no' alternatives. At school 2, teachers had to prepare individual descriptive reports for each child; but when the researcher examined these reports, she could see that what was actually described was the pedagogical planning for the group of children and not the individual child's participation in the activities. Both kinds of assessment reports had spaces for parents to add personal comments.

In the beginning of the intervention, the researcher promoted study moments with both groups, when they read some papers about conceptions of childhood and assessment in early childhood education.[5] When the teachers were asked about how they registered children's voices and initiatives in the classroom, they said how difficult this task seemed to them.

The researcher then observed and videotaped some of the situations teachers experienced with children and these images and dialogues were discussed with each group. She could see that it was difficult to register the children's voices and participation because of different reasons: the classroom organisation did not foster children's initiatives and individual choices in the daily routines; teachers did not observe and register individual children's behaviour and voices during daily activities; teachers did not know how to motivate children to talk about their play and learning experiences.

After the first discussions, each group tried to find solutions for their practical difficulties: at school 1, teachers organised themselves in a better way during the story telling time and when children chose books to take home, in order to make observations and take notes on the children's participation at these activities; at school 2, classrooms were already organised in different 'small corners' and children could choose where to play, but teachers did not know how to deal with the high number of children in order to observe and interact with small groups or one individual child and register children's participation. They also developed different thematic projects, but failed to register children's reactions and contributions to these projects along the way. The researcher made suggestions for them to try out in order to overcome these difficulties and the school team decided to engage other teachers to stay in their classroom, allowing them more time to observe and interact with individual children. At this point, small changes started to be observed in each school.

School 1. Children selecting books to take home

(Two teachers stay near the bookcase and groups of five children take turns to go there and choose books)

Teacher M:　　Carlos, you got the book *Who is afraid of wolves?* Why did you choose this book?

Carlos:　　Because I like wolves.

Teacher A, looking at her notes:

　　Look, he is reading all the collection. Carlos, you already took *Who is afraid of ghosts*, *Who is afraid of monsters* and now *Who is afraid of wolves*.

Carlos:　　Who is reading them are myself, my mother and my father.

(Colasanto, 2014, p. 104)

School 2. Story telling moment

(Teacher with all the children together at the classroom)

Teacher J:　　Today I brought two stories to tell you about. This book title is *Lucia, I'm going in a moment*. (Showing some pages from the book) Who can read this kind of writing?

Children:　　Rogério! (It is a book written in Braille)

Teacher J:　　Look, the two books are the same, but this one is written in Braille. Mariana is going to help Rogério read the book. (Teacher helps Rogério put his hands on the book pages)

(Colasanto, 2014, p. 113)

In these two examples, it is possible to identify some small but important changes: at school 1, teachers made questions and used their notes to interact with the child at the moment of his choices; the researcher had suggested that instead of asking a child 'Do you like the book?' (a question that leads to a pattern of yes or no answers), teachers could ask 'Why did you choose this book?'; at school 2, teacher J explained her choice to children, showing them how to respect and help a schoolmate with a visual impairment. The researcher evaluation of this moment points out that it is not possible to foster children's participation if one does not include all children in the activities.

But even if teachers started to create the necessary conditions for a more active participation of children in the daily activities, with more adult/child interactions, the researcher observed that they did not bring those changes into their written reports.

A researcher observation about this phase

> When watching the videos, we could observe children's interactions, their questionings, the teacher's interventions; but we could not find these experiences in the written registers, either on a piece of paper or on a notebook, and on the children's assessment reports.
>
> (Colasanto, 2014, p. 80)

Different strategies were planned with the two groups of teachers to help them make notes and organise their registers. Some of these strategies had to do with the written reports' logical structure. Most teachers did not have access to a good basic education and needed help to improve their writing abilities. The researcher's Master's degree was obtained within a Linguistic programme, where she learned to apply a special methodology to analyse the text organisation of written assessment reports (Colasanto, 2007). This methodology helped her in the process of improving the teacher's written registers logical structure, using 'premises, arguments, counter arguments and solutions'.[6]

School 1. Examples of teacher registers

> *Teacher J:* 'I've noticed that Julia does not like to retell stories, she seems very shy, keeps her head and eyes low and does not answer me. I ask: Julia, what book did you take home? I show her the images, but she maintains the same attitude. But I observe that at table she talks to her classmates about different subjects . . .'
>
> *Teacher O:* 'Renato pays attention when his friends are telling the stories that they took home. He knows how to retell the stories he takes home. Once he took home the book *Marcelo, Marmelo, Martelo*[7] and he said: "Tell the part that milk was called cow's juice" . . .'
>
> (Colasanto, 2014, pp. 142–143)

School 2. Examples of teacher registers

> *Teacher F:* 'Jonathan showed progress when it comes to following rules and agreements, like for instance, he stays in the football team for which he was chosen, waits for his turn to be the goal keeper . . .'
>
> *Teacher J:* 'Ryan very much likes table games, like chess, puzzles (. . .) At the beginning of the year he started to learn about how to move the chess pieces, he invents ways to move the queen, he can seize the other player pieces. . .'
>
> (Colasanto, 2014, pp. 148 and 150)

In her analysis, the researcher shows how these registers were improved with the use of concrete examples about each child's learning experiences, providing evidence for teachers' appraisal in the assessment reports.

Additionally, the two groups of teachers decided to make interviews with individual children, to explore their opinions and register their own evaluation about their school experiences. After reading Oliveira-Formosinho and Azevedo's (2008) discussion on how important it is to encourage children to review their experiences and gain conscience about their own learning, each group planned their questions and how to organise children for the interviews.

School 1. Interview reports

Teacher E: 'Fabiana liked most the story "How to catch a star". Then I asked her: Which part of the story did you like most? She said: I liked most when the boy saw the star reflection on the water at the beach. (. . .) Francisco named the same story, but the part that he remembered was different: I liked most when the boy could catch the star and started to play with it'.

Teacher V: 'Felipe, what did you learn with the stories you took home? Felipe: I learned that when mother and father tell stories you have to keep quiet, otherwise they shout and stop telling the story. I learned that stories are more interesting than video games. I also learned that even when the book cover is boring, the story can be cool and it is fun to get another book.'

(Colasanto, 2014, pp. 162–163)

School 2. Interview reports; answers given by children to questions about the 'animals' project[8]

Gabriela: I learned that sloths sleep upside down and that the Guará wolf has long legs.[9]

Rodolfo: There are animals that are born from eggs: ducks, chickens, and alligators.

Willian: I learned that lions have bones; ants don't have bones; snake has bones; Guará wolf has bones and jaguar has bones.

Jean: Dinosaurs lay eggs; volcanoes have that chimney that gets fire and burns everything in its way. I learned that animals that are born from eggs don't suck from their mother's breasts and the ones that lay eggs are not mammals.

(Colasanto, 2014, p. 165)

Teachers were very pleased with their achievements. They planned how they could continue to use what they learned in their pedagogical practices. During the year, other teachers joined the action research group at each school, revealing their need to learn more about observation and assessment methodologies. These accomplishments were acknowledged at the end of the intervention, when teachers could assess what they learned in the process.

School 1

Teacher O: I very much liked the proposal of registering what the children say as a support for the assessment reports; I am going to take that with me from now on.

Teacher V: In the next year I am not going to use weekly registers; I am going to have an individual sheet for each child. I am looking for ways to organise myself . . .

(Colasanto, 2014, p. 171)

School 2

Teacher P: First, the child[10] assessed herself, told us about what he or she learned; a new thing was to register teachers' interventions.

Teacher J: We do things, (. . .) but we do not register them . . .

Teacher F: Our interventions, you told us that we do not value our work when we do not register our contribution to the children's progresses.

(Colasanto, 2014, p. 176)

Teachers also answered about what they learned from children, when they could hear and register their voices. The example given by teacher P from school 2 is very meaningful.

Teacher P: We always pay attention to the most talkative, the most active, the most aggressive. And there is the group of the ones who are not very salient, the quiet ones; when I called each one at a time, I was surprised with those that do not talk, those that like to make drawings, but do not comment on them. Children surprised me. One of them told me that he wanted to learn who took care of sick and abandoned animals. I stayed without words . . . sometimes we come with everything already prepared, but what do they want to learn?

(Colasanto, 2014, p. 178)

Another result of the improvements introduced in the assessment practices could be observed in the parents' reactions, expressed in their written comments at the end of their child assessment reports. When teachers gave concrete examples of their child's participation on the reports, they could recognise their own child's characteristics and not only the teachers' general information on the classroom activities as before. Some of their comments helped teachers to better assess each child's changes during the school year.

> Father A: I like the way activities are done, and to be able to participate in the readings, plays and drawings. This has a positive impact at home. Thank you!
>
> Mother B: Fabiana has developed a lot during this year. Her drawings gained new forms. She can talk about everything; she uses some words that get me admired. (. . .)
>
> Mother C: Jean is eating better now; before he did not eat vegetables, but because he serves himself at school, he learned to like it . . .
>
> (Colasanto, 2014, pp. 158–159)

Teachers acknowledged these changes: teacher V, from school 1, observed that 'the assessment got nearer the parents, they started to read the reports and to talk more with us'. The researcher could see that the improvements introduced in the language employed at the assessment reports made it easier for parents to understand the school pedagogical proposal (Colasanto, 2014, p.172).

In her thesis conclusions, Colasanto summarises the most important results of the whole process developed at both schools. She starts by recognising that at first it was necessary to change the focus of her research, from 'the children's participation in their assessment' to 'the previous conditions' that have to exist to enable this participation to occur.

> I proposed a formation process, starting with the analysis of practices, working with some of the video taped activities, pointing out the teachers' important role while interacting with children, as well as the children's participation, which had to be registered, in order not to be forgotten and in this way could help them in the assessment process.
>
> (Colasanto, 2014, pp. 182–183)

The research also shows that the democratic kind of practices already in place at both schools permitted the kinds of changes that were promoted during the action research. Before, children's participation practices happened at a few occasions during the school year; it was necessary to learn how to adopt them in the daily activities.

Colasanto also tells about other results obtained with the changes introduced in the assessment reports: they helped the pedagogic advisors to provide a more objective orientation to teachers and they helped teachers to change their planning to fit the children's needs and interests. She finishes her conclusions with comments on her own learning process:

> My involvement with the teachers and the schools contributed to my formation as a teacher and as a researcher . . . This experience made

my conviction that children must participate in their own assessment even stronger. . .

(Colasanto, 2014, pp. 188–189)

Challenges and possibilities

These two experiences show that, given certain conditions, it is possible to change teachers' assessment practices in a way that each child's participation is encouraged and registered at daily activities, as well as documented and recognised in the assessment reports. It is possible to conclude that a transformation process has started at both schools, motivated by the teachers' participation in the action research. It was not only their practice that was changed: their conceptions about children's potentials were transformed in the process.

We can recognise in the case studies many important assessment and documentation features that were analysed by Carla Rinaldi (2012). She argues that documentation is important when it is embedded in the learning processes; its value does not reside only as a memory of something that has already happened and can be revisited, however important this can be. When Colasanto started her research, she saw how far the assessment documentation prepared by teachers was from the children's daily experiences. Hearing others is not easy, it requires that we suspend our judgements and stay open to changes, according to Rinaldi; it is necessary to develop a 'hearing context', where we learn to hear and to make narratives (Rinaldi, 2012, p. 125). The development of this quality needs support, comprehension and time: 'time that children have but that adults do not have or do not want to have' (Rinaldi, 2012, p. 127). The process of change described in this case study took one year and it was only going through its first steps at both schools at its end. When this process is experienced within a group, adults and children become conscious of their experience, they can develop their own representations and narratives. The pedagogical documentation becomes a 'visible hearing'; this is essential to teachers' and children's metacognitive processes (Rinaldi, 2012, p. 130). It is possible to recognise some traces of these achievements in Colasanto's narratives. Other aspects of documentation and its role in children assessment, according to Rinaldi, also could be observed in the research data: in order to build an effective documentation, teachers must have good reading and writing abilities; documentation must be legible to others, like parents; teachers must cultivate their sensibility and their understanding in order to be able to be part of this 'hearing context' at schools (Rinaldi, 2012, pp. 134–138).

However, it is not possible to foresee how long these changes can last or lead to other kinds of positive changes in the pedagogical practices adopted at the two preschools. It is necessary to consider some of the characteristics of the São Paulo education municipal system that can explain, on the one hand, why this process of in-service formation was possible and, on the other, what kind of structural obstacles could hinder the adoption of similar experiences at other early childhood education centres in São Paulo.

Professionals can leave a specific school and go to work in another one if they wish, at periodical transference moments defined by the system; these transferences can cause instabilities at schools that can interfere with the pedagogical work and with the children's well-being. The principals' and the pedagogic advisor's leadership can play a role in this context, making some school teams enjoy more stability than others, as could be verified in the two schools where the reported intervention was made. But many decisions that can have important impacts at individual schools are taken at other instances of the Municipal Education Department power structure.

An important feature of public preschools in São Paulo is the teachers' right to a planning period of time at their work place. This was a required condition for the development of the action research at both schools. It is a basic condition for the 'in context' kind of teacher formation described by Oliveira-Formosinho and Formosinho (2002). This author proposes a contextualised methodology of in-service formation that integrates teachers' professional development with institutional development and innovation. This conception is based on Bronfenbrenner's ecological perspective on human development; Oliveira-Formosinho and Formosinho acknowledge the various spheres of reality that contextualise a teacher's professional formation (Oliveira-Formosinho and Formosinho, 2002, pp. 11–18). This means that teachers' professional development has to be supported by the organisational development. In the case of the two São Paulo preschools, this organisational development was made possible by the existence of a planning time, the presence of the pedagogic advisors, the support of the principals and the researcher's intervention.

However, these conditions are not present at all early childhood municipal centres: the not for profit subsidised crèches do not offer the same work conditions to their teachers and they represent the majority of all municipal centres. On the other hand, many public centres do not benefit from the teachers' planning time like the two preschools described in Colasanto's research: either they do not have the support of a positive pedagogic leadership, or they can suffer from a high staff turnover. In a huge school network such as this, it is not easy for the administration to monitor, support and guide all centres with a shared pedagogical conception.

To conclude, it is important to comment on something that determines a basic condition for this kind of educational experience: democracy. Dewey's concept of a democratic school was part of the theory basis for the Colasanto thesis. The recent history of the São Paulo education system includes the period when Paulo Freire[11] was the municipal secretary of education and another period when the municipality adopted participative methodologies at the city administration; the pedagogical and political experiences developed in these two former periods were still present in the educators' memories and in the practices adopted at both preschools, like children's assemblies. But democracy needs to be built at all levels and in everyday life. Democratic practices have to be nurtured and cared for; they can easily be lost.

204 Campos and Colasanto

Acknowledgements

The authors are grateful to Marina Célia Moraes Dias and Beatriz Oliveira Abuchaim for their remarks on the first drafts of this chapter.

Notes

1. This research was described and analysed in the Doctoral Thesis of Cristina Aparecida Colasanto, who is a pedagogic advisor at the São Paulo municipal educational system. Maria Malta Campos was her supervisor at the Graduate Programme on Education and Curriculum, at the Catholic University of São Paulo.
2. This document was prepared by the National Education Council and applies to all ECE centres in the country: public, private, and not for profit subsidised.
3. Pedagogic advisors are hired for each municipal school in São Paulo; at the 13 regional administrative offices, there is also a group of pedagogic supervisors, who have to visit and monitor all schools.
4. In Brazil, the October 'children's week' is a week of celebrations mainly promoted by the mass media and adopted at most school systems. Children receive gifts from their families and enjoy many kinds of celebrations. This week includes a 'teachers' day' when schools do not open.
5. They were texts from the following authors: Sarmento (2007); São Paulo, Municipal Department of Education (2007); Colasanto (2007); and Oliveira-Formosinho and Azevedo (2008).
6. Text planning and organisation based in Bronckart's 'argumentation sequence' (2003).
7. The title in Portuguese has three words with the same sound: *Marcelo*, a name, *Marmelo* (a fruit) and *Martelo* (hammer).
8. This project was developed after the children found a *paca* youngling (a wild herbivorous rodent) in the sand pit at the schoolyard.
9. The maned wolf – *Lobo Guará* – is found in Brazil's central and southeast regions.
10. Child is a feminine word in the Portuguese language (*a criança*).
11. Paulo Freire (1921–1997) was an important Brazilian educator and author; he was persecuted by the military regime and exiled; he returned to Brazil with the democratization process and became again an important actor in the Brazilian education scenario.

References

Ação Educativa (2013) *Educação e desigualdades na cidade de São Paulo*. São Paulo: Ação Educativa/Rede Nossa São Paulo.

Brazil. Ministry of Education (2010) *Diretrizes curriculares nacionais para a educação infantil*. Brasília: MEC.

Bronckart, J.-P. (2003) *Atividade de linguagem, textos e discursos: por um interacionismo sócio-discursivo*. São Paulo: Educ.

Campos, M.M., Fullgraf, J. and Wiggers, V. (2006) Brazilian early childhood education quality: some research results. *Cadernos de Pesquisa* 36, 127: 87–128.

Campos, M.M., Esposito, Y. Bhering, E., Gimenes, N. and Abuchaim, B. (2011) Quality of early childhood education: a study in six Brazilian state capitals. *Cadernos de Pesquisa* 41, 142: 20–54.

Colasanto, C.A. (2007) *A linguagem dos relatórios: uma proposta de avaliação para educação infantil*. Master's Dissertation, Catholic University of São Paulo.

Colasanto, C.A. (2014) *Avaliação na educação infantil: a participação da criança*. PhD thesis, Catholic University of São Paulo.

Oliveira-Formosinho, J. and Azevedo, A. (2008) A documentação da aprendizagem: a voz das crianças. In J. Oliveira-Formosinho (ed.), *A escola vista pelas crianças*, pp. 117–143. Porto: Porto Editora.

Oliveira-Formosinho, J. and Formosinho, J. (2002) A formação em contexto. A perspectiva da Associação Criança. In J. Oliveira-Formosinho and T.M. Kishimoto (eds), *Formação em contexto: uma estratégia de integração*, pp. 1–40. São Paulo: Pioneira/Thomson Learning.

Rinaldi, C. (2012) *Diálogos com Reggio Emilia: escutar, investigar e aprender*. São Paulo: Paz e Terra.

Sarmento, M.J. (2007) Visibilidade social e estudo da infância. In M.J. Sarmento and V.M.R. Vasconcellos (eds), *Infância (in)visível*, pp. 25–49. Araraquara, Brazil: Junqueira & Marin.

São Paulo. Municipal Department of Education (2007) *Orientações Curriculares: Expectativas de Aprendizagens e Orientações Didáticas Para Educação Infantil*. São Paulo: MDE.

Thiollent, M. (2004) *Metodologia da pesquisa-ação*. São Paulo: Cortez.

12

CASE STUDY 5

The Effective Early Learning (EEL) Programme: evaluation and assessment in a private daycare setting

Sue Ford and Christine Pascal

The case study examines the challenges and benefits of using a supported and participatory self-evaluation and improvement programme within a private daycare setting located in a large, metropolitan city in England. It demonstrates how the Effective Early Learning (EEL) Programme (Bertram and Pascal, 2006) was implemented as a quality improvement tool by practitioners as part of the city-wide early years quality improvement programme and the impact of this programme on the quality of children's experiences and outcomes. The case study also shows how the data from this setting-led, self-evaluation and improvement programme has been used to inform the city's wider strategic planning process for supporting quality improvement within its wider range of early years settings. It demonstrates that ethically robust, participatory, self-directed evaluation and improvement processes are capable of supporting significant shifts in the quality of practice offered in early childhood settings and have the capacity to evidence this across a large metropolitan authority in a way that informs strategic planning and development.

Context: pedagogical and cultural location of assessment and evaluation work

The case study is located in the south of a large local authority in the Midlands, England and is a well-established private daycare setting. The ward where the case study is located is supported by a further 9 private, voluntary and independent (PVI) nurseries, 1 children's centre nursery, 1 maintained nursery school and 24 childminders. The city has a diverse and growing population and includes some of the most deprived areas in the country. The estimated population growth in the case study ward from 2011–2013 is 0–10.5 per cent. Within the ward, and across the city, there is a longstanding history of partnership working to provide childcare and education for children from birth to school age in order to offer places for all eligible children. Providers in the PVI sector offer the majority of places for pre-school age children, with most of them receiving Early Education Entitlement funding from the local authority. The case study nursery receives funding for children aged 3–4 years; it has been registered since 1989.

The nursery is purpose built and set within the grounds of the owner's home. There is a safely enclosed garden for outdoor play and access to a further area where a mud kitchen/forest school can be found. Access to the premises is on a level at the front and there is a drive at the side for wheelchair users. The nursery is registered to care for 17 children on the Early Years Register. The setting is able to support children with special educational needs and is able to care for children who speak English as an additional language. The staff team consists of six practitioners, all qualified to level 3 or above. It is a well-established team and there have been few staff changes. It also accommodates students on placement from the local Further Education college. The nursery consistently strives to offer the best quality care for children and has participated in a number of quality assurance and quality im-provement programmes offered by the local authority.

Assessment and evaluation praxis: Description of assessment and evaluation programme of work and practice

Following the election of the Labour government in England in 1997 there were a number of changes at a national level within the early years and childcare sector, along with an increased level of funding which enabled local authorities to invest in an increased level of support for the early years and childcare sector. This brought with it a higher level of responsibility to ensure that 'affordable, accessible, quality childcare' was available for all children and families (National Childcare Strategy; DfEE, 1998) In response to this the local authority produced a city-wide quality assurance framework which was used to raise quality in early years settings across the city. The quality framework offered bronze, silver and gold awards for quality and, over time, was expanded into a country-wide quality framework used by five other counties/metropolitan boroughs. In 2002 the quality framework was accredited under the national 'Investors in Children' scheme, along with a number of other national and local quality assurance programmes, including the Effective Early Learning (EEL) Programme.

The quality assurance programme worked effectively in the city from 2000 to 2006 when it was decided to evaluate its effectiveness and to produce new documentation to reflect ongoing changes in policy and practice. From 2006 there was a period of analysis, evaluation and consultation resulting in the production of a single quality improvement tool which could be used in a variety of early years settings. This quality improvement tool was launched in 2009 at the same time as the government produced the Early Years Quality Improvement Support Programme (EYQISP) which added further capacity and impetus to this quality improvement work. Using EYQISP as a guideline the local authority designed a support programme for early years and childcare settings. This programme identified nine criteria which operated as a set of quality indicators and comprised:

- Welfare requirements
- Staffing and leadership
- Leadership and development requirements
- Outcomes for children
- Partnership with parents, carers and partner professionals
- SEN provision/inclusion
- Training and continuing professional development
- Transition
- Sustainability issues in business planning.

These criteria were used to assess all settings that received city funding and to identify the level of support needed (whether they were high, medium or low priority). The local authority team of development workers visited settings on a regular basis to discuss what level of support they required, recorded on the 'traffic light' basis – with 'red' settings needing the most support. The team of development workers, support workers and advisers met on a monthly basis to identify what support was needed and who/which team would be responsible. A variety of tools were available to assist settings which included the local authority quality improvement tool, a SEN/Inclusion framework and a healthy eating/physical development programme. These programmes fulfilled the needs of the majority of settings within the local authority, however a number of settings – those who were rated as 'green' and needing little support – were identified as needing or wanting an alternative, more self-directing route to raising quality. The local authority then decided that the most appropriate tool for these settings was the EEL programme, particularly as there was also the Baby Effective Early Learning (BEEL) Programme specifically designed for children from birth to three years, where often quality was more variable.

EEL is a programme of supported self-evaluation and improvement for all settings that provide early education and care. It has three key aims:

1. To offer a manageable strategy to evaluate and improve the quality of early learning and development and the effectiveness of outcomes for young children in a wide range of settings.
2. To achieve this through a collaborative, systematic and rigorous process of self-evaluation, which is supported and validated externally.
3. To generate evidence which feeds directly into quality and inspection processes.

EEL begins with an intensive training programme, followed by an extended process of setting-led, but well supported, self-evaluation. The self-evaluation involves the systematic collection of evidence which demonstrates how the setting meets the English Early Years Foundation Stage (Curriculum) Framework, the statutory Safeguarding and Welfare requirements and the new inspection framework and, in addition, assesses the quality of learning and development experiences offered to, and experienced by, the very young child. This self-evaluation is carried out by the team of practitioners within the setting, and also involves parents/carers and children.

The evidence gathered allows the identification of good practice and highlights what is needed to improve the quality of provision. A portfolio of evidence is put together into an Evaluation Report, which provides the basis of an agreed action plan to improve the quality of services. Settings are then supported in the implementation of an action plan for quality improvement. The success of the action plan is reviewed through reflection and further evaluation, leading to the next cycle of action and improvement. The BEEL programme works in exactly the same way as EEL but with a specific focus on children from birth to three years. The training programme covers both programmes and settings are able to choose which programme they want to work on, they can do either EEL or BEEL or a combined EEL/BEEL programme.

We have found that the portfolio of evidence gathered through the EEL self-evaluation process not only provides settings with the information required to demonstrate compliance with the Early Years Foundation Stage Framework, the statutory Safeguarding and Welfare requirements, Ofsted inspection and quality improvement requirements, but also encourages settings to undertake a process of deep level, and longer term, organisational development. In this way the EEL programme provides a clear and targeted strategy for change, which builds upon, and extends, the existing skills and expertise of those who work with young children in a range of early childhood settings.

All of the settings throughout the duration of the quality improvement support programme were sponsored by the local authority for the three-year accreditation programme. Initially two settings attended the EEL/BEEL training, followed by a further seven a few months later. In total 79 settings in 11 separate cohorts completed the EEL/BEEL training programme between 2009 and 2015.

The training programme is delivered over two days. They begin with an introduction which includes:

- the rationale for the programme;
- what the programme offers;
- identification of the theoretical underpinning of the programme;
- how the programme works.

It then identifies the 10 Dimensions of Quality (Pascal and Bertram, 2006):

1. Aims and Objectives
2. Learning Experiences/Curriculum
3. Learning and Teaching Strategies
4. Planning, Assessment and Record Keeping
5. Staffing/Volunteers

6. Relationships and Interaction
7. Inclusion, Equality and Diversity
8. Parent/Carer Partnership and Community Liaison
9. Physical Environment
10. Leadership, Monitoring and Evaluation.

The principles of operation and the Quality, Evaluation and Improvement Cycle are explained:

- Evaluation and Improvement are viewed as inseparable.
- The process of Evaluation and Improvement is shared, democratic and collaborative.
- The process promotes equality of opportunity and acknowledges cultural diversity.
- The process is opted into and not imposed.
- The framework for evaluation is rigorous but flexible and non-judgemental.
- The Action Plans are followed through.
- The process is intended to empower and develop practitioners, not to threaten or judge.

During the training practical exercises are used to introduce the methodology, and types of data collection, barriers, benefits and ethics are discussed. Three sets of observations are also introduced:

- Child Tracking
- Child Involvement
- Adult Engagement.

The final part of the training involves discussing and agreeing the way forward for each of the settings and planning an 18-month timeline.

The case study setting

The case study setting was part of the second EEL/BEEL cohort, commencing in November 2009 with a target completion date of May 2011. The owner/manager of the setting attended the training programme, facilitated by an EEL/BEEL trainer. Initially participants found it difficult to understand how to implement the programme within the setting, particularly managing the process and engaging staff, parents and children. The local authority then implemented an ongoing support structure for settings which included regular cluster group meetings and visits from an EEL Adviser (a local authority officer). Due to the difficulties at the beginning of the programme the setting had an extension until March 2012.

Following the training programme the setting owner, also the nursery manager, was responsible for cascading the training within the setting – informing and training the staff, parents and children. The implementation of the programme benefitted from the commitment of a pro-active manager who felt that she needed to lead by example, drawing on her own academic development of leadership and evaluation skills as identified by Moles (2010) who describes an early years manager as ideally having leadership and management qualities in equal measure. During the introduction of the EEL programme, although the manager was a little overwhelmed by the amount of paperwork it seemed to require, she was committed to the programme, knowing that it would benefit the setting and enrich staff's, children's and parents' early years experiences and development.

The introduction of the programme to the staff was the first objective, followed by the introduction to parents, ensuring that they were fully informed of the rationale, process and participation needed. It also included agreement for their children to be involved in the child observations. This initial information sharing was later built on to include discussions with parents to explore what they felt about the setting and the experiences of themselves and their children during their time at the nursery.

Discussions with parents, staff, volunteers, students, management or governing bodies and children provided substantive data for the Evaluation Report. Parent and family partnership working is an important part of the EEL programme and one of the identified dimensions of quality. It identifies that settings should actively work in partnership with parents to meet the needs of the children. Collection of data and evidence of partnership working is used to evaluate its effectiveness and areas for improvement. The introduction of EEL to parents at the beginning of the programme was important, giving them the opportunity to ask questions and to voice any concerns. One of the main concerns was confidentiality and parents needed to be reassured that sensitive information would not be shared. The explanation of what information was needed, how it would be used and who would have access to it was important to ensure their peace of mind. The knowledge that the focus was on collective data rather than individual children, and that they would be able to read the final report, proved to be reassuring. This was proved by the practical support that was offered by parents when compilation of data proved to be a challenge. The discussions with parents then produced another set of useful data which contributed to the action planning. Parents stated that the EEL process had developed the nursery and enabled them to be more involved in their children's learning and play. Being a part of the process displayed to parents how they operated and how they drew conclusions from their observations. Parents noted a change to the planning and application of targets and development. Questionnaires confirmed that parents were very happy with the setting 'I can't think of anything that would make it better'. Data confirmed that parental partnerships, home and community liaison was productive, using comments such as 'supportive', 'discovery', 'expanding experiences at home from the nursery day'.

It was important to get the views of the children to ensure that they were able to comment on their experiences within the nursery. They collaborated well and enjoyed answering questions and participating in compiling photographic evidence. Children were unable to answer some of the questions asked by staff; however as they broke them down and used skills to ask the same question in different ways, they were able to participate fully. Their views recorded and supported the notion that children in the setting clearly understood the concept of learning and were able to recall morning focus time with their key person. Children's comments highlighted their knowledge of practitioners' roles, stating that the manager was 'in the staff room writing' (particularly during the collection of the EEL data). One member of staff helped children to tidy up and supported them to 'learn sounds' (using a phonics box during key group times) and another 'talked to mommies and daddies' and 'playing outside'. This third member of staff was the parent co-ordinator and therefore spent a lot of time with parents.

As shown in Figure 12.1, the collection of written data was important when looking at all aspects of nursery practice. For staff, one of the first tasks was to complete a professional biography. These biographies provided information about staff's knowledge and experiences within the nursery and explored the reasons for entering the profession and further aspirations. The EEL methodology is designed to reflect an emphasis on the importance of process, acknowledging its role in the development of positive attitudes to learning, which are critical to academic

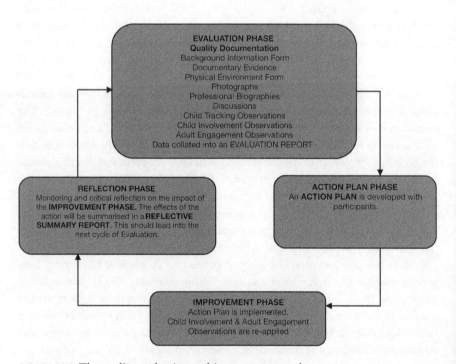

FIGURE 12.1 The quality evaluation and improvement cycle

success in the long term. The assessment focuses on the way the child engages in the process of learning and the way in which the adults who work with the child support and facilitate that learning. The Child Involvement and Adult Engagement Scales used to complete the child and adult observations, which follow the Child Tracking observations, provide the data to inform the evaluation and action planning process. This Evaluation Phase of the programme is designed to take between 9–12 months, but due to difficulties at the beginning of the programme it took a little longer.

The next phase was action planning. Following the analysis and evaluation of all of the data and completion of the Evaluation Report which examined the ten dimensions of quality within the setting, the action plan detailed what was to be put into practice within the Improvement Phase. This included a second round of child and adult observations. The final phase of the programme was the Reflection Phase when the data collected over the Improvement Phase was again analysed and evaluated and a reflective summary completed showing the progress and improvement in quality as a result of participation in the programme. Once complete the whole report was submitted for accreditation to the Centre for Research in Early Childhood and this was achieved in March 2012. The accreditation was granted for three years, dependant on an Annual Report being completed each year. The setting maintained their accreditation and achieved their final accreditation in March 2014. At this stage the setting were in a position to decide how they wanted to move forward – to either complete the full accreditation programme again or to implement EEL to achieve the best outcome in the setting, with the flexibility to expand or adapt specific aspects of the programme or resources.

Three principles into practice: paradigmatic; theoretical, methodological principles within the assessment and evaluation practice

The process of the 18-month programme was a continuous journey of professional development for the whole staff team. During the initial stages of the programme staff were very sceptical with comments including 'More paperwork and what is it all for?' and 'We are outstanding anyway so why do we need to change our method of observing, and give ourselves more writing to do?' The manager, although sympathetic to practitioners, was autocratic in initiating the process and led by scaffolding how to complete the observations, by example and by explaining that the method would provide explicit and informative data and would enhance personal development and the development of the children and the environment. Staff needed a period of time to adjust, observations had been an everyday experience for them but EEL observations were more intense and required certain skills from all participants. Use of the training video included in the programme resources was beneficial and the nursery also sourced support from the local authority development worker. Using observation skills during play was paramount to the nursery's success in producing honest and clear data. For the manager it provided an opportunity to reflect on her previous studies regarding theories of play, in particular Froebel who suggested that play is the way children integrate and bring together what they know, understand and feel into a whole. The manager shared this with staff and highlighted that it was this type of play that enabled staff to complete observations where children's involvement levels were high as they were very involved in what they were doing and practising what they already knew. The process of the EEL programme demonstrates a number of the principles discussed in Chapter 7, for example, that 'assessment and evaluation should be meaningful and useful for each child, supporting individual learning journeys'. The practitioners were experienced in completing observations and learning journeys for each child; however the EEL programme enabled them to look further and to identify levels of involvement and well-being for each child. The information gained from data enabled the practitioners to create an environment where children could become competent learners, providing the space, opportunities and stimulation with adults who were sensitive to their needs.

Analysing data proved to be a challenge but the manager, as the EEL Support Worker, used skills gained during her early years degree along with assistance from parents, who had volunteered their support following their initial introduction to the programme. Following the first data analysis and evaluations, practitioners were able to see the benefits of the observation methods and developed a more committed attitude to the EEL programme, eagerly mentoring new students and contributing confidently to peer observations.

The nursery identified a number of benefits from participating in the programme:

- The collection and analysis of data has enabled them to gather invaluable information which has been used to inform areas for development.
- They have been able to celebrate good practice and to uphold their outstanding Ofsted rating at their recent inspection.
- Most importantly, it has given them the tools and confidence to always do better.

It has also been identified that this demonstrates the principle: 'assessment and evaluation should promote confidence and participation, following a rights based approach'. The EEL programme, with its structured approach, gives practitioners the tools to evaluate their practice and to become more confident individuals. The tools identify why, what and how they are evaluating and then support the collection, analysis and evaluation of data leading to action planning and quality improvement. This process is led by the practitioners themselves giving them ownership of the programme and decision making. In completing the programme skills and knowledge are increased resulting in more competent and confident practitioners.

The EEL programme was a collective adventure for the whole of the case study setting, including staff, parents and children. It supported professional development for all the nursery practitioners; the manager particularly recognised her own personal and professional development which was supported by the EEL External Adviser throughout the programme. One of the benefits of EEL was to have someone who could discuss data analysis objectively as well as advise on the practical aspects of completing the programme.

This objectivity is important and supports the principle that 'assessment and evaluation should be informed by available knowledge, rigorous, reliable and valid'. The EEL programme has two key aims:

1.   To develop a participatory, manageable strategy to evaluate and improve the quality of early learning and development, and the effectiveness of outcomes available to young children in a wide range of education and care settings.
2.   To achieve this through a collaborative, systematic and rigorous process of self-evaluation, which is supported and validated externally, and which feeds directly into the quality and inspection process.

This process of self-evaluation exemplifies the principle; practitioners gather the required data, complete a process of data analysis and evaluation to produce an action plan. The evaluation is discussed and challenged by the EEL External Adviser to ensure that it is reliable and valid.

Reflections: what learned? Challenges and possibilities within the practice described

In the setting

The manager has developed more self-confidence, she now feels that she is able to support staff in reaching the very highest level of caring for and educating young children. She also has the management skills to meet the needs of the practitioners and the nursery as a whole. Practitioners have attended training courses, and as the Graduate Leader and leader of the EEL programme the manager has been able to guide and support them. As a team they piloted the *Early Years Foundation Stage* (EYFS; DfE, 2012) which proved invaluable during the transition period. Organising training was accomplished by research and collaboration with other good practices, as the local authority did not offer courses until after the EYFS was implemented. By using skills learnt from completing the EEL Quality Assurance Programme they were able to use observation documents such as tracking, engagement and involvement to gain a clear and informative analysis of where the children were within the EYFS during their first few weeks and where they were after a full term. Data informed them that all children had progressed well, and that every child was working within their age development band. They had a high percentage of children working above their age band confirming that they were accommodating high achievers and also children who had special educational needs, who were being supported by Individual Education plans. This data provided the evidence that their understanding of delivery of the new EYFS (DfE, 2012) was indeed positive, which gave them the incentive to continue with training and development to further support every child in their learning environment.

As part of the EEL programme planning was evaluated, resulting in the key person planning on a daily basis for each child. Completing the research, data analysis and evaluation was a great accomplishment and the team were able to celebrate with the evidence that the process worked well and that everyone around the child had a part to play in their learning and development. As a direct result of learning how to analyse data the manager was able to collect informative data at the start of the September term which clearly identified which children were working below, which ones were working within and which ones were working above their age band. This concurred with observations from the EEL Project and gave practitioners a clear pathway to progress and to provide opportunities for development in specific areas.

Another positive outcome of the programme was working in partnership with parents. Parents' involvement was enhanced by assisting them to identify and recognise the prime and specific areas of learning and showing them how they could support their children's development. The key person worked hard with parents to help them understand the EYFS and how they could assist their child's learning at home. Documents were developed with collaboration with parents and children. The children's interests from home and at nursery were in particular a great asset in providing individual planning for each child focused on where they were and how could move forward. Parents were also involved in tracking where their child was within the EYFS, this was recorded on an individual target sheet which was used as a guide for each child. Parents had a copy and were able to see what their child could experience to develop each target. The focus on play and interests made the new curriculum a fun tool to use for parents as they were able to use familiar toys which the child enjoyed. As a setting they were able to show parents how to use equipment and activities in different ways to encourage children to think critically, or to change strategies to accomplish a task.

The nursery environment was constantly evaluated and assessed for effectiveness and during the programme they were able to acquire some land adjacent to the setting that accommodated an allotment. Parents worked with staff and children in order to plant and grow their own vegetables and this introduced a more 'forest school' approach to the outside experiences. They had an artist attend for three full days who introduced self-expression in the outside environment e.g. children were able to create with natural resources and mix them with paints and recycled items to create a weaving area. Having the allotment and increasing the practitioners' ability to offer a widening learning environment endorsed the opportunity for children to experience and develop by enabling them to learn using their own abilities, thinking and exploring with guidance from practitioners and parents who were very involved in the venture.

The impact of EEL was instrumental in some practitioners' qualification development. The deputy manager was keen to complete her Foundation Degree and used her observation skills within her group of children, to give her a clear understanding of individual needs and interests. The observations learnt from EEL were linked very closely with the EYFS (DfE, 2012), offering a detailed dialogue of engagement and how children were involved in their play and learning experiences. She also led staff training and supported the implementation of the EYFS. Another practitioner chose to develop her skills in implementing the EYFS by completing an E-Learning course; this gave her the opportunity to work at her own pace and use the internet at home. She used her skills and knowledge gained from EEL, putting into practice her studying of theorists and the part they play in observations and teaching strategies. This led her further, to consider how she could reflect on her own professional development, and how she could continue her studies. For the manager it proved that EEL had inspired her to go forward and to want to understand the part professional observations can have on individual children's learning.

All of the practitioners have continued with their professional development; one has developed her skills in being parent co-ordinator, compiling questionnaires and providing data so that parents could see the benefit of their involvement in their child's learning. She also led parent stay and cook and play and learn sessions, which were very successful and continue to develop. All practitioners have completed individual courses to support their personal and professional development.

As an Outstanding rated setting it was at times challenging to inspire staff to reflect upon their practice; however the peer observations continued to be a key to their success. At the end of the three-year accreditation programme they were able to reflect on their learning and decide how to use EEL as a tool within the nursery. They developed the adult engagement observation sheets to include teaching strategies, environment and resources and added a summary box. They also adjusted child involvement observations to inform them how the child was learning, specifically linked to the characteristics of effective learning. Having confidence as a Graduate Leader has enabled the manager to change documentation and to use research as a key to her findings, she states that this is as a result of completing the EEL programme.

The wider impact

The local authority ceased the quality improvement programme following changes in government legislation which identified Ofsted as the sole arbiters of quality. The primary focus of local authority support was directed towards settings rated as Inadequate or Requiring Improvement following Ofsted inspections. Support for these settings also needed to be focused on the identified Ofsted actions. No new settings were able to join the EEL programme but settings who had commenced the programme continued on their journey and regular cluster group meetings were also maintained to ensure that they had the necessary support. An evaluation of EEL and BEEL was also completed at this time. The first settings who commenced in 2009 have completed the three-year programme of accreditation and annual

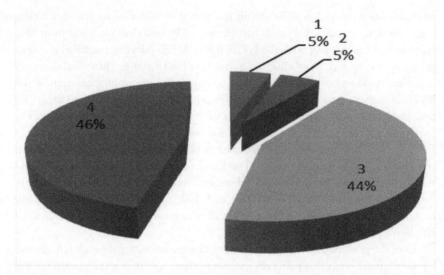

FIGURE 12.2 Settings' Ofsted ratings after implementation of EEL programme

reviews and continue using EEL/BEEL in their ongoing cycle of planning, observation and assessment. Settings who commenced in 2010–2013 are at various stages of the three-year programme.

An evaluation of the programme shows that of the original 79 settings, 10 of the 20 settings who withdrew from the programme were children's centres or nurseries attached to children's centres – a number withdrawing because of closure and others due to them participating in other programmes. Five were schools (either LEA or independent) and five were private, voluntary and independent (PVI) nurseries, the majority of whom had a change of staff or ownership and were unable to continue with the programme.

An audit of early years providers registered to receive Early Years Entitlement funding in January 2015 revealed that of the 372 providers registered, 67 providers were rated as Outstanding by Ofsted and of those, 21 had completed the EEL/BEEL programme (31 per cent). When looking at the settings who were actively involved in the programme, Figure 12.2 illustrates that following Ofsted Ratings, 2 settings had 'Satisfactory', 2 settings had 'Requires Improvement', 18 settings had 'Good' and 19 settings had 'Outstanding'.

This result of 90 per cent of EEL/BEEL settings having a good or outstanding Ofsted rating suggested that the programme had a positive outcome for settings participating in the programme. This was complemented by the outcomes of Ofsted inspections for a number of nurseries who had participated in EEL and/or BEEL:

> Planning and assessment documents ensure children's interests are planned for very effectively. Plans are comprehensive, and shared with parents to keep them up-to-date with topics and activities children are currently engaging in.

There are excellent systems in place to evaluate and reflect upon practice and set plans for future improvement. Highly focused self-evaluation and close monitoring of the educational programme are evident. The management team and practitioners show a very strong commitment to improving outcomes for all children.

Staff engage well in developing good partnerships both with parents and other professionals, to ensure that children's individual needs are recognised and given the utmost priority.

Two of the nurseries had only one Ofsted action to 'further extend the arrangements to share the setting's inspirational practice with other providers.'

Based on this evidence, the local authority made a decision to pilot the Baby Effective Early Learning Programme in a small number of targeted settings. The criteria for eligibility was primarily that the setting should be able to increase access for two-year-old children who were entitled to receive two-year-old funding by moving from Requiring Improvement to a Good Ofsted rating. An introduction session, followed by the two day training programme, took place in February 2015 and the first cohort of three settings in the south of the city began at the end of that month. The BEEL training package also included reference to each of the setting's Ofsted Report and actions, identifying how each aspect of the BEEL programme would address their Ofsted actions. This pilot programme will continue to be monitored and evaluated.

References

Bertram, T. and Pascal, C. (2006) *Effective Early Learning (EEL) A Handbook for Evaluating, Assuring and Improving Quality in Early Childhood Settings.* Amber Publishing: Birmingham.

EYFS (2012) *The Statutory Framework for the Early Years Foundation Stage: Setting the Standards for Learning, Development and Care for Children from Birth to Five.* Revised and published March 2014 and effective from September 2014, UK Department for Education, HMSO: London.

Moles, J. (2010) *The Excellence of Play*, 3rd edn. Open University Press: Berkshire.

National Childcare Strategy (1998) *National Childcare Strategy Green Paper: 'Meeting the Childcare Challenge'*, May 1998. Department for Education and Employment, HMSO: London.

13

CASE STUDY 6

Participatory assessment with parents: the Accounting Early for Lifelong Learning (AcE) Programme

Donna Gaywood and Christine Pascal

This case study reveals the challenges and benefits of using a participatory model of assessment and evaluation within a network of Children's Centres. It demonstrates how the AcE programme (Bertram, Pascal and Saunders, 2008) was adopted as an assessment tool by practitioners and how it has operated as a catalyst for staff to fundamentally reconsider and reshape their relationships with both parents and children within the learning process. The case study also reveals how the data generated by the participatory assessment process is used to inform the planning process and ensure learning in the settings and at home is individualised and meaningful for both children and parents.

Context: pedagogical and cultural location of assessment and evaluation work

This case study is located within a group of five Children Centres in South West England. Children Centres were established by the last Labour government (1997–2010) to ensure that all children under five could access universal health services, high quality groups, funded daycare and early education with the aim to promote children's development and early learning. Children Centres were initially built within areas of high deprivation around England and aimed to offer services to the most vulnerable children and their families, with a clear remit to identify issues early and offer support to families. As a result, Children Centre services developed a skilled workforce that was able to build and sustain relationships with families who were often managing difficult life events which may include workless-ness, domestic violence, bereavement, drug and alcohol dependency and complex family relationships. The current British government is keen for Children Centre services to become a key player in narrowing the attainment gap between the children from the poorest families and their peers, who seem to consistently perform better at the end of their primary school reception year at aged five (Child Poverty Strategy, 2014) As a result, the work undertaken by the service has developed a clear approach to promoting children's learning and engaging parents in this process.

The local authority area is known to be a wealthy, thriving place; however there are pockets of deprivation across the county which are often hidden to the general public. Therefore, the Children Centres within the local authority serve a varied demographic. Most families who access the services are living within poverty, many from workless households but there are a growing number of families who can be considered 'the working poor'. The majority of the families who access the service are white working class, although in two of the centres there is a higher rate of black, minority and ethnic families accessing services, including both economic migrants and asylum seekers. There are also a number of travelling families who access services across the county. The Children Centres each have areas where deprivation, rural isolation, poor maternal mental health, rates of childhood obesity and child accidents are high. Regular stay and play groups are delivered in each of these areas.

The work, regarding assessing and evaluating children's learning within the Centres' services, has been ever developing and has grown organically through listening to and reflecting on staff, parents and children's responses. Our approach was initially implemented within one busy daycare setting which accommodates children predominately living within an area of high deprivation, with over 80 per cent considered 'vulnerable' according to the national inspection criteria. We now use similar assessment and evaluation methods throughout the Children Centre services. These include: two local authority Children Centre nurseries, universal and targeted groups for parents and children, and family support and safeguarding work within the five Children Centres. Currently, the original five Children Centres are merging with another four, so these processes and pedagogy are being shared with our new colleagues.

The senior staff, who were the catalyst for this work, are a multi-disciplinary team, drawing from health, social care, early years and education, who share a vision of the overall aims and goals of the service. Philosophically and pedagogically, they are passionate about children remaining at the centre of any assessments and take the position that the voice of very young children should be heard, taken note of and can be elicited through sensitive and well-interpreted observations.

Equally, there is an explicit understanding that for children to be 'school ready' they need to have the skills, attributes and attitudes that allow them to become competent and independent learners. This goes beyond solely being prepared to read, write and grasp basic arithmetic. The team believe that children need to have the capability to rebound from disappointments, to understand how to conduct themselves within a social world and are keen to explore new things.

In addition, the management team have a strong commitment to the empowerment of parents, believing that parents are the most important participant in a child's outcome. Underpinning this is the belief that children need warm, responsive and reciprocal relationships with their care givers to be enabled to achieve well beyond the early years. When working with parents who are often stigmatised because of their socio-economic status, it has been important to create a co-constructed model of service that embodies these principles and brings the parent's perspective and experience to the assessment process.

Driving this work is a strong commitment to lifelong learning and a participatory pedagogy; in addition is the belief that children and their families who are empowered thus will be better equipped to bridge the attainment gap. This approach has become fundamental to the delivery of services for children and their families across the Children Centre network.

Assessment and evaluation praxis: description of assessment and evaluation programme of work and practice

In January 2010 the local authority made a decision to adopt the AcE programme (Bertram, Pascal and Saunders, 2008) as a method to engage parents in their children's learning at home. This programme is a strength based, participatory model which helps parents and staff to identify what children are able to do rather than what they are unable to do, through the parent's knowledge of their child, conversation and observation of the child at play. It is based on research findings which we find is extremely powerful when engaging parents. The observations and conversations form the basis of an initial assessment that places the child and their competencies at the centre, ensuring any plans to promote learning are child centred building on what the parents know and can see. This allows the learning to develop individually, organically and through relationships. The AcE programme identifies five areas or domains covering the prime areas of learning identified by the Early Years Foundation Stage curriculum in England. However, the indicators give parents a clearer understanding about the specific competencies their children need to develop in order to be competent lifelong learners. Once parents and staff have made a clear assessment of the child's current capacities, they develop a plan to promote further learning. Parents agree to play with their children in a certain way or support them differently to ensure progress in all areas of learning. Staff also agree to provide extra activities which will also support this development, either in the Children Centre, the nursery or on a home visit. After a period of time parents and staff have a follow-up meeting to discuss any developments or progress, again based on parent and staff observations of the child.

The Flying Start programme of early support is offered to parents whose children are entitled to an allocated two-year funded nursery place. This programme means that prior to the child starting nursery, an early years practitioner visits the child at home and supports the parent to play with their child, keeping a play diary. A 'team around the child' meeting, which includes professional staff from education, health and social care, is subsequently held and the child would then be supported into nursery by this multi-professional team. The results of this programme have been encouraging as there seems to be less parental disengagement and more children stay in nursery to go on to take up the universal early years entitlement at three. The AcE participatory approach to assessment and learning has been adopted across the whole range of Children Centre services as detailed below.

In the nursery: birth to 5 years

Aware of the success of the Flying Start programme, the staff at one of the Children Centre nurseries were keen to build on this model and use the AcE programme as a way to strengthen their parental participation in children's learning. After trialling this approach, the decision was taken to use the learning indicators and domains in the programme to inform the children's summative assessments. These indicators include empathy, resilience, responsibility, emotional literacy and language exploration.

These assessments have enabled staff to track individual children's progress and also make clear analysis of the developmental process of the cohort of children. In addition, staff have been able to reflect upon the learning environment and the opportunities offered to the children, considering the quality and impact of these on the learning process.

For example, for one cohort it became clear that a high number of children were experiencing delay in their emotional literacy. As a result, the Pain Assessment Tool (Baker and Wong, 1987), which is used in children's nursing to help children assess their own levels of pain, was introduced during welcome time each session. Very young children quickly became able to indicate how they were feeling that day and soon could link these feelings to experiences e.g. 'miss Mummy'. The children's emotional literacy levels swiftly rose.

Using the assessments of individual children to consider the well-being and learning of the whole cohort has become established in practice. Practitioners have begun to identify patterns in children's learning. For example, it has been observed that children who have experienced domestic violence tend to struggle to be assertive. Therefore, all the children are taught the first stages of being assertive with one another. They are encouraged to say, 'Stop I don't like it' and use a hand gesture to indicate that they are uncomfortable with how a peer or an adult is relating to them. The children have become more confident and changes in their attainment levels can be seen more clearly.

The paperwork which is used to document children's learning is kept under continual review to ensure that it is fit for purpose and manageable for both staff and parents.

Parents have been introduced to the AcE indicators through regular parents' meetings and are encouraged to contribute. However, it is recognised that within the nursery setting, parents need to have more input and be more intimately involved in their child's learning, particularly within the initial assessments. As a result, staff are beginning to visit parents and children at home after their settling in period in nursery, so that they can complete an initial assessment of the child's learning with the parents.

Universal and targeted groups

The principle of using the AcE programme to support the learning and development of a group of children and their parents has been developed further by staff who are using it to enhance children's learning through both universal and targeted groups in the Children Centre. A three pronged approach has been developed:

*   using the indicators for planning in the group;
*   using AcE programme to engage parents;
*   using the individual assessments for tracking children's progress.

Parents are introduced to this lifelong learning approach through displays and through conversations with staff. As a group they are encouraged to choose one indicator within the AcE programme that resonates for them and their children.

Staff may steer this selection as a result of their observations of the group or the Children Centre data for the area, which may include health statistics, crime indicators or data gathered from local schools at the end of reception year when a child is five. This data is then used by local authorities to analyse the learning needs of children who are preparing to go to school (under fives). For example, within the group it may have been noted that the children have very little opportunity to exercise choice and be independent. Staff may discuss this with parents and then possibly make changes to the snack time – re-structuring it to actively promote independence. So children are encouraged to prepare snacks, pour their own drinks and clear their own plates.

Medium term plans are created which set the direction of the group and parents are given the opportunity to make individual assessments for their children in the chosen learning area with staff and then encouraged to support their children's learning both in the group and at home. Following this a later assessment is made to see the progress of the children.

Diaries are kept by staff and parents to document the children's learning. Parents are encouraged to participate by taking photos, sticking them in and recording their child's learning.

Data is generated from these individual child assessments which clearly evidences the distance travelled by individual children within the group in one area of learning. We have begun to use this data to produce single page reports that highlight the positive impact the group has on children's learning and outcomes. Examples of these reports are given below.

IMPACT REPORT
TA stay and play
November 2014

Timescale: 19.9.14 – 24.10.14

TA is a stay and play group which runs weekly, term time only, within the children centre targeted area

The families who attend are generally already working with children centre services.

The group is a stable group, currently there are six families attending.

This group also acts as a bridge for local families who may struggle to access groups or services at the Children Centre.

The staff have been trying to engage parents using the Accounting Early for Lifelong Learning. Two of the six parents were able to make an assessment of their children's resilience in September. The children whose parents took part in the AcE programme are 16 months, 18 months and 3.

Through conversations about this indicator, staff and parents have worked together to support the three children at home and through the activities of the group.

Summary
100% of children involved were with the recognised vulnerable groups.
67% were BME
33% were girls
67% were boys
100% of the children had witnessed domestic abuse.

Within just one month

Assertiveness: Ace Indicator Distance travelled			
	September 2014	October 2014	Distance travelled
Child A	25%	50%	25%
Child B	50%	75%	25%
Child C	25%	50%	25%

25% – at risk of significant delay
50% – at risk of delay
75% – within normal range
100% above expected level

FIGURE 13.1 Impact report stay and play

The parents' voice

'She is more sure of herself – more confident. She knows there's consequences to actions. She tries and gets her own clothes on – shoes and socks.' (24.10.14)

'He is more playful and looks at mum, smiles and runs away with toys, comes back and plays with mummy again' (24.10.14)

'Helps with chores, negotiates and asks mum for help saying, 'please' and 'thank-you'' (24.10.14)

Analysis

1/3 of the parents attending TA have taken part in assessing their children and through this assessment it can be demonstrated that the children's long-term outcomes have been significantly and positively affected.

Staff have shown that through their relationship with the parents, it is possible in a targeted universal group to support parents to become more focused on their children's outcomes and be more effective in their role as first educator.

The piece of work was only measured over a short piece of time. One of the children is currently on a child protection plan. Her improved levels of assertiveness through such a small piece of work will make a significant difference to her outcomes.

Parents are beginning to understand how their input can affect their children's long-term outcomes.

Learning for the staff

- Using AcE in a universal targeted group is possible.

- The success of engaging parents to understand their role as their child's first educator is dependent on the strength of the relationships which are formed.

- A significant change for children is possible over a short period of time, if all staff and the parents decide to work together.

- Capturing the parent voice as part of the assessment is crucial.

- Being confident to break the AcE programme down to bite sized, manageable chunks is important.

- Converting the assessment process into data is simple but a powerful method of showing the impact of the work and outcomes achieved.

FIGURE 13.2 Capturing the parents' voices

Family support

Staff use a similar strategy to this in family support. The team believe that the AcE model is a 'can do' approach to assessment which is an extremely positive way to make assessments for children and their families. Parents, who may be experiencing negative feelings about a child and their behaviour, have responded well to it. Children are not assessed according to their age and stage, and so cannot be seen to be 'failing'. Equally, the emphasis is clearly on how to support the child to develop skills so that the parents feel less blamed and more enabled, therefore becoming more engaged in supporting their children's learning. This way of working has been so successful that family support staff are including it in Common Assessment Framework (CAF) plans. These are used as a way of planning multi-agency involvement with a child to ensure that parents have a clear plan from each agency involved and each professional is held to account by this plan. This helps everyone to act consistently on behalf of the child. These plans stop families becoming overloaded with professional input and advice, ensure the child's needs are central and are reviewed regularly to maintain momentum.

Children's groups

More recently, the Children Centre service has developed children's groups. Senior staff decided to re-name the crèche provision 'children's groups' because of an underlying feeling that a rich learning experience should be a key priority, providing the opportunity for children to improve their outcomes. It was agreed that where possible children should have similar learning outcomes to their parents, but differentiated according to their age.

It was felt that in order to ensure the children's groups remain true to our pedagogy where possible there should be a home visit. Ideally, staff should use these home visits to work with parents to make initial child assessments using the AcE programme. However when this has been too challenging practically, staff make observations of the children's play and then make an initial practitioner assessment, once the child is settled. Using the same principles of planning for a group of children, staff plan dynamically, responding to the children's behaviour, development and their social interactions. At the end of the course a final assessment is made and staff are able to share these assessments with parents alongside their learning diaries which pictorially evidence the children's learning. Using the AcE programme in this way has proved to be an invaluable tool to evidence the positive impact of the groups on children's outcomes. Figures 13.3–13.5 are an example of a report submitted to an advisory board following the completion of a children's group which was supporting the Incredible Years parenting course.

AB CHILDREN CENTRE
Incredible Years Children's Group
SEPT – DEC 2014

This children's group was the first children's group that was run to the new children's group standard.

Staff used the Accounting Early for Lifelong Learning Programme (AcE) to assess children's learning and development.

Making an assessment

Three indicators from AcE were selected which most closely reflected the adult outcomes:

• Resilience
• Empathy
• Emotional literacy

Staff made an assessment of the children's learning at the beginning and at the end of the group, based on their observations of the children within the group and at play.

This assessment enables the Children Centre to measure the positive impact of the group for the children.

Information about the children

9 children attended the group. (1 child only attended one session.)

Of the 8 who were regular attendees:

100% are within the vulnerable categories as outlined by Ofsted

63% girls

37% boys

37% spoke English as a second language

25% BME

FIGURE 13.3 Using AcE to assess children's learning and development

Initial assessment	Resilience	Empathy	Emotional literacy
At significant risk of delay	37%	50%	50%
At risk of delay	63%	37%	37%
At the level expected		13%	13%
Ahead of expected			

Final assessment	Resilience	Empathy	Emotional literacy
At significant risk of delay			
At risk of delay	25%	50%	25%
At the level expected	75%	13%	62%
Ahead of expected		37%	13%

Analysis of data in tables

At the start of the children 100% of the children who attended were experiencing some form of delay in their levels of resilience.

The majority of the children, 87%, were experiencing delay in their empathy skills and in emotional literacy (the ability to understand and manage their emotions)

As a result of their parents attending the Incredible Years parenting course and the children attending the children group the majority of the children, 75%, had improved their levels of resilience and were able to operate within the expected levels.

50% of the children had increased their empathy skills so that they were within the expected level and ahead.

75% of the children were no longer experiencing any delay in their emotional literacy.

FIGURE 13.4 Initial and final assessment of children's group using AcE

Individual children's distance travelled in %

Child	Resilience	Empathy	Emotional literacy
A	25%	50%	25%
B	25%	25%	25%
C	25%	25%	25%
D	25%	25%	50%
E	25%	25%	50%
F	25%	25%	25%
G	25%	50%	25%
H	50%	25%	25%

All the children made a 25% increase in all areas as a result of attending the children's group.
Some children in some areas made significant distance travelled by 50%.
There were no children who remain static in their attainment.

Summary
The children's group for the Incredible Years parenting group was run according to the new children's group standard which is based on strong attachment practice. It ensures each aspect of the group is set up to provide the richest of learning experiences for the children and the characteristics of effective learning (EYFS) are promoted throughout.

Children are assessed using skills, attitudes and attributes which are essential for lifelong learning.

All assessments are made through staff observations in accordance with high quality early years practice.

The children's group is run by senior early years practitioners to ensure that the children experience the highest level of early years skill.

As a result, this group has been an extremely positive learning experience for the children who attended. All the children have increased their resilience, their capacity for empathy and all have become more emotionally literate as a result of attending this group.

Strong baseline assessments were made and the distance each child travelled can be tracked. Positive impact of the group can be evidenced.

Recommended next steps
• To increase the level of involvement of the parents in making both the initial and final assessment so that they can more fully understand their role in supporting their child's learning at home.
• To improve the children's understanding of their own learning in the groups by sharing learning diaries and talking about what they have learnt.

FIGURE 13.5 Assessment of individual 'distance travelled'

Parenting groups

The Children Centre offers regular opportunities for parents to attend the Incredible Years parenting course. While the parents are attending the groups, the children are cared for at the children's groups led by the senior early years practitioner. As staff have become more convinced of the importance of supporting parents to become confident first educators of their children and seeing the positive outcomes when using the AcE programme a session has been added to the course to incorporate the principles of supporting lifelong learning at home, where the pedagogy of the service is shared with parents. Parents have responded well and are keen to take home the indicators to think about and begin to offer further opportunities to their children to develop. For example, one parent returned the next week and shared how she had begun to approach learning through play. She said, 'It was actually fun'. Other parents have chosen to complete a Home Learning Plan to act as a reminder of what they want to achieve with their children.

After-school provision

The Children Centres offer an after-school club in four out of the five centres where primary schools are able to refer children who are experiencing emotional or behavioural difficulties. This is supported by an educational psychologist. Staff use two of the five domains in AcE to assess and evaluate the children's learning: 'Emotional Well-being' and 'Social Competence and Self Concept'.

As with the universal groups, medium term plans are used to support the social development of the group as well as individual children's development. To do this, a relevant indicator is identified, from within the two domains, based on the staff's observations of the group. For example if the children in the group are all experiencing difficulty being able to regulate their emotions, the indicator Emotional Literacy would be selected. Staff then create a medium term plan which encompasses any therapeutic interventions which ensures the environment is enabling for the children to learn how to begin to become competent in the individual competencies within the indicator.

When a child is referred to the group, the practitioner makes contact with the parent and arranges an initial meeting, usually without the child being present. Staff explain about the group to the parents and introduce the AcE indicators. The parents are encouraged to use the indicators to make an assessment of their child at home, supported by the staff member, in order to identify whether the child demonstrates the attributes, attitudes or skills described rarely, sometimes, often or consistently. Children then begin to attend the group. Staff allow a term for the children to settle and begin to feel comfortable. Once the child is settled, the one to one work begins. Staff introduce the AcE indicators to the child and together they make an assessment of the child's development. The child is encouraged to understand their own development and work with the staff to create a plan to help them to develop the skills they need. This one to one work continues throughout

AcE Home Learning Plan

Name of Child: All of them! (family of four children)

Start date: October 2014   Review date: January 2015

AcE indicator: Independence

What you have noticed	What are you going to do at home	How did it go	Any differences you have seen in your child	What could you do next
Mum does everything around the house. Cleaning, cooking, washing, tidying bedrooms, etc. etc.	Set rules. Use charts/rewards. Stop doing things for them when I know they are capable. Talk to them about new rules. Reward & praise.	B now offers to make me a cup of tea whilst making his own breakfast. S said 'Mum we couldn't cope without you as you do everything.' J does put away one thing before getting out another. O likes to help with the washing.	S can see all what mum has to do and now offers to help.	Keep to routines. Don't take over, let them help. Reward them for helping.

FIGURE 13.6 An AcE home learning plan

their time in the group. Reviews are held with the parents when the initial assessment is re-visited each time, so progress can be tracked.

Children do not attend the group indefinitely. There is an understanding that this group is to support their emotional and social development, helping them to manage their behaviour in a safe group, and once the children have made good progress, their need for the group diminishes, so they move on. A final assessment is made using the AcE indicators in order to track their learning gains as a result of attending the group.

Although the outworking of using the AcE programme varies across the service, there are a number of common elements throughout. Assessments are made from observations of children's play and behaviour, with parents contributing from their own knowledge and relationship with their child. These assessments are based on what children can do rather than what they can't. The learning environment and the 'way we do things' is expected to adapt to promote learning rather than the children adapting to fit in. The meaningful engagement of parents is fundamental and needs to be pursued relentlessly, through positive relationships. The initial assessment and subsequent assessments are vital in order to evidence learning. Data from these is used as evidence of impact of the service on real children's real lives.

Three principles into practice: paradigmatic, theoretical, methodological principles within the assessment and evaluation practice

Many of the principles outlined in Chapter 7 are central to the work of the Children Centre service team. In particular we fundamentally believe that:

- assessment and evaluation should facilitate the encounter of voices, allowing for collective learning;
- assessment and evaluation should promote competence and participation, following a rights based approach;
- assessment and evaluation should be meaningful and useful for each person, allowing for individualisation.

Parents' voices

Much of our journey has been about creating a new model of partnership with parents which is both meaningful and where parents are seen and treated as equal partners. There have been and continue to be many challenges, including staff confidence, time to make relationships and parents' perceptions of the service. For example, for staff to feel confident to have a meaningful conversation with parents about their children's learning, they need to understand how children learn and feel confident themselves in making assessments. A lot of time has been invested into staff across the whole of the service to support their own understanding of pedagogy and how to interpret observations of a child's play and behaviour.

Children's voices

Involving children in considering their own learning has also been and continues to present a challenge to the team. Within the nursery settings, where strong early years practice of child centred observations and the key person approach is firmly established, it has been easier to begin the process of involving children in reflecting and directing their own learning. Currently, the key people regularly share learning diaries with the children, giving opportunity for them to reflect and comment on their play. The children's comments are recorded in the diaries. Ownership of the learning diaries is encouraged so children can draw or mark make to enhance the learning stories already documented. The child's voice is added to displays and photographic learning stories which capture specific pieces of group learning e.g. woods trips or outdoor teddy time.

'Learning' giraffe puppets are used daily in small group time. Children, from two years old, are encouraged to talk to their giraffe about what they have been doing and what they have been thinking during the session.

Staff within the nursery settings are currently discussing new ways to promote children's participation in assessing their own learning and development.

Introducing this child participatory model more widely in the Children Centre services remains challenging. The reason for this, as yet, is unclear. It may be that both parents and staff are unsure of children's capacity to reflect and direct their learning or it may be that the culture of universal stay and play groups has no room to offer this opportunity to children.

Senior staff remain firmly committed to ensuring the service considers the child's voice at all levels. There has been a re-orientation of focus of the last few years which has resulted in Family Plans being written from a child's perspective (Figure 13.7). Case chronologies clearly recording the child's voice and children's views are being sought as part of the recruitment process. However, this needs to be developed further through staff having times to reflect and plan how to involve children more fully in considering their own learning.

Promoting competence, participation and a rights based approach

Adopting a participatory approach to assessing children's learning and development, the team has worked on the assumption that all parents, irrespective of circumstance, want their children to do well in school and achieve much in life. In order to ensure that assessments are child centred, made with parents and that parents are given a voice, both staff and parents have had to make a shift in their understanding. This has been a cultural shift in the organisation, which continues to date. The results have enabled us to incorporate the child's voice in plans used in multi-professional meetings. The re-writing of documents in this way has provided the impetus for both parents and professionals to ensure the work remains clearly centred on the child's outcomes.

Example of a Family Plan

Priority Area/Child's voice	Next Steps/Actions	By Who	By When	Completed (date)
Promoting good health 'For mum to keep talking about her feelings and keep taking her medicine until she feels better'	A to keep attending her doctor's appointments Keep taking anti-depressants until she is told otherwise by her doctor	To keep A feeling positive so she doesn't relapse	A on-going BC social worker to try charities by Nov '14	DE got funding from CC budget to fund the carpets Quote – Oct '14
'To have carpets to keep our house warm and stop dust coming in our house'	To try charities to get money for carpets	To stop the children from becoming poorly	DE to organise a quote	Carpets fitted Jan '15
Social networks 'I would like to play with some children of my own age, especially when I feel better'	For A and F to try and attend groups especially when F feels better	F to socialise with other children A to meet new friends and see other parents	A on-going	
Supporting Learning 'I would like to have some positive touch to keep the bond between us'	DE to do baby massage in the home	DE to organise dates for this	Nov '14-Jan '15	Dates organised and completed course

FIGURE 13.7 An example of an AcE family plan

One of the biggest challenges still facing the team is around the observation and interpreting of children's behaviour. Both parents and staff, at times, still interpret children's play and behaviour negatively. The assessment approach that we have adopted uses observation and relationships as the foundation. Senior staff believe and are committed to providing reflective opportunities for staff to think together about how we understand and interpret children's play and how this can be related to their learning and development.

Meaningful, useful and individual assessments

This principle is clearly embedded within all areas of the service, mainly due to the fact that many of the staff team come from an early years background that embodies the need for an individual learning journey. However, it has taken staff some time to fully embrace the need for assessments to be meaningful. In a busy group or early years setting, it is easy to regard assessments as a providing a piece of paper which needs to be filled in either for 'management' or for the government inspectors. There seems to be a sea change of opinion amongst staff with many understanding the importance of good assessments and how a carefully planned learning journey can significantly and positively impact a child's learning and development. Senior staff have worked hard to consistently send this message and have provided much support, training and reflection time to the staff.

Reflections: what learned? Challenges and possibilities within the practice described

Much has been achieved by the staff team who have invested hard work, time and energy as the service has sought to re-model our systems and processes of assessing and evaluating children's learning to become more inclusive, participatory and rights based for all involved. We believe it is now more cohesive and is ethically more reflective of the pedagogy of the organisation. As already described, this has been an evolving journey and a great deal has been learned along the way, as set out below.

The need to have a flexible approach

We have learned that to make the AcE model work on the ground, there needs to be a high level of flexibility. For example through trial and error, staff have found that using the whole range of the AcE indicators at the same time, to make an assessment of the child's learning, can be overwhelming for families who are already in a vulnerable position. The decision was taken to create more manageable 'bite sized chunks' for groups, families and staff. By identifying one or two indicators through discussion with the parents, incorporating observations of the children and taking into account the felt needs of the parents meant that all concerned were able to engage in conversations about children's learning in a new way. One staff member commented, 'It has been important for us working with individual families, because they are all so different. The fact that we have been able to use AcE flexibly means we can tailor it to every family we work with.' A family support worker also noted,

> When a family has a child with additional needs, they may have a lot of professionals working with them with loads of different assessments. Being able to discuss AcE and pick just a few indicators has stopped people feeling overwhelmed.

Whilst aiming to remain true to the principles of our beliefs about children and their learning, we have found it has also been necessary to classify the outcomes indicated on the Likhert scales so that staff and others can be clear about what the data generated means. Senior staff have chosen to classify children who achieve:

- Rarely – At serious risk of delay
- Sometimes – At risk of delay
- Often – Within expected development
- Consistently – Ahead of expected development.

There are problems with this as many young children may well be achieving at the level of 'Rarely' across the board. However, the expectation is that there is movement or progress in their achievement, rather than the child reaching a defined level of developmental outcome. There is also a philosophical issue as many staff find this labelling of such young children challenging. Being flexible has meant that a pragmatic view has needed to be taken. The benefit of using the AcE programme has been weighed against the consequences of this type of categorisation. Despite these reservations, it is agreed that assessing and evaluating children's learning in this way has given the service an evidence based model which has fundamental ethical principles at its core, a professional language for staff and clear positive steps for parents to support their children's learning. In addition, the ability of the service to track children's learning and generate robust data which clearly records the impact of the service far outweighs this problem.

The dynamic nature of children's learning.

Developing this new participatory way of thinking about children's learning has highlighted the fact that children's learning is not static, that children learn in different ways and that both individuals and groups experience learning journeys. Parents and staff are also part of this dynamic. Whilst most early years staff would know this, it has become very visible through the programme. Service delivery is never boring or repetitive but it does require staff to have the skills and confidence to respond to each new situation. This may mean re-modelling the learning environment or the delivery of a group according to the emerging learning needs of the children and parents. This has at times presented a huge challenge to staff at all levels.

We are now more aware that senior staff have to remain alert, and responsive to the changing relationships within a living structure, to ensure the closely held values and principles remain central to service delivery. The practitioners who work daily with families need to have opportunities to reflect on their practice and also remain flexible within a developing continuum.

The challenge of changing the way we see things

One of the significant challenges that has faced the senior team was the need to change the way staff understand children's learning in order to implement this participatory style of assessment. To be most effective, staff needed to view children and their parents as equal partners. This is a world view, a way of doing things rather than a set of assessment criteria with boxes that can be ticked. Change can be challenging and because of the evolving nature of the learning and assessment process, which is based on relationship with parents and children, it can sometimes feel too loose, never ending and subject to various possibilities. Therefore staff need to feel confident in their abilities, and it has become important to ensure that they are provided with monthly practice supervision to talk about children's learning and how they are making assessments with parents in a variety of situations.

Being able to make assessments that are rigorous

Learning how to ensure that the assessments are rigorous has been vital in this process. The team have found that both parents and staff working closely with children, either in a family support role or as a key person, are keen for the children to be represented in the best possible light. This initially proved to be a barrier to making realistic and authentic assessments which were useful in identifying next steps of learning. In order to address this staff have spent time considering the concepts of *Rarely, Sometimes, Often, Consistently* used in the assessment process so they are more confident in making judgements and more able to present these to parents.

Inclusive of children with special educational needs and disability

One of the strengths of using the AcE programme has been the positive impact when working with parents of children who have additional needs. Often when these children are assessed using other methods, little progress is seen. Parents are faced with endless professionals telling them all the things their child is unable to do or may never be able to do. We have found that by using the AcE indicators it is possible for children's development and learning to be captured and recorded in a positive way. Take, for example, a profoundly deaf child who remained in an extremely passive state, not only unable to make contact with his peers but showing no drive to do so either. At each 'Team Around the Child' meeting, his parents were told about how he had made no gains in development by the many other professionals involved. By using the AcE programme, the nursery was able to support this child as he learned to become aware of his peers and eventually would go up to them and tap them to gain their attention. By the time he moved into school, he was chasing around the garden with his peers, banging on windows to catch their attention and waving to recognisable members of staff. By making clear concise assessments, planning for his needs, considering the environment and offering intense family support, Children Centre services we were able to evidence his learning in a manner other forms of assessment failed to do.

Ofsted (Office for Standards in Education)

Since 2010, the Children Centre service has been visited for inspection by Ofsted five times. It has been our experience that each Ofsted inspector understands and appreciates the method of assessment and evaluation of children's learning that has been adopted throughout the service.

Our experience has reinforced our strong belief that the AcE programme elicits robust data and enables staff to not only track individual children's learning and attainment, but allows a critical analysis of that data which can easily be translated into strategic and service delivery planning. Patterns of behaviour can be identified and the corporate learning of larger groups of children can be understood and developed. Importantly, it also is an authentic experience for both children and parents of their rights within an assessment process which enhances their capacity to self-assess and evaluate their own lifelong learning journeys. The ethical approach is very much appreciated by all involved.

At a recent core group a parent commented, 'If it wasn't for the Children Centre, I definitely wouldn't have achieved all that I have with my children'. Another parent said, 'It's not until you start looking at things like this, it really makes you think about what you do at home and how children learn'.

References

Baker, C. and Wong, D. (1987) Q.U.E.S.T. A process of pain assessment in children, *Orthopaedic Nursing*, 6(1): 11–21.

Bertram, T., Pascal, C. and Saunders M. (2008) *Accounting Early for Life Long Learning (AcE), A Handbook for Assessing Young Children,* Amber Publishing, Birmingham.

Child Poverty Strategy (2014) *UK Government Child Poverty Strategy 2014–17*. Presented to Parliament by the Secretary of State for Work and Pensions pursuant to section 9 of the Child Poverty Act 2010, June 2014, HMSO, London.

14

CASE STUDY 7

A participatory model of assessment across a network of children's centres

Elizabeth Fee and Christine Pascal

The case study examines the challenges and benefits for children, parents, practitioners, settings and local authorities of using a participatory child assessment programme for children from birth to three years within a large city in the south-west region of England. It demonstrates how the Accounting Early for Lifelong Learning (AcE) Programme (Bertram, Pascal and Saunders, 2008) was implemented as an authority wide assessment process as part of the city-wide focus on improving child outcomes for all its children and evidencing this progress. The assessment process has enabled a significant shift in the involvement of parents in their children's learning and is also making progress in ensuring the active voice of the child in the assessment outcomes. This case study also shows how the data from this participatory assessment programme is being used to inform the city's wider strategic planning process for improving child outcomes within its wider range of early years' settings. It demonstrates that ethically robust, participatory assessment processes are capable of supporting significant shifts in the quality of practice offered in early childhood settings and have the capacity to evidence this across a large city in a way that informs strategic planning and development.

Pedagogical and cultural location of assessment and evaluation work

This case study is located in a large city in the southwest of England. The city council has a proud history of investment in developing and sustaining high quality early years provision which is recognised nationally and internationally. The Early Years Service's commitment to introduce an assessment for children from birth to three, in 2012, was underpinned by a strong aspiration to improve the quality of early education and childcare provision for the youngest children using an assessment process that provides consistent, reliable and valid information about children's progress which can be shared with parents/carers, the local authority and external agencies. The city's early years values and principles are rooted in equity, empowerment, positivity and authenticity. Early years (EY) leaders have worked hard to promote a shared understanding, amongst the early years community, that assessment is a dynamic process that reflects the child's context and is collaborative, involving practitioners, parents/carers and relevant external agencies, with the child at the heart. Above all, the city's cultural and racial diversity should be reflected in an assessment that is inclusive, embracing personal history and heritage and a celebration of the unique child. Margaret Carr's (2002) words regarding assessment resonate closely with the city council's aspiration that, 'the child has ownership of the assessments; it (the assessment process) encourages reflection, analysis and interpretation, it follows unscripted pathways'.

Catalysts for the introduction of a birth to three assessment process were the emerging national policy drivers in 2012. Key innovations proposed by the Department for Education (DfE) included the extension of Free Early Education Entitlement (FEEE) funding for 40 per cent of the most disadvantaged two-year-olds; the government's intention to introduce an integrated progress check for all children aged between 24 and 36 months in 2015; and the strong incentives offered to families to take up childcare so that more women can return to work. The rapidly changing demographic context in the city also influenced decisions regarding assessment practice. The city has experienced an unprecedented period of population growth and demographic change over the last decade. The increase in the number of under-fives in the city (35 per cent) is one of the highest in the country with an increase of more than 1,000 children in each single year of age. The city now has more children than at any time in the last 30 years; the number of children aged five and under is now approximately 30,700.

In addition, the population of the city has become increasingly diverse and some local communities have changed significantly. The proportion of the city's population who are not 'White British' has increased from 12 per cent to 22 per cent over the last ten years. The percentage of births to mothers who were not themselves born in the UK has increased from 16 per cent to 28 per cent in ten years, with the greatest increase in the number of births to Somalia-born mothers. One in four children (24.9 per cent) lives in low income families compared to a national average of 1 in 5.

In planning an assessment programme for the youngest children, the early years team carefully considered the needs of practitioners across the city's diverse range of early years provision. This includes 12 nursery schools of which 11 are now integrated into children's centres, 24 children's centres, 42 nursery classes attached to schools, 99 reception classes in LA maintained schools and academies, 114 voluntary playgroups, independent settings and private day-nurseries and approximately 439 childminders. The qualifications of practitioners are variable across the different types of provision. The city has a high level of graduates in early years settings, most are in children's centres, maintained and independent schools. Over the past ten years the government's steady investment in EY qualifications training has increased the number of graduates in playgroup and day care nursery provision, where currently the highest statutory requirement is for level 3 qualified practitioners. The city council has strongly promoted and supported practitioners to gain higher qualifications and currently approximately 70 per cent of settings have a graduate leader but there are still many private and voluntary early years settings with only one graduate which, particularly in larger settings, limits their capacity to impact on quality improvement.

A key determinant in the city council's choice of a birth to three assessment programme was to support practitioners to develop a reflective learning culture which genuinely promotes children's deep-level learning and their creative and critical learning dispositions. The assessment had to support the development of practitioners' pedagogic knowledge, skills and understanding, as well as providing a principled approach to monitoring children's progress.

Despite the government's severe budget reductions in recent years, the city council has maintained a clear focus on improving the outcomes for the youngest children and their families, recognising the moral imperative of early intervention on educational attainment, social cohesion, and on the economic and emotional well-being of the city's communities. Innovative and progressive early years strategic decisions were made to secure high quality provision universally with an increased focus on targeted provision for children and families that need it most. This has been achieved in the context of a developing national education strategy for system leadership in schools whereby quality improvement of provision and practice is led by the schools and early years providers themselves.

The city council's decision to maintain a thriving network of 24 children's centres, 11 of which are integrated with nursery schools, 12 with primary schools and 1 which is managed by a small local voluntary organisation, has secured the quality of early education at a good level, enabling positive engagement with families and strong capacity for leadership of learning across the whole of the city's early years provision including leadership of an assessment process for those children under three years of age (U3s).

The city council was faced with an additional significant challenge to develop 2,400 good quality places to meet the government's policy for early education funding for 40 per cent of the most disadvantaged two-year-olds by 2014. It was this context that prompted the introduction of an assessment process which has a three-fold purpose, namely to:

• measure the progress of funded two-year-olds using a programme which reflects the city's values and principles;
• ensure that the assessment process adds value to the quality of a child's learning and development and includes his/her family's participation in the assessment process;
• support practitioners in their own learning journeys as they develop a deeper understanding of how children learn and acquire the skills of making reliable and valid assessment.

Assessment and evaluation praxis: introduction of the Accounting Early for Lifelong Learning (AcE) Programme

The city's EY team is committed to an assessment process which is underpinned by a value base and principles which reflect the city's quality improvement strategy and journey. In previous years, the EY Service had involved early years settings in small scale assessment projects using Effective Early Learning (EEL) and Baby Effective Early Learning (BEEL), assessment programmes developed by Professors Christine Pascal and Tony Bertram at the Centre for Research in Early Childhood (CREC) (Bertram and Pascal, 2004, 2006).

Furthermore, for almost 20 years the city's quality assurance process has included the use of the 'City Standard', a framework which enables practitioners to reflect on their provision and practice using ten dimensions of quality to self-evaluate and identify improvement priorities. Professors Pascal and Bertram gave permission for the city council to adopt the ten dimensions of quality, which underpin the EEL assessment programme. Our sustained connections with the CREC team and our knowledge and respect for the team's research work contributed to the decision to implement CREC's Accounting Early for Lifelong Learning (AcE) Programme (Bertram, Pascal and Saunders, 2008). AcE meets the city's priority for an ethically based U3s assessment process that emphasises the development of children's skills for lifelong and life-wide learning.

The AcE programme introduces a strategy for the systematic recording of evidence on the progress of children's development and well-being. It offers a manageable but rigorous means of assessing children on entry to provision and tracking their progress through the statutory (DfE, 2014) Early Years Foundation Stage (EYFS). The programme and its assessment scales were developed with and for practitioners and parents to provide evidence of outcomes for children and to support planning for effective EYFS practice, both within the setting and the home. The AcE programme grew out of a national research project which was designed to support the planning and assessment of young children's development initially in two key areas of learning; Personal, Social and Emotional Development (PSED) and in Communication, Language and Literacy (CLL). The city council worked with CREC to develop assessment indicators for Physical Development (PD) thus including all three prime areas of the revised Early Years Foundation Stage requirements (2012). The programme sets out practical strategies to rigorously assess PSED, CLL and PD development in children from birth to five years old.

The AcE programme has the following features:

- It combines assessment of children's well-being (social/emotional) and cognitive (language and dispositions) and physical development.
- It provides assessment which is formative (assessment for learning) and summative (assessment of learning).
- The process is both diagnostic and evaluative.
- It is based on a collaborative and informed dialogue between practitioners, parents and children about the learning and development of unique children.

• The data generated provides a developmental profile of the child which is built collaboratively over time.

The Early Years Service implementation strategy and methodology

During 2011/2012 the Early Years Service funded an AcE pilot project involving three children's centres. The pilot began with a three-day AcE course, commissioned from the CREC team, and targeted at lead teachers and the practitioners responsible for leading the U3s provision. Members of the early years team also attended the course to enable high quality support as AcE assessment was introduced to more settings. The AcE course was followed by an extended process of setting based implementation of the strategies and actions introduced during the training. Each term, the pilot centres attended a support session led by a CREC mentor (six sessions in total).

A key factor in the pilot's success was the regular meetings of the pilot group to discuss progress and share implementation strategies. The group quickly recognised that it was crucial to establish a strong infrastructure of support for future AcE leaders in settings to secure consistent and embedded practice which adhered to AcE principles and methodology. The pilot settings also trialled CREC's AcE data management system but found it did not meet their information needs, so discussions began with the city's EY data officer to upgrade the system taking account of the pilot settings' findings.

An AcE steering group was established comprising the children's centre lead teachers, EY Consultant team members and the data officer who took a significant role in developing a city AcE data management system. The steering group planned the next phase of development and the lead teachers agreed to act as mentors to newly trained settings during their AcE implementation stage. The lead teachers and local authority officers were given further training from CREC to enable them to facilitate the three-day training. This group has continued to meet regularly to share information about settings that are doing well and others who are in need of support. This is primarily worked out by feedback from the AcE mentors who visit the settings as well as the city's Performance, Information and Intelligence team who collect and analyse AcE data from all the participating settings.

In 2012, lead teachers and U3s room leaders from 13 children's centres formed the first AcE cohort to be led by the pilot project lead teachers and local authority officers. Their training costs and AcE training materials were funded by the local authority. Centres funded their own supply cover costs. A key finding from the pilot was the importance of strategic planning for effective AcE implementation following the three-day training. The course included time for action planning, detailing when and how the assessment programme will be introduced to the setting's wider team and how the process will be carried out by all practitioners who care for two-year-olds, working collaboratively with parents/carers and children.

Mentor support visits to settings clearly showed that purposeful leadership was crucial to engendering a strong sense of collective responsibility in the setting for monitoring children's learning and development and encouraging active partici- patory practice. Importantly, where headteachers and managers were supportive of the assessment programme and enabled their lead teacher or practitioner to implement AcE, there was greater commitment from the whole staff and as time went on for deeper understanding of the assessment process and its impact on teaching and learning. The following extract from a setting's annual AcE review report describes how an AcE lead practitioner supported practitioners to fully understand the AcE domains and indicators.

> During this year I ensured there was moderation and discussion of AcE, but I became slowly aware of several strands that were inhibiting the pace of change. The first was that whilst the practitioners were familiar with the language used in the AcE tool, it was still not apparently being used in their observations. Our stated aim was, that while we might not be able to use AcE with all observations we made of a child, every observation should be good enough to use with AcE. Some of the observations were still too short, or contained information that was subjective ('He enjoyed playing in the water area'), or of a very superficial level. This opened a whole debate amongst staff as to what was a 'short observation', 'long observation' or a 'learning story'. The arguments and justifications of different styles and ways of making observations seemed at first to be slowing the forward momentum of embedding AcE. However, reflecting on this after a year it was a slow, but wholly necessary step. The difference in staff understanding and their pedagogy was enhanced by this process and the subtle, but profound shift in their working methods show this, as they now produce observations that are fewer in number, but higher in quality.

In the next two years, a further three AcE training programmes took place involving more children's centres and private and voluntary settings caring for funded two-year-olds. By the end of 2014, 70 settings and 170 practitioners had attended the training. Many of the children's centres and private and voluntary settings requested additional training places for staff to promote stronger dissemination of the AcE assessment process building capacity to embed the principles more securely in practice. The steering group mentors noted that most early years settings needed at least six months to introduce AcE to the team and to begin to make AcE observations and collect data. Setting leaders arranged regular staff meetings to discuss and agree consistent interpretations of the AcE indicators.

The following description from an annual AcE review report of the early implementation phase of AcE by a senior leader in a children's centre is typical of a process through which practitioners pass to fully understand the possibilities of the assessment.

My initial impression of AcE was how the overall observation form could be seen in two different ways: in one it is a good way of focussing the observer so they could 'see' the skills possessed by the child, and in another it became a reflective tool that can be used for consideration when planning or discussing learning in more general terms. The simplicity of the tool is beguiling; while a practitioner who knows AcE and their child well enough can make a very accurate assessment in a very short amount of time, it is also possible to have an entire moderation session with a large team of practitioners spending an hour discussing what 'connectedness' or 'self worth' really look like, and why they are vital for lifelong learning opportunities. This flexibility of AcE is very apparent and avoids superficial snapshots of children's learning. The apparent simplicity of the AcE observation tool belies its depth and breadth as a way to not just observe and assess children, but to strengthen an underlying ethos of a setting and drive forwards practitioner knowledge.

As settings became familiar with the indicators and began to share their observations with parents they reported that discussions with parents were more meaningful, informative and celebratory of the child's progress and their own understanding of a child's learning and development was deeper and more highly attuned to individual needs.

During this intensive period of AcE implementation in settings the local authority Information and Data team continued to refine the AcE management system as participating practitioners made suggestions for improving the data collection and presentation. The city now collects AcE data for approximately 900 children. Figure 14.1 provides an example of city-wide data analysis and its visual presentation.

AcE settings return their data to the local authority Performance, Information and Intelligence team three times a year in October, February and July by a given date. The AcE observations that practitioners make from day to day inform the summative judgements that they record as a score on the AcE management system. The data officer has dedicated 'AcE time' to collate, process and present the information. The data is then returned to settings and a network meeting is held to help settings to interpret their data, to answer their queries and to take feedback on how the AcE management system can be improved.

The use of the AcE data is still variable across the city as some of the settings are inexperienced in analysing data. However, in some settings data analysis has had a powerful impact, especially in supporting practitioners' communications with parents about their children's progress. The sharing of progress data has helped to build relationships and partnership in children's learning and development. By exploring the data practitioners are developing an understanding of looking at data for individuals, cohorts, free school meals, gender and ethnic groups. For example, one setting was surprised to find a wide gender difference in children's outcomes and used the AcE data to monitor and evaluate their interactions, resources, indoor and outdoor provision to improve boys' progress.

As part of the strategy for implementing the use of the AcE assessment tool across the city there was an investment in AcE mentors and AcE moderation groups. Strong settings from the first AcE cohort facilitated these moderation meetings. Hargreaves describes this emerging joint professional development model as,

> less about attending conferences and courses and more about school-based, peer-to-peer activities in which development is fused with routine practice. Professional development becomes a continuous, pervasive process that builds craft knowledge, rather than an occasional activity that is sharply distinguished in time and space from routine classroom work.
>
> (Hargreaves, 2012, p. 8)

He refers to this form of professional development as 'building social capital'. Although the sessions were advertised as moderation, initially they were used more like group supervision or coaching, where issues and difficulties were raised and others' experiences or materials were then shared to enable the group as a whole to learn and grow.

One of the frequently cited issues in network meetings was that of engaging parents in the AcE process in a meaningful and sensitive way. Two children's centres (StA and CP) worked hard to develop a set of materials aimed at parents, which they shared with the rest of the network. This 'social capital building' of sharing strengthens the trust and relationships that are necessary for networks to grow and prosper. Parental leaflets that were initially developed by SW Nursery and Children's Centre were used in other settings, and in return others developed posters and additional materials to engage parents in the AcE assessment process.

The following extract from an annual AcE review report from KW Nursery School and Children's Centre illustrates the challenge of enabling genuine parent partnership.

> The real breakthrough occurred as practitioners took on the ideas of the Pen Green Loop. In the two-year-old room each key person had a poster outside the room where they asked parents what the children had been doing at home or at the weekend. The response at first was poor and the practitioners reflected that writing on a wall was maybe not the most natural way of writing, and they also considered that levels of literacy also had a big effect on some parents' participation. The fact that the feedback was in written form also excluded the children from this process. However, slowly there was an increased amount of writing on each of these posters, and the practitioners themselves added things they had done outside of the centre. Other practitioners laminated learning stories for all parents to read, and they also made a 'book' about each of their key children illustrating their families and

(a)

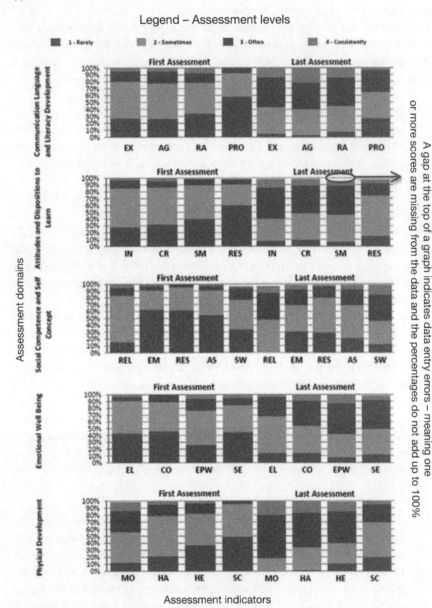

FIGURE 14.1 AcE data analysis and visual presentation

(b)

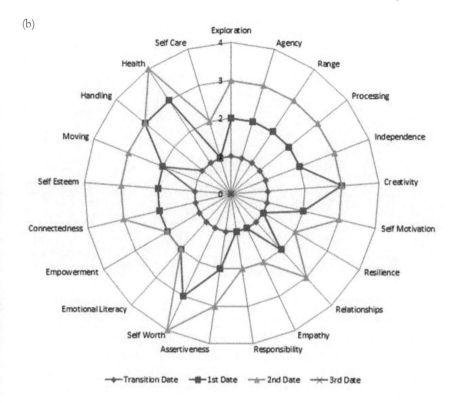

FIGURE 14.1 *continued*

Notes for Figures 14.1 (a) and (b)

(a) These graphs are showing the same group of children and the percentage of the group who are at each level at their first assessment and at their last assessment. Each child will have had at least two and up to three assessments over the period of an academic year. A small number will have been assessed using AcE in the last academic year and we are comparing their progress from this point. The graphs show the distance travelled at a glance visually. For example in the block diagram, under the Physical Development domain along the bottom line of boxes, the SC (Self-care) indicator shows the percentage of the group assessed as 'Rarely'(coloured red) starts at nearly 50% of all children assessed and reduces to 20% in the Last Assessment of SC on the extreme right. You can also see that initially at First Assessment, no children in the group were scored at 'Consistently' (coloured blue) whereas at the Last Assessment around 5% had this reached this level.

(b) This second graph visually displays another individualised form of 'distance travelled'. This distance travelled graph is used to show individual children's progress and can be used in review meetings with parents. It is another helpful visual representation of distance travelled which also tells a story about the child's journey. All the AcE indicators are on each 'spoke' of the circle, assessment levels are indicated by the different sized circles and each assessment date is indicated by the different line colours and marker shapes. You can see that this child was assessed last year so has a 'Transition' assessment date (the inner blue line) – this would have been their last assessment scores in the previous academic year. Their first assessment in the current academic year is shown by the red line and their second assessment is shown by the green line. You can see that this child has made improvements in every area as the coloured 'web' lines get larger and larger.

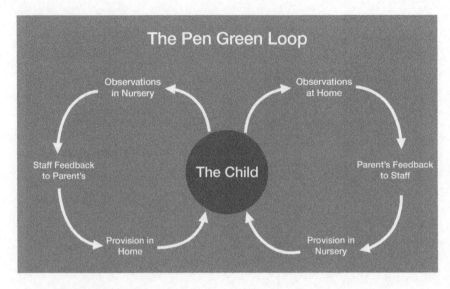

FIGURE 14.2 The Pen Green loop

their interests. Each room had a display board containing photos and a summary of children's interests that week and included language from the EYFS and AcE in order to make learning visible. These weekly updated displays were popular amongst the parents and created a buzz of interest when they were changed each week.

Carrying on the idea of the Pen Green Loop (Pen Green, 2007; see Figure 14.2) to its natural conclusion and ensuring nursery staff create opportunities for parents to initiate and sustain an ongoing, open dialogue, staff in the three-year-old room used video to capture observations of children and used these as the basis of the parent meetings. Several of these meetings were videoed as part of our whole centre research question around problem solving. What was immediately noticeable was that the balance of dialogue between parent and practitioner was nearly equal and the comments being made were more reminiscent of a dialogue than of merely passing on information.

The use of video had been revolutionary and had happened over a very short space of time. Parents, practitioners and children enjoyed watching and sharing these clips and what was noticeable was the way in which it brought the child to the centre, with parents and practitioners commenting and reflecting on what they had seen. This democratic process gave ownership of the learning back to the family with the practitioner as facilitator of learning rather than a keeper of learning. The need to provide genuinely meaningful information has improved practitioners' knowledge and skills but more importantly has involved parents much more directly with their child's lifelong learning skills. Whether this is video clips, posters for parents to add to outside the room, learning stories in the corridors or just more regular, meaningful verbal exchanges, the result has been the same: a greater understanding of how life is full of potential learning experiences.

Principles into practice

The following learning stories of three children involved in the AcE programme at KW Nursery School and Children's Centre and FA Nursery School and Children's Centre provide profiles of their competencies at the beginning of the programme, and how work with parents and children helped assess and develop children's PSED, CL and PD competencies, and evaluate the impact for parents and children. The first case study illustrates the principles that 'assessment and evaluation should take into account children's holistic learning' and 'assessment and evaluation should contribute to the identification of children's needs, purposes and voices, that is, individualising education'. The keyworker's sensitivity to the child's family context and physical development was central to the effectiveness of the assessment and evaluation process.

Case study 1

LB is three years and nine months at the time of this narrative and has been at KW Children's Centre since November 2012. She has two older brothers (five years old and eight years old) and one younger brother (a one-year-old) as well as three half siblings (who are all considerably older than LB). Her father has contact with her but does not live in the family home. Her mother is profoundly deaf and has moved to this part of the city, away from her own extended family of seven sisters, and has told us that she feels quite isolated and lonely. There have been health concerns raised by her mother, as LB was gaining weight rapidly as a baby. The health visitors have monitored her diet and exercise and she has been referred to regular appointments to monitor her weight gain and investigate the cause.

She arrived during our pilot year of working with AcE, and it was evident that given her complicated family life that both LB and her mother needed as much support as we could give her. We always pay particular care with our home visits, but even more so if we suspect a child or family are vulnerable and we believe that 'home visits help to break down stereotypes as practitioners gain knowledge about varied family practices, cultures and histories' (Wheeler and Connor, 2006, p. 108). Her keyworker was one of our most experienced and the fact that she had also worked with the family previously and was a 'local' was welcomed by mum and as stated, 'parents are less likely . . . to feel comfortable and develop trust in a setting that makes little attempt to reflect their background or represent difference in the make-up of its staff' (Wheeler and Connor, 2006, p. 78).

LB's keyworker was very sensitive to both mum's deafness and her socio-cultural background so she was never patronised but it was important that communication had to be made accessible. 'The language used should be free of jargon, acronyms or phrases that may seem ambiguous . . . for example, parents may not consider a child who is deaf to have a "hearing impairment", but may refer to the child's "deafness" instead' (Brodie, 2013, p. 114). This was helped with the use of text messaging which was mum's preferred way of communication, because even though her lip reading was very good: 'Communication should be considered from various points of view . . . the tone of what is said can alter the perception of the listener' (Siraj-Blatchford et al., 2009, p. 164).

LB presented as a quiet and wary child but one who was attentive and keen to watch other adults and children. Her overall assessment needed to be seen as a child who lived with a deaf mother and who tuned into non-verbal communication and although she did not fulfil the requirements of the EYFS assessment criteria in CLL, she had some very interesting assessments in AcE which showed much stronger levels of communication. This was also in line with mum's assessment of LB who knew that her comprehension was very strong as she herself was tuned in to this way of communicating. Carr states that 'parents' perceptions of their children's ability and effort predict children's self-concepts of ability and perceptions of task difficulty' (Carr, 2002, p. 141) and even though LB spent nearly a year producing no language, when she did it was easily in line with her EYFS age and stage as well as showing a child who was 'consistently' showing language range and agency in her AcE assessments.

Working with vulnerable children and families can be a very delicate and subtle act. The relationship is key, especially where parents have had negative experiences of other organisations and institutions as was the case with LB's family. As Bruce stated, 'educators who look below the surface of what parents/carers are saying can find a shared basis for work on which trust can be built' (Bruce, 2005, p. 177). LB's keyworker quite openly discussed LB's weight and how difficult it was for her to do many of the activities in our very outdoor driven setting and curriculum. Because mum knew we were working with health professionals and were trying to help LB rather than criticise her parenting she also helped encourage LB to be as physically active as she could be at home. Mum brought her along to additional 'Gym Tots' exercise classes and the whole team were encouraging towards LB. As Bilton observed: 'there is strong evidence to suggest that it is the quality of physical activity that has a lasting impact: when students leave school with positive attitudes towards . . . their own ability, they are more likely to be physically active as adults' (Bilton, 1998, p. 24).

By the end of the year, her physical attainment in PD (Physical Development) in the EYFS was just within her age and stage according to Development Matters, and her AcE 'Moving' and 'Self-Care' went from 'sometimes' to 'often' over the course of the year. Although she was still on a high percentile of weight, she had lost some overall, and more importantly had developed new skills and a growing self-confidence. (Self Motivation: 'sometimes' to 'consistently', Resilience: 'rarely' to 'often' and Empowerment: 'sometimes' to 'consistently'). LB had made very good progress whether using the EYFS or AcE assessment tool, but AcE also showed she was still only 'sometimes' for Connectedness and Positive Self-Esteem. This was shared with mum and we discussed why this might be, producing more discussion and insight into her home life which we could use to signpost mum to some relevant services which she could access.

Summary of AcE assessment:

- LB had made solid progress in all of her CLLD skills, particularly Language Range and Language Processing as she had started off her year being selectively mute, but finished the year being a language producer.
- Attitudes and Dispositions to Learn showed very good progress, mostly towards 'often'.
- Social Competence and Self-Concept were either 'often' or 'consistently', showing LB's very strong sense of empathy and forming effective relationships.
- Emotional Well-being was the one area where LB's skills were not as developed, as discussed above, and probably an area that would be 'masked' in the future by her other well-developed social competencies.
- Physical Development, as discussed above, was 'often' by the end of the year.

Case study 2

The second case study from KW Nursery School and Children's Centre illustrates the principle that 'assessment and evaluation can be supportive of learning journeys both for children and professionals' that is, it needs to be *praxeologically oriented*.

OW is two years and six months at the time of this narrative and has been in the Children's Centre since January 2014. He had a typical transition into the centre, in that he had a home visit and then his settling visits with no anxiety from child or family. His keyworker is relatively new to our centre and had recently received a promotion from one level of pay and responsibility to another. This has been a good challenge for her as she has taken on more key children and there was a greater expectation of her skills.

Her first few observations of OW were shorter observations and contained photographs as well as text and she made sure she showed the learning diary to his parents regularly. The keyworker here used the learning diary *as 'a catalyst for discussion and a record of dialogue'* (Carr, 2002, p. 134) and this was evident in the first parent meeting feedback where it was reported: 'O is doing really well at the centre, he had a little phase of hitting us, but his behaviour has changed and he's much better. O loves nursery!' The conversations between the keyworker and the parents had relieved their anxiety about his behaviour, which the parents saw as alarming, but which the keyworker put in context of a child's normal stages of development and showed them evidence that his AcE observations, and that his effective relationship overall was 'often' when it came to these skills.

It was interesting that the parents' other comment was that 'The centre is fabulous and I'm really pleased at how they help with O's development' as they have purposefully used the word 'development' as Bruce states, 'teachers need to share what they know about child development and curriculum provision, rather than to guard their knowledge' (Bruce, 2005, p.1 77). The parents were very happy to discuss aspects of language, personal and social development and physical development, and the keyworker reported that it was easy to explain areas in which OW was very secure and other aspects of his development that needed some further strengthening. As Siraj-Blatchford et al. reported: 'our findings suggest that where staff shared educational aims with parents, and encouraged pedagogic efforts at home, good child outcomes were established' (Siraj-Blatchford et al., 2009, p. 7). This is very clear in the AcE assessments which show OW moving from 'sometimes' and 'usually' to 'usually' and 'consistently' in the space of six months.

His keyworker reported at the end of his settling period that:

> O has settled into nursery really well, he explores the whole environment and will access resources independently. He has a lovely curiosity and interest in most things. He is confident to approach adults and will join in with his peers. His communication with speech and language is excellent.

She has specifically used AcE language with the report which shows an understanding of the need to communicate effectively with parents, but maybe words like 'peers' and 'environment' could be further clarified so that language does not get in the way of true communication.

The observations of OW became more detailed and more of them were learning stories as the time went on. This was partly due to OW and the keyworker building a closer relationship but also through supportive observations by colleagues and team leaders in the room. His particular interest in the mud was one of the starting points for the development of a 'mud kitchen' and this interest was shared in a relaxed and humorous way as practitioners and parents swapped stories of how OW was often seen to be covered from head to toe in mess whilst at the same time valuing the learning opportunity inherent in this.

His keyworker's feedback to parents, four months later, concluded:

> O has made great progress in EY2. He loves to explore the outside garden and loves getting wet and muddy. He shows interest, care and concern for living things. He loves books and will always join in with singing and actions at circle time.

She also stated: 'His next steps are support in forming new effective relationships.' As AcE had been shared with the parents so successfully, the next steps were understood to mean even better, stronger relationships with a wider variety of adults and children.

The response from the second parent meeting was that: 'O enjoys coming to Nursery every morning and we (mum and dad) are pleased with the progress he has been making.' They also reported that: 'I think the Centre is wonderful and the workers and O's care worker do a lovely job. My son is very happy here!!! . . . a very welcoming atmosphere and all staff are pleasant and happy.' In conclusion, using AcE enabled the relationship between keyworker, child and family to be strong and trusting with a totally transparent understanding of OW's learning and development and how his skills are preparing him for life in the rest of his education and then life beyond. His keyworker has shown a high level of impact and 'put simply, we learn by communing with and connecting to others. The Communicator might just as easily be named the Connector' (Rose and Rogers, 2012, p. 51). The keyworker, child and family have been shown to have this deep connection which has been shown to have made a measurable difference.

Summary of AcE assessment:

- OW showed marked improvements in CLLD and by the end of his year he was 'consistently' in all areas apart from Language Processing.
- Attitudes and Dispositions to Learn were again 'consistently' in evidence.
- Social Competence and Self-Concept went from 'rarely' and 'sometimes' to more 'often' in line with his parent and keyworker's discussion of Effective Relationships.
- Emotional Well-being was 'often' or 'consistently' across the indicators.
- Physical Development was deemed to be 'consistently'.

Case study 3

The third case study from FA Nursery and Children's Centre reflects the principle that 'assessment and evaluation should be contextualised and situated, that is, should be ecological'. The learning and development of the child in the case study was compromised due to the child's social and emotional context. The case study illustrates how AcE assessment supported the skilled practitioners to meet the needs of the child and parent.

Child A started nursery provision in the two-year-old room funded by the local authority following an assessment of complex needs and global developmental delay. The child also displayed behavioural and emotional difficulties. Professional support from agencies had been inconsistent and uncoordinated. There were concerns around the child's home situation regarding parenting style and possible emotional abuse.

The child's AcE assessment on entry showed a varied picture but low scores on social competence and self-concept and on emotional well-being. Mid-year AcE scores across all domains went down or remained static. Staff awareness was raised at a team meeting around data causing concern. Attitudes and dispositions and emotional well-being scores had dropped. Physical development scores were also down while the scores for communication and social competence remained static.

The EY team felt that the area of most urgent concern was Child A's emotional well-being. Child A's behaviour had become more challenging and required considerable adult time and support to manage. Staff looked closely at the emotional well-being domain which showed that Child A's indicator of most concern was positive self-esteem. Empathy and assertiveness scores were mostly 'rarely'.

Improving Child A's emotional well-being was a priority in order to raise scores in these two indicators.

Concerns were discussed with mum and strategies were agreed to support Child A's emotional well-being at nursery. An Individual Education Plan (IEP) was agreed which centred on social interaction and emotional literacy e.g. naming feelings. Staff continued to liaise closely with professionals and mum who also worked with Child A's speech and language and occupational therapists.

Individual planning centred on improving Child A's self-care and positive self-image. A dressing-up area was created in nursery so that self-care and role play could be modelled by peers. A multi-disciplinary team meeting was arranged to reflect on help that could be provided for mum. The case was referred to social services to assess the home situation. A follow-up meeting which brought the professionals back together was a good opportunity to share positive outcomes.

A series of home visits which focused on improving Child A's self-esteem was put in place for the last two terms of the academic year. Mum worked collaboratively with professionals to improve outcomes for Child A and used strategies that were modelled to her.

In order to support transition from the two-year-old room to the pre-school class, strategies were put in place to support Child A's social competence. Child A moved across with a close friend from the two-year-old group. On transition Child A was scoring 'often' for emotional well-being. All exit scores were higher than the baseline. Child A's individual assessment had no 'rarely' scores on exit from the two-year-old group.

Reflections: what learned? Challenges and possibilities within the practice described

The city has made significant progress in implementing AcE assessment at a local authority level. Feedback from participating settings to the steering group and monitoring through mentor visits and regular network meetings indicates that practitioners are not only using the assessment with increasing confidence and reliability, they report that their understanding of children's learning and development has grown and the involvement of parents in children's learning has been transformed. Practitioners are delighted with the increasingly sophisticated analysis of AcE data they receive three times a year from the local authority Intelligence and Data Team and many settings are now using the information to drive their improvement agenda. The city cannot yet use the data to reliably monitor progress of two-year-old children at a local authority level as new settings continue to be introduced to AcE. However, data analysis takes place at an individual setting level to identify anomalies and additional support needs.

The local authority's strategic decision to initially introduce AcE to children's centres strengthened the implementation plan. As children's centre staff became familiar with AcE they supported the private and voluntary settings within their reach areas. Cross pollination of ideas and a collectivised way of organising resources can only happen when social capital is high and one of the fascinating aspects of AcE is how some private and voluntary nurseries have taken it on board. Some of the larger private chains have used AcE to streamline their two-year-old assessment across their different nurseries and what has been even more encouraging is the sense of cooperation and climate of sharing that goes on between different nursery companies despite many being in direct competition with each other. For some practitioners and managers, the AcE training and moderation meetings were the only times they had spoken to colleagues outside their settings, in what can be a very isolated working environment.

One of the most challenging aspects of implementing AcE is that it usually requires a cultural and professional shift in practice within a setting. Practitioners, using AcE in the manner in which it was intended, have to accept responsibility for their own actions and especially their interactions with the families of their key children. During the initial training, there was a strong focus on the critical and intrinsic partnership with parents and on practitioners' own role as change agents. Subsequent mentor visits and network meetings facilitated the exchange of effective strategies for dissemination of AcE in their settings and for promoting successful parent partnership.

In many settings, particularly in the private and voluntary sectors, parent partnership in AcE assessment is still an area for development. Practitioners cite the difficulty of finding time to meet with parents and working parents find it difficult to meet with practitioners. Practitioners are becoming more innovative in using electronic devices to communicate with parents but understand that this does not provide the opportunity for the rich dialogue that face-to-face meetings offer.

The shift in practice needed to create a participatory culture when implementing AcE is a continuous process that has varied in pace depending on the pedagogic understanding and leadership capacity in the setting. For the most part, this has been a smoother process in settings where there are more teachers or early years' graduates. Here, AcE systems and processes were embedded more quickly with all practitioners taking responsibility for AcE assessment. In some settings the leadership of AcE resides with one or two practitioners and the whole learning community is uncertain of its purpose and benefits. These settings receive more sustained support from the AcE mentors to promote a shared understanding of why they should use an assessment such as AcE and why there needs to be a shared goal with the parents and families of children involved in this process. Siraj-Blatchford et al. (2009, p.163) note that ultimately 'success depends on the willingness of staff to acknowledge parents' values and beliefs, as well as the staff's commitments to accept changes that may be necessary within themselves.'

The city's goal to introduce AcE assessment, in settings which care for the most socially and economically disadvantaged children under three, is almost fully implemented. The challenge now and in the future is to draw on the AcE expertise in settings that has grown over the last three years, to enable practitioners through ongoing mentoring to fully realise the potential of AcE. To this end the Early Years

Service has recently commissioned two children's centres to become AcE Hubs which have well-developed AcE practice and will be open to other settings to visit and observe AcE assessment in practice.

The city council's goal to introduce an ethically based assessment has now become a shared aim with the city's early years community. Together we aspire to firmly embed AcE in practice as a reliable and meaningful assessment and the vehicle for working in an equal and genuine partnership with parents to support children to become competent, self-motivated and resilient lifelong learners.

Acknowledgements

The authors gratefully acknowledge the contributions of: Matthew Caldwell, Knowle West Children's Centre; Elizabeth Williams, Filton Avenue Nursery School and Children's Centre; Jo Sloggett, Compass Point Children's Centre.

References

Bertram, T. and Pascal, C. (2004) *Effective Early Learning (EEL): A Handbook for Evaluating, Assuring and Improving Quality in Early Childhood Settings*, Birmingham, Amber Publishing.

Bertram, T. and Pascal, C. (2006) *Baby Effective Early Learning (BEEL), A Handbook for Evaluating, Assuring and Improving Quality in Settings for Birth to Three Year Olds*, Birmingham, Amber Publishing.

Bertram T., Pascal C. and Saunders M. (2008) *The Accounting Early for Lifelong Learning Programme*, Birmingham, Amber Publications and Training.

Bilton, H. (1998) *Outdoor Learning in the Early Years*, Oxford, David Fulton Publishers.

Brodie, K. (2013) *Observation, Assessment and Planning in the Early Years*, New York, McGraw Hill Education.

Bruce, T. (2005) *Early Childhood Education*, Oxford, Hodder Education.

Carr, M. (2002) *Assessment in Early Childhood Settings*, London, Paul Chapman Publishing.

DfE (2014) *Statutory Framework for the Early Years Foundation Stage (EYFS); Setting the Standards for Learning, Development and Care for Children from Birth to Five*. Published March 2014, Effective September 2014, UK Department for Education, London, HMSO.

Hargreaves, D. (2012) *A Self Improving School System: Towards Maturity*, Nottingham, National College for School Leadership.

Pen Green Research, Development and Training Base (2007) *Parents Involved in Their Children's Learning (PICL) Materials*. Corby: Pen Green.

Rose, J. and Rogers, S.(2012) *The Role of the Adult in Early Years Settings*, Maidenhead, Open University Press.

Siraj-Blatchford, I., Wheeler, H. and Connor, J. (2009) *Parents, Early Years and Learning*, London, National Children's Bureau.

Wheeler, H. and Connor, J. (2006) *Parents, Early Years and Learning*, London, National Children's Bureau.

INDEX

Note: Page numbers in **bold** are for figures, those in *italics* are for tables.

Aboud, F. 170
abstractness, and transmissive pedagogy 16, *17*, 97
accountability xxviii, 62–63, 140–141, 178
Accounting Early for Lifelong Learning (AcE) programme 60, 77, 84, 87; case studies 220–239, 240–258; data analysis and visual presentation **248**, *249*; Family Plans 234, **235**; flexible use of 236–237; Home Learning Plans **232**; learning indicators 223, 231, 236, 238; parental participation 230–239, 247, 250–256, 257; *see also* Children Centre service (England)
action plans 67, 70, **71**, 88, 89, **212**, 213, 214
action (praxis) 61, 64, 89
action research 182, 192, 193–202, *203*
Adult Engagement Scale 86, 89, 210, 213
Adult Styles 86
affordances, learning experiences as 59
Aga Khan Foundation Portugal 26–27
agency 29, 30, 98; of children 41, 45, 80, 111, 183; of teachers/professionals 45, 109
Andrade, H.H. 51n5
anthropology of education 94
applicationist view on assessment and evaluation 93–98; curricular dimension of 97; evaluative dimension of 97;

inadequacy of 98; organisational dimension of 97; pedagogical dimension of 97; and positivist paradigm 94–95, 98; as reductionism 95–98
Araújo, S. B. 8, 32, 33, 35, 43, 45, 49, 51n5, 63, 103, 116, 158, 169, 170, 182, 183, 288
artistic language 162
assertiveness 44, 223
assessment and evaluation 59–73; applicationist view on *see* applicationist view on assessment and evaluation; ethics *see* ethical principles for assessment and evaluation; focus of 68–70 (pedagogic context 68, 69, 83–85; pedagogic outcomes 69, 87–88; pedagogic processes 68, 69, 85–87); methods *see* methods of assessment and evaluation; nature of 66–67 (democratic approach 66–67, 134–135, 165; inclusionary approach 66, *99*; multiple perceptions and voices 66); process of 70–72 (action plan phase 70, **71**; engagement in 90; evaluation phase 70, **71**; improvement phase 71; reflection phase **71**, 72); purpose of 62–66 (knowledge generation 64–65; liberation and transformation 65–66)
Associação Criança see Childhood Association
attainment gap 220–221, *222*

attention 40; children's and teacher's joint 30; as element in active listening 79
attitudes and dispositions 87
attunement, pedagogical 168–180
audio records 77, 84
audit trail 90
autonomy 35, 45, 75, 86, 133
Azevedo, A. 48, 49, 113, 116, 136, 158, 188, 199

babies, as curious beings 111
Baby Effective Early Learning (BEEL) Programme 208, 209, 217, 218, 219, 243; Child Engagement Scale 85
Bachelard, G. 51n2
Bahktin, M.M. 81
Baker, C. 223
banking concept of education 12, 13, 144
Barnett, W.S. 66
behavioural psychology 95–96
being/feeling/thinking (pedagogical axis) 32–33, 38
beliefs 27, 131
belonging 33–34, 37, 38–39, 44, 112, 144, 169
Bennett, J. 21, 132, 134, 143
Berger, P.L. 109
Bertram, T. 21, 30, 41, 45, 59, 63, 64, 66, 69, 75, 77, 78, 83, 84, 85, 86, 87, 98, 104, 113, 124, 132, 140, 145, 163, 170, 182, 206, 220, 222, 240, 243
Bettelheim, B. 41
Biesta, G.J.J. 80
Bilton, H. 252
Blatchford, I. 158
body language, and active listening 79
bonds 39; pedagogy of 33
Bortoft, H. 100–101
Bourdieu, P. 45, 113
Bradbury, A. 145
Bradbury, H. 65, 82, 182
Brazil, curriculum 193; *see also* São Paulo
Brodie, K. 252
Bronfenbrenner, U. 41, 70, 101, 102, 117, 203
Bruce, T. 79, 252, 253
Bruner, J. 27, 36–37, 47, 51n4, 59, 112
bureaucratic management of education 6–8, 19
bureaucratic pedagogy 7

Campos, M.M. 193
care: and education, as dual system 19–20; provision 19, 20, 132, 133
Carr, M. 36, 113, 145, 241, 252, 253

Centre for Research in Early Childhood (CREC) 113, 213, 243, 244
The Child and the Curriculum (Dewey) 10, 11
Child Engagement Scale 85
Child Involvement Scale 85–86, 89, 210, 213, 217
Child Poverty Strategy 221
Child Tracking 83, 124, 163, 165, 210, 213, 215
child-centred pedagogy 11
child/children: agency of 41, 45, 80, 111, 183; as citizens 63–64, 79–80; and decision-making process 44; democratic participation 75, 79–80, 81; image of, in participatory pedagogies 110–111; involvement xxvi, 85–86, 89, 124, 135, 177, 178, 210, 213, 217; listening to 74–75, 79–81, 138; as observers 77; participation in own assessment 192, 194–205, 234; purposes of, harmonisation with educators' intentionalities 111–112; rights of 30, 41, 43, 63–64, 75, 80, 81, 82, 109–110, 133, 135, 179, 183; as socio-cultural beings 40–41; voice of 63, 75, 81, 134–135, 192–205, 234; well-being of 69, 86–87, 134, 136, 177, 178, 181–191
Childhood Association (*Associação Criança*) 26, 31, 51n1, 107, 113, 114, 142, 168, 183, 188
Children Centre service (England): AcE programme within 220–239, 240–258 (and after-school provision 231, 233; and children's groups 227, **228–229**; and family support 227; mentors 247; moderation groups 247; and parenting groups 231; and TA stay and play groups **225–226**; universal and targeted groups 224)
circle time 61
citizenship 63–64, 79–80
Clark, A. 63, 84
Clough, P. 23n1
co-construction: of knowledge 108, 109, 125, 139; of learning 48, 49–50, 59, 125, 184; of meaning 79, 125
Colasanto, C.A. 198, 199, 200, 201–202
collaboration xxviii, 35, 50, 67, 141
collaborative learning 15, 30–31, 35, 43, 44, 108
Common Assessment Framework (CAF) (England) 227
communication 35, 37, 39, 87, 109, 112, 144, 169

Communication, Language and Literacy (CLL) 245
communities of practice 64
companionship, learning in 30
complexity of educational process 107; applicationist perspective rejection of 94; holistic assessment/evaluation acknowledgement of 98–102; transmissive pedagogy minimisation of 96–97
compulsory education, development of 3
confirmability of assessment/evaluation findings 89, 90–91
conformity 34; and transmissive pedagogy 19
conjunction, principle of 102
connectedness 39, 85, 104
Connor, J. 251
conscientisation 183
consciousness raising 61
contextual approach xvii, 15, *16*, *18*, 19, 68, 69, 102, 118, 137, 178, 189, 255
contextual professional learning 114–116
contextualisation, absence of, and applicationist perspective 94
Copernican revolution in pedagogy 109, 139
Costa, H. 51n5, 183
Craveiro, M.C. 116
CREC (Centre for Research in Education) 113, 213, 243, 244
Crèche and Preschool Albano Coelho Lima 168
credibility of assessment/evaluation findings 89–90
critical self-evaluation 61
critical thinking 4
Csikszentmihalyi, M. 86
cultural capital 133, 134
cultural circles 84
cultural difference: respect for 183; transmissive pedagogy blindness to 8
cultural diversity: of public mass schools 8–9; respect for *17*, 67
cultural relevance xxvii, 139, 165, 178
cultural sensitivity 80
cultural situatedness of human action 102
curriculum: Brazil 193; bureaucratic model of formulating 6–7; horizontal segmentation of 5; integrated 4; standardisation of 5; vertical segmentation of 5–6

Dahlberg, G. 63, 80
Damásio, A. 99

daycare provision 19, 20, 132, 133
decision-making, children and 44
democracy 3, 12, 28-30, 41, 47, 65, 183, 203; learning 80
Democracy and Education (Dewey) 10
democratic approach to assessment/evaluation xxvi, 66-67, 134–135, 165
democratic participation 75, 81
dependability of assessment/evaluation findings 89, 90
development: as complex, non-linear process 59; institutional setting 69; parent 59, 69, 88; physical 87, 243; practitioner 59, 67, 69, *see also* professional development; as socio-cultural process 59
developmental psychology 94, 95, 96
Dewey, J. 3, 4, 5, 9-12, 13, 20, 23n6 and 10, 28, 30, 44, 47, 51n4, 94, 97, 112, 125, 151, 203; *The Child and the Curriculum* 10, 11; *Democracy and Education* 10; *Experience and Education* 10-11, 12, 108–109; `My Pedagogic Creed' 10, 11, 23n2; *The School and Society* 10
Dewey School *see* Laboratory School (University of Chicago)
dialogue 13-14, 60, 61, 67, 79, 112, 125, 138, 139, 243; reflective 83; support for open 61; symmetrical 61, 78
difference: respect for 16, 60, 183; *see also* cultural difference; ethnic difference; racial difference
disability 238-239
discovery learning 4, *18*, 96
disjunction, principle of 94, 102, 104
distance travelled graphs **249**
distinction, principle of 102, 104
diversity 29; racial 170; respect for 16, *17*, 60, 170; social 8–9, 16; understanding 61; *see also* cultural diversity
documentary analysis 83
documentation *see* pedagogic documentation
Dubiel, J. 145
Dunne, J. 113

Early Years Foundation Stage (EYFS) framework (England) 208, 209, 215, 216, 217, 222, 243
Early Years Quality Improvement Support Programme (EYQISP) (England) 207-208
ecological approach xxvi, 15, *16*, *18*, 19, *99*, 102, 137, 189, 203, 255

economy of education 94
educational assembly line 5–6, *18*, 97
educational environment, organisation of 40-45; integrated pedagogical dimensions 41–42; learning groups 44–45; pedagogical materials 43-44, 169, 171, 183, 185–186, 188; pedagogical space 42–43, 171, 183, 185–186, 188; pedagogical time 44, 183, 185, 186, 188
educational environment, quality of *see* quality of educational environment
educational freedom 22
educational intentionalities 16, 30, 31-37, 49, 111-112, **113**, 144, 165
educational psychology 94
Effective Early Learning (EEL) Programme 60, 66, **68**, 69, 132, 243; case study 206-219; observational instruments (Adult Engagement 86, 89; Child Tracking 83, 124, 163, 165, 210)
Emilson, A. 114
emotional intelligence 87
emotional literacy 223, **229**, 231
empathy 40, 223, **229**, **230**
employment, families right to access 132, 133-134
empowerment 61, 64, 67
engagement: adult 86, 89, 210, 213, 215, 217; in assessment/evaluation process 90; child 85, 86
England: case studies (Accounting Early for Lifelong Learning (AcE) programme 220-239, 240-258; Effective Early Learning (EEL) Programme 206–219); Children Centre service *see* Children Centre service; Common Assessment Framework (CAF) 227; Early Years Foundation Stage (EYFS) framework 208, 209, 215, 216, 217, 222, 243; Early Years Quality Improvement Support Programme (EYQISP) 207-208; Flying Start programme 222–223; Free Early Education Entitlement (FEEE) funding 241; Incredible Years parenting course 227, **228–230**; Investors in Children scheme 207; National Childcare Strategy 207
environment, educational *see* educational environment
equality: of opportunity 7, 67; and respect for difference 16; as uniformity 7, *17*

equity 29, 133, 134, 143
ethical principles for assessment and evaluation xxv-xxviii, 131–141; paradigmatic stance 131; praxeological stance 132; theoretical stance 131–132
ethnic difference: respect for 183; transmissive pedagogy blindness to 8
ethos of participative pedagogies 107, 108–112
European Early Childhood Education Research Association (EECERA), Ethical Code 185
European Early Childhood Education Research Journal 182
Evaluation Reports 70
examinations, final 5
Experience and Education (Dewey) 10–11, 12, 108–109
experiential learning 30, 35, 37–38, 46, 47, 112, 114, 116, 169; motivation for 30; organisation of educational environment for 40–45
exploration 35, 39, 85, 109
expressive activity 82

families: belonging 33-34; co-construction of learning with 49–50; participation 152; right to access paid employment 132, 133-134; well-being 50, 134; *see also* parents
Family Plans, AcE programme 234, **235**
Faundez, A. 134
feedback 90; and active listening 79; reflective 84
feeling(s) 32, 38, 133, 136
Figueiredo, I. 143
Fink, D. 97
Fleet, A. 113
Flying Start programme (England) 222–223
Flyvbjerg, B. 94
focused improvement cycles 88-89
Folque, M.A. 115
Ford, H. 3, 5
formative assessment 243
Formosinho, J. 1, 3, 7, 8, 19, 21, 23n8 and 11, 26, 28, 30, 31, 33, 34, 35, 40, 49, 50, 51n5, 64, 94, 98, 102, 103, 107, 110, 111, 113, 114, 131, 132, 134, 140, 143, 145, 152, 169, 170, 182, 184
Foucault, M. 41
Free Early Education Entitlement (FEEE) funding, England 241
Freinet, C. 23n10, 51n4

Freire, P. 4, 9–10, 12–14, 30, 42, 47, 51n2
and 4, 61, 64, 65, 78, 84, 96, 97, 110,
134, 144, 171, 174, 183, 203; *Pedagogy
of the Oppressed* 12-13, 60
Froebel, F. 5, 20, 23n10, 214

Geertz, C. 90
gender awareness and identity 170
generosity 40
Ghandi, M.K. 60
Giardello, P. 23n1
Gibson, J.J. 59
Giddens, A. 98
Gill, D. 84
Gladwell, M. 65
Goethean science 99-100
group work 4-5
groups, learning 44-45
Guba, E.G. 89, 185

habitus 45, 46
Hargreaves, A. 97
Hargreaves, D. 247
HighScope Educational Research
Foundation 185
history of education 94
holistic assessment and evaluation 93, 98-
105, 118; aims of *99*; ethical principles
for xxv-xxviii, 131–141 (paradigmatic
stance 131; praxeological stance 132;
theoretical stance 131–132); processes of
100
holistic learning xxvi, 136, 165, 251
Home Learning Plans, AcE programme
237
human rights 30, 135
human understanding 40

identification 40
identities/identity development 30, 32–33,
37, 38–39, 41, 109–110, 110–111, 112,
133, 134, 135, 144, 162, 169, 177;
gender 170; plural 139; professional 138
imagination 40
inclusionary approach to
assessment/evaluation 66, *99*
Incredible Years parenting course 227,
228–230
inquiry audit 90
Institute of Child Studies (University of
Minho) 168
integrated curriculum 4
integrated learning *99*, 133
integration of method and content 47
intelligence 40

intelligent senses 35, 37, 111, 112, 174
intentionalities, educational 16, 30, 31–37,
49, 111–112, **113**, 144, 165
interactivity 15, 30, 35, 45, 47, 110, 188
intercultural relevance xxvii, 139, 165, 178
intersubjectivity 30, 40, 104–105, 118, 177
intrapersonal learning 103
Investors in Children scheme (England)
207
involvement, child xxvi, 85–86, 89, 124,
135, 177, 178, 210, 213, 217
isomorphic pedagogy 26, 103–104, 114
isomorphism 105n6

James, A. 80
joint attention, children/teachers 30
journaling 84–85, 91
just community concept 44

Kilpatrick, W.H. 23n10, 47
kindergartens, progressive 20, 21
Kishimoto, T. 51n4, 182, 183
knowing and knowledge: co-construction
of 108, 109, 125, 139; complexity of
96–97, 98–99; experiential learning as
co-construction of 37, **38**; expressive
forms of 82; generation of 64–65;
pedagogical 27–28
knowledge society 134, 138
knowledge-in-action 47
Knowles, M.S. 59
Kohlberg, L. 34, 44, 95
Kozulin, A. 95–96

Laboratory School (University of Chicago)
10, 12
Laevers, F. 43, 85, 86, 87, 124, 177, 181,
185, 186, 188
Langsted, O. 75
language development 87
language exploration 223
languages 37, 38, 39–40, 133, 162, 169,
177; *see also* one hundred languages
Lave, J. 115
learner identities 133, 135
learner-in-action 136, 137
learning: assessment for (formative
assessment) 243; assessment of
(summative assessment) 243; by doing,
experiencing and discovering 4, *18*, 96;
co-construction of 48, 49–50, 59, 125,
184; collaborative 15, 30–31, 35, 43, 44,
108; in companionship 30; complexity
of 59, 96–97, 98–102; context of 102;
dynamic nature of 237–238;

engagement in 85, 86; holistic xxvi, 136, 165, 251; integrated *99*, 133; intrapersonal 103; meta- 50, 184; motivation for 8, 15; narration of 35–37, 39, 112, 136, 144, 169; parent 59; process of 212–213; reproduction of, and transmissive pedagogy 7–8, 15, 17, *18*, 96; rote 4; situated 115, 117, 137; as socio-cultural process 59; solidary 29–30, 48, 108, 121–125; of teachers 114–116; uncovering 123–125; *see also* experiential learning; lifelong learning
learning communities 75
learning democracy 80
learning diaries 224, 234
'learning' giraffe puppets 234
learning groups, organisation of 44–45
learning how to learn 47, 49, 97, 103, 111, 136, 137, 144, 165
learning indicators, AcE programme 223, 231, 236, 238
learning journeys xxvii, 35–37, 39, 103, 122, 133, 137, 138, 139, 178, 214, 236, 253; plural 139; professional 138, 139
learning stories 77, 113
Lee, W. 36, 113
Lehrs, E. 100
Lessard-Hébert, M. 185
Leuven Scales for Emotional Well-being 87, 124, 186
Lewin, K. 41
Lewis, A. 63
liberation 60–61, 65–66, 134
lifelong learning 21; *see also* Accounting Early for Lifelong Learning (AcE) Programme
Lincoln, Y.S. 89, 185
Lindsay, G. 63
Lino, D. 116, 183
listening 46, 60, 74–75, 76; active 61, 64, 78–79; body language and gestures 79; with humility 78; providing feedback when 79; to children 74–75, 79–81, 138; with/to parents 74–75, 77–79
listening circles 61
Lloyd, E. 132
Lloyd-Smith, M. 63, 64
localism 64, 65, 118
Luckman, T. 109

Macedo, D. 14
Machado, J. 3, 8, 30, 51n5, 116, 181, 183, 184

MacNaughton, G. 170
McNiff, J. 61, 65, 89
Mairs, K. 113
Malaguzzi, L. 23n10, 35, 38, 51n4, 64, 94, 96, 111, 113, 139, 145, 315
mass production 5, 18
mass schooling 3
materials, pedagogical 43–44, 169, 171, 183, 185–186, 188
mathematic language 162
Máximo-Esteves, L. 182
Maybin, J. 80
meaning: co-construction of 79, 125; creation of 36, 37, 38, 39–40, 85, 109, 112, 144, 162, 169, 177, 178
member checking 90
memorisation 4, 7, 15
memory 35, 40, 184
metacognition 36, 48, 131, 158
meta-learning 50, 184
methods of assessment and evaluation 74–92; AcE Scales 87; action planning 88; documentary analysis 83; focused improvement cycles 88–89; journaling 84; observational instruments 83–84, 123 (Adult Engagement 86, 89, 210, 213, 215, 217; Child Engagement 85; Child Involvement 85–86, 89, 124, 210, 213, 215, 217; Child Tracking 83, 124, 163, 165, 210, 213, 215; Leuven Scales for Emotional Well-being 87, 124, 186; Program Quality assessment (PQA) 185); parent outcomes 88;practitioner outcomes: professional development 87; questionnaires/surveys 84; reflective dialogues 83; rigour and trustworthiness of 89–91; setting outcomes {—} quality improvement; 88; visual/digital images or audio records 84
Mezirow, J. 59
migrant communities 63
migration 8
Miller, J. 79–80
Modern School Movement 115
Moles, J. 211
Moll, L. 33, 51n6
Monge, G. 50
Montessori, M. 5, 20, 23n10
Morin, E. 31, 37, 39, 40, 43, 47, 50, 51n2, 94, 97, 101, 102, 104, 105n1, 109
Mosaic Approach 84
Moss, P. 20, 21, 63, 84
motivation for learning: participatory pedagogy 15; transmissive pedagogy 8

multiple intelligences 43, 125, 133
music baskets 170–177
'My Pedagogic Creed' (Dewey) 10, 11

narration of learning 35–37, 39, 112, 136, 144, 169
narrative thought 36–37
National Childcare Strategy (England) 207
National Curriculum for Early Childhood Education (Brazil) 193
nature/nurture 40–41, 96
negative case analysis 90
Niza, S. 115
Noffke, S. 182
non predictability of human action 102–103
Novo, R. 116
Nutbrown, C. 23n1

observation 46, 74–77, 183, 213–214; by children 77; parents involvement in 77; peer 76, 217; persistent and regular 90; planned 76–77; recording of 76, 77; regular/systematic 77; skills 76; spontaneous 76
observational instruments 83–84, 123; Adult Engagement 86, 210, 213, 215, 217; Child Engagement Scale 85; Child Involvement 85–86, 89, 124, 210, 213, 215, 217; Child Tracking 83, 124, 163, 165, 210, 213, 215; Leuven Scales for Emotional Well-being 87, 124, 186; Program Quality Assessment (PQA) 185
Ofsted (Office for Standards in Education) 209, 217, 218–219, 239
Olivais Sul Children Centre 27, 142, 143
Oliveira-Formosinho, J. 8, 15, 21, 23n8, 26, 28, 31, 32, 33, 34, 35, 40, 45, 48, 49, 50, 51n5, 63, 64, 94, 98, 103, 107, 108, 110, 111, 113, 114, 116, 131, 132, 140, 144, 145, 158, 169, 170, 182, 184, 188, 189, 199, 203
one hundred languages 35, 37, 38, 39, 40, 111, 112, 125, 144
ontological isomorphism 103–104
Opening Windows project 84
oppression, transmissive pedagogy as 12–14
organisational theories 3, 5
outcomes of educational processes 137, 178; medium and long term evaluation of 103

Pain Assessment Tool 223
Parente, C. 116

parents: co-construction of learning with 49–50, 59; dialogues with 60, 61; introductory meetings with 78; listening with/to 77–79; and observation 77; own learning and development 59, 69, 88; participation of xxvi, 136, 152, 165, 211, 216 (AcE programme case studies 220–239, 247, 250–256, 257); voices 233; *see also* families
participation 33–34, 37, 39, 41, 43, 44, 47, 48, 65, 67, 112, 134–135, 144, 152, 165, 169; democratic 75, 79–80, 81; *see also* parents, participation of
participatory belonging 37, 169
participatory pedagogy 4, 9–14, 19, 21, 28; active role of teacher/learners in 15, *16*, *18*; comprehensiveness, respect for complexity of knowledge 16, *17*; concrete character of curriculum/teaching *17*; and diversity, respect for 16, *17*; ecological and contextualised approaches in 15, *16*, *18*, 19; ethos of 107, 108–112; evaluation, concept of *18*; human equity, concept of 16, *17*; image of the child in 110–111, 136; main goals of education in 15, *16*; schools, conception of 15, *16*, 19; and transmissive pedagogy, contrast between 14–19; *see also* pedagogy-in-participation
Pascal, C. 21, 41, 45, 59, 63, 64, 66, 75, 77, 78, 83, 84, 85, 86, 87, 98, 104, 113, 120, 124, 132, 140, 145, 163, 170, 182, 206, 243
passivity: education for 34, 184; and transmissive pedagogy 15, *16*, *18*, 19, 184
pedagogic creed for assessment and evaluation xxv–xxviii, 131–141
pedagogic documentation xxvii, 36, 48–51, 107–128, 139–140, 184, 197–202; and co-construction of learning with parents 49–50; pedagogical attunement case study 168–180; praxis of 112–114; as process of constructing meaning for pedagogic situations 48–49; as process for sustaining pedagogy-in-participation 50–51; project work case study 142, 144–165
pedagogic isomorphism 26, 103–104, 114
pedagogical attunement 168–180
pedagogical materials 43–44, 169, 171, 183, 185–186, 188

pedagogical space 42–43, 171, 183,
185–186, 188
pedagogical time 44, 183, 185, 186, 188
pedagogy: Copernican revolution in 109,
139; praxis as the locus of 27–31,
143–144
pedagogy of bonds 33
Pedagogy of the Oppressed (Freire) 12–13, 60
pedagogy-in-participation 26–55, 107,
132; activities and projects development
47–48; anchors for evaluation 118;
beliefs, values and principles 27, 28; case
studies (Portugal) (pedagogical
attunement 168–180; project work 142,
144–167; well-being of children
181–191); and democracy 28–30;
documentation 48–51, 112–121, 142,
144–165, 168–180; educational
environment 40–45 (learning groups
44–45; pedagogical materials 43–44;
pedagogical space 42–43); experiential
learning 30, 35, 37–38, 40–45, 46, 47;
interacting with the child(ren) 45;
learning areas 38–40, **39**, 123 (identities
and relationships 38–39; languages and
meanings 38, 39–40); pedagogical axes
31–38, 123 (being/feeling/thinking
32–33, 38; belonging and participation
33–34, 38–39, 44; exploration and
communication 35, 39; narration and
learning journeys 35–37, 39); planning
in 46
peer review/observation 76, 217
Pen Green Centre 113
Pen Green Loop 247, **250**, 250
Penn, H. 132
Personal, Social and Emotional
Development (PSED) 243
Pestalozzi, J. H. 20, 23n10
physical development 87, 243
Piaget, J. 51n4, 96
Pinazza, M.A. 51n4, 182
Pires, C. 116
planning 46, 183, 203; solidary 46,
121–122, 125, 151, 158
play 133, 213–214, 216, 236
portfolios 48, 122, 163; professional
development 50, 122
Portuguese case studies: pedagogy-in-
participation (pedagogical attunement
168–180; project work 142–167; well-
being of children 181–191)
positivism 93–94; and applicationist view
on assessment and evaluation 94–95, 98;
and psychological research 95–96

poverty reduction 133, 142–143
*Practice Guidance for the Early Years
Foundation Stage* (DCFS) 76
practitioner(s): learning and development
59, 67, 69; outcomes 87; reflective 72;
selfhood 61; *see also* professional
development; teacher(s)
praxeological research 182
praxis 61, 64, 65, 89; as the locus of
pedagogy 27–31, 143–144
pre-schooling: and bureaucratic mode of
education 8; as preparation for primary
school 21
problem solving 4, 96
process of learning 212–213
professional biographies 212
professional development 66, 76, 87, 203,
214–215, 247; assessment/evaluation
process as vehicle for 67; portfolios 50,
122
professional identity 138
professional learning journeys 138, 139
Program Quality Assessment (PQA)
185
progressive education movement 4–5, 10,
12
project work 47–48, 96; pedagogy-in-
participation case study 142–167
projection 40
Prout, A. 80
psychological approach to
assessment/evaluation 138, 139
psychological isomorphism 104
psychological reductionisms 95–96
psychology: behavioural 95-96;
developmental 94, 95, 96; educational
94
psychometric assessment 96, 138, 139
purpose of assessment and evaluation 62;
knowledge generation 64–65; liberation
and transformation 65–66

quality of educational environment 66, 67,
88, 134, 143; case studies (Effective
Early Learning (EEL) programme
206–219; traditional versus participatory
pedagogic environment 181–191);
conceptual framework for evaluating
and developing (Effective Early
Learning (EEL) programme) **68**, 69
Quality, Evaluation and Improvement
Cycle 210, 212-213; action plan phase
212, 213; evaluation phase **212**, 213;
improvement phase **212**, 213; reflection
phase **212**, 213

questioning observations 76
questionnaires 84

racial awareness 170
racial difference 170, 183
rational uncertainty, principle of 97
Reason, P. 65, 82, 182
recording observations 76, 77
reduction, principle of 94, 102
reductionist evaluation 15–16, *17*, 95–98,
    105n3; aims of *99*; processes of *100*
reflection 61; and learning 35, 37, 40; as
    phase of evaluation/assessment process
    71, 72, **212**, 213
reflective dialogues 83
reflexivity 91, 109
Reggio Emilia 113, 193
relational identities 37, 45, 109–110,
    110–111, 112, 144, 162, 169
relationships, development of 33, 37,
    38–39, 45, 47, 169, 177
reproduction of learning, as core activity in
    transmissive pedagogy 7–8, 15, 17, *18*,
    96, 97
resilience 223, **229**, **230**
responsibility 223
rights based approach 23, 49–50, 74, 135,
    214, 233, 234
rights of children 30, 41, 43, 63–64, 75,
    80, 81, 82, 109–110, 133, 135, 179,
    183
Rinaldi, C. 111, 113, 145, 202
Roberts, R. 79
Rogers, S. 255
Rogoff, B. 41, 59, 109
Rose, J. 255
rote learning 4

Salamanca Statement (1994) 9
Samuelson, P. 114
São Paulo: case study: children's
    participation in own assessment 192,
    194–205; educational and social
    contexts 192–194
Saunders, M. 77, 84, 85, 87
The School and Society (Dewey) 10
schoolification of early years education 21,
    22
schools, conception of: and participatory
    pedagogy 15, *16*; and transmissive
    pedagogy 15, *16*
scientific language 162
scientific management of education 3, 4–5,
    9, *18*
segmentation of education 4–9

self-evaluation 208–209, 215
self-regulation 144
selfhood, development of 61
sensitive intelligences 35, 37, 111, 112
sensitivity: adult 75, 86; cultural 80
simplification, applicationist
    view/transmissive pedagogy 15–16, *17*,
    97–98
Siraj-Blatchford, I. 252, 254, 257
situated learning 115, 117, 137
social capital 247
social competence 87
social control 7
social diversity 8–9, 16
social justice 133
social regulation 144
socio-cultural environment 69–70
sociology of education 94
solidary learning 29–30, 48, 108,
    122–125
solidary planning 46, 121–122, 125, 151,
    158
solidary teaching 30, 105
Somekh, B. 182
Sousa, J. 51n5, 116
Sousa-Santos, B. 16, 23n9
space, pedagogical 42–43, 171, 183,
    185–186, 188
special needs children 9, 215, 238–230
standardisation 5, 8, 15, 97
Steiner, R. 5, 20, 23n10, 100
stimulation 75, 86
subject content 4; and prior experiences
    11; standardisation of 5
subjectivism, control of, and applicationist
    perspective 95
subjectivity 104
summative assessment 243
surveys 84
sympathy 40

Tarr, J. 63, 64
Taylor, F.W. 3, 5, 23n3
teacher education 189; academicisation of
    21, 23n11
teacher(s): agency of 45; contextual
    professional learning 114–116; and
    participatory pedagogy 15, *16*, *18*;
    professional development *see*
    professional development; and
    transmissive pedagogy 8, 14, 15,
    16, *18*
teaching, solidary 30, 105
temporal teaching time units 6
tests/testing 5

theory of mind 36
thick description 90
thinking 32, 36, 37, 38; shared 158; *see also* metacognition
Thiollent, M. 192
time, pedagogical 44, 183, 185, 186, 188
togetherness 30, 44
Tomasello, M. 30
tracking: as assessment method 83, 124, 163, 165, 210, 213, 215; vocational/academic 23n5
transferability of assessment/evaluation findings 89, 90
transformation 65–66
transmissive pedagogy 3, 4, 8, 9–10, 17–19, 21, 28, 47, 110; abstract character
of 16, *17*, 97; and conformity 19; evaluation, concept of *18*; human equity, concept of *16*; main goals of education in 14–15, *16*; minimisation of complexity 96–97; motivation for learning 8; as oppression 12–14; and participatory pedagogy, contrast between 14–19; passivity (student/teacher) as feature of 15, *16*, *18*, 19; prevalence in mass schools *16*, 17–18; reductionism and simplification in 15–16, *17*, 97–98; reproduction of learning as core activity in 7–8, 15, 17, 96; schools, conception of 15, *16*; uniformity approach *17*, 184; and well-being of children 181–191
Trevarthen, C. 177
triangulation 90–1

understanding, human 40
UNESCO 9

uniformity, assumptions of, applicationist view/transmissive pedagogy *17*, 97, 184
United Nations Convention on the Rights of the Child (UNCRC) 63, 82
universalism 64
University Primary School *see* Laboratory School (University of Chicago)
usefulness/usability of assessment/ evaluation information xxviii, 140, 165, 236

Valsiner, J. 117
values 27, 131; clarifying 61
Vieira, F. 116
visual records 77, 84
voice(s) 65; children's 63, 75, 81, 134–135, 192–205, 234; parents' 233
Vygotsky, L. 39, 40, 51n4, 59, 65

we-ness 120–121, 125
Weber, M. 5, 6, 23n4, 23n7, 105n3
well-being 50, 69, 86–87, 112, 124, 134, 136, 177, 178, 243; pedagogy-in-participation versus transmissive pedagogy 181–191
Wenger, E. 31, 64, 75, 115, 152
Wertsch, J.V. 33, 109, 131
Whalley, M. 34, 113
Wheeler, H. 251
whole-part relationship *17*, 104
Wong, D. 223
Woodhead, M. 63, 80, 81–82
working mothers, support for 132, 133–134

Zaslow, M. 66
Zelan, K. 41
Zone of Proximal Development 65, 86